Praise for *Saving the American Dream*

"*Saving the American Dream* is a powerful exploration of what binds—and divides—America and Americans today. John K. Roth reminds readers that democracy, equality, and opportunity are not guaranteed. They must be renewed by every generation. *Saving the American Dream* challenges complacency, offers a warning and a way forward, and calls 'We the People of the United States' to civic responsibility and moral courage. I highly recommend it."

—**Carol Rittner**, RSM, Professor Emerita of Holocaust and Genocide Studies, Stockton University, New Jersey

"Having dedicated more than a half century toward exploring the American Dream, John K. Roth has a mastery of American history, literature, philosophy, poetry, culture, and music to understand the Dream's nuances and its aspirations. Roth has risen to the defense of the American Dream and offers an accurate, anguished, and searing condemnation of those now in power who seem determined to destroy it. The question of our age is can the American Dream be preserved. Roth cannot answer that question, but he does tell us why it should be preserved and offers sagacious guidance as to how it can be preserved. This work must challenge us all, arouse our conscience, and inspire us to action."

—**Michael Berenbaum**, Distinguished Professor of Jewish Studies, American Jewish University

"John K. Roth has spent over five decades challenging students to wrestle with the import and meaning of the American Dream and inspiring them to fulfill its promise. In *Saving the American Dream*, he uses that lifetime of philosophical and historical exploration as the lens through which to view the actions of Trump 2.0. This book is for policy makers, patriots, and anyone feeling overwhelmed by the past year. More than a mere indictment, it delivers an urgent and inspirational call to action and a path forward, guiding 'We the People' toward resilient resistance and communal action to meet the needs of our nation's moment."

—**Steve Bullock**, Montana Governor (2013–21) and former student of Prof. Roth

"In a time when it is hard to keep up with all the ways democracy and the American Dream are under attack, this book skillfully provides analysis of key events, actions, and positions of both those attacking democracy and the Dream and those defending them. Written with refreshing candor, *Saving the American Dream* weaves together the US Constitution, the Declaration of Independence, the Pledge of Allegiance, notions of patriotism, political philosophy, history, literature, and more to both inform and inspire the reader to action. Roth warns us all to 'watch what Trump does and remember what he keeps doing. He consolidates power and advances oligarchy.' Roth helpfully reminds us that 'if we want more democracy, we must be more democratic—now. If we want the rule of law, we must practice it—today. . . . We have to defend and support—with no wasted time—a free press and schools and universities that teach students to inquire critically, follow where evidence leads, and respect truth.' Roth writes with a passion and urgency that capture the reader's attention. This is an important book for our times and should be read and taught widely."

—**Erin McKenna**, Professor of Philosophy, University of Oregon

"In this moment of constitutional crisis, *Saving the American Dream* is essential reading. It sounds the alarm, provides wisdom from sages past and present, and ultimately invites us to embrace hope as we face hard truths about our nation. Whether the American Dream can be reclaimed and redeemed is still to be determined, but John K. Roth makes strong arguments for why and how we should save it. This book is both a meditation and call to action."

—**Elizabeth Wydra**, President, Constitutional Accountability Center, Washington, DC

Saving the American Dream

Saving the American Dream

Meditations for Dark Times

JOHN K. ROTH

CASCADE *Books* • Eugene, Oregon

SAVING THE AMERICAN DREAM
Meditations for Dark Times

Cascade Books
An Imprint of Wipf and Stock Publishers
199 W. 8th Ave., Suite 3
Eugene, OR 97401

www.wipfandstock.com

PAPERBACK ISBN: 979-8-3852-4920-6
HARDCOVER ISBN: 979-8-3852-4921-3
EBOOK ISBN: 979-8-3852-4922-0

Cataloguing-in-Publication data:

Names: Roth, John K., author.

Title: Saving the American dream : meditations for dark times / John K. Roth.

Description: Eugene, OR: Cascade Books, 2026. | Includes bibliographical references and index.

Identifiers: ISBN 979-8-3852-4920-6 (paperback). | ISBN 979-8-3852-4921-3 (hardcover). | ISBN 979-8-3852-4922-0 (ebook).

Subjects: LCSH: Ethics. | Democracy. | Political philosophy. | Trump, Donald J., 1946–.

Classification: E169.1 R75 2026 (print). | E169.1 (ebook).

VERSION NUMBER 03/09/26

To
Keeley
and
Her Yale College Gen Z Friends

Send out your light and your truth.

—Psalm 43:3

It has been frequently remarked that it seems to have been reserved to the people of this country, by their conduct and example, to decide the important question, whether societies of men are really capable or not of establishing good government from reflection and choice, or whether they are forever destined to depend for their political constitutions on accident and force. If there be any truth in the remark, the crisis at which we are arrived may with propriety be regarded as the era in which that decision is to be made; and a wrong election of the part we shall act may, in this view, deserve to be considered as the general misfortune of mankind.

—Alexander Hamilton, *The Federalist Papers*, No. 1

Contents

Acknowledgments

Saving the American Dream depends on freedom of speech and freedom of the press. I thank my editor, K. C. Hanson, and his stellar team at Cascade Books, especially Jeremy Funk, for encouraging me to write this book and for publishing it in dark times that endanger the United States and put the Dream at risk. Wipf and Stock Publishers defends American democracy by publishing books that raise critical questions, invite dialogue about them, and inspire much-needed ethical commitment and spiritual resilience. I am grateful that *Saving the American Dream* can advance that mission.

The American Dream: I am grateful for that idea and ideal. I believe that I am not alone in saying that my life would be diminished and impoverished without it. The chapters ahead explain and justify that conviction, partly by showing how the Dream became pivotal in the teaching and writing I have done for decades. That work always involved students, mostly at Claremont McKenna College but around the world too. I thank them for inspiring me to pursue the Dream, for helping me to discern how my life and my country are inseparable from it. Respect for that relationship leads me to capitalize the American Dream, as I have done in the pages that follow except where fidelity to accurate quotation requires a different style.

The book is dedicated to my granddaughter, Keeley Brooks, a recent Gen Z college graduate. Born between 1997 and 2012, Gen Z mostly came of age during the COVID-19 pandemic and the Trump contagion. Those disruptions understandably discourage that group, which some call the "rejection generation," because, as the journalist David Brooks says, "It's just phenomenally hard to be young right now."[1] Earlier generations have not had easy times, but for Gen Z, mainstays of the American Dream—home ownership, job security, work-hard-and-get-ahead, better life chances than previous generations had—cannot be taken for granted. More obvious instead are obstructions: the dysfunction of American politics, disruption caused

1. Brooks, "'Most Rejected Generation.'"

by artificial intelligence (AI), lie-enabled corruption, resurgent cultural division and disrespect, environmental deterioration, and feeling priced out of the future. Gen Z is not alone in feeling that the American Dream may not be for them. Only half of the country thinks it is still possible.[2]

Gen Z, however, is not in the doldrums. It is not going away or giving up. Adaptability, resilience, resistance, ingenuity, social justice concerns—those are Gen Z characteristics and American Dream virtues. *Saving the American Dream* is for Gen Z, whose light and truth can put the United States back on track. That's hard work, but as the American leader Kamala Harris likes to say, "Hard work is good work. Hard work can be joyful work."[3]

This book highlights gifted American writers old and new who have taught me about the American Dream. One of them is Annie Dillard. Her small book, *The Writing Life*, a guide for living, is a favorite of mine. It never mentions the American Dream, but Dillard writes about hard and joyful work in ways that help me to concentrate on what it means to make the Dream the best it can be.

Dillard tells a story about an artist friend, Paul Glenn, who was experimenting with new styles and techniques at his studio on an island in the Haro Strait off the coast of Washington state. When Dillard asked him how the work was going, he answered with a story about an old friend, Ferrar Burn, "a joyful man, . . . a calm and determined one."[4]

Glenn told Dillard that Burn had been building a house before he died twenty years ago. He used driftwood timber when he could. One evening, he saw a choice log floating in the channel. It looked like good Alaskan cedar.

Burn rowed out, roped the log, started home, and then the tide turned. It strongly sent him south when home was north. Determined not to lose, Burn kept rowing, even as he was pulled farther from where he needed to go. A night's dark hours passed while he worked hard, hoping the tide would turn.

Burn made it home with his log. Learning about the struggle, Glenn asked his friend how he had felt about it. "He said he had a little backache," Glenn told Dillard, but "I didn't see the palms of his hands." Burning, blistered, even bloody—surely that way, Burn's hands brought the treasure home.

"That's how my work is going," Glenn told Dillard. "The current's got me. Feels like I'm about in the middle of the channel now. I just keep at it. I just keep hoping the tide will turn and bring me in." *Saving the American*

2. Borelli, "Americans Are Split"; Burch, "The American Dream?"
3. Harris, Address Conceding the 2024 Presidential Election.
4. Dillard, *Writing Life*, 85–88.

Dream is about hard work, joyful work like that. Keeping at it. Hoping the tide will turn.

"When you write," Dillard begins *The Writing Life*, "you lay out a line of words. The line of words is a miner's pick, a woodcarver's gouge, a surgeon's probe."[5] You follow where the words lead, where the evidence points, looking for what's true, rejecting what's not. You will not find out until tomorrow or next year if you have been on the right track.

Writing this book has been work like that, because so much of it, so much of the American Dream, is about aspirations and hopes for the future that unavoidably face hostile currents and tides moving away from where we need to be. But *Saving the American Dream*, both the book and its goal, are well worth the struggle, a joyful one for me. If that message is conveyed, then I am glad for how my work is going.

5. Dillard, *Writing Life*, 3.

Preamble

We the People

The American Dream at its best is an ethical ideal and a moral compass. It aspires to make the United States more just, equitable, and inclusive, which will make the country stronger and more prosperous as well. If respected and sustained, the Dream can guide the United States through dark times.

Governed by the US Constitution, *Saving the American Dream* contains seven chapters, one for each of the Constitution's seven articles. The book's conclusion reflects the Constitution's amendments. A preamble starts the inquiry.

> We the People of the United States, in Order to form a more perfect Union, establish Justice, insure domestic Tranquility, provide for the common defence, promote the general Welfare, and secure the Blessings of Liberty to ourselves and our Posterity, do ordain and establish this Constitution for the United States of America.

No American words are more beautiful, aspirational, and challenging. They anchor these meditations.

Meditations are intentional acts of focused attention. They seek insight—clear, accurate, and deep-down understanding—about critical issues of our time: What, for example, is good, right, and true, and what's not? What is most important for the United States today, and what isn't? Are we Americans doing the best we can? How may inquiry about the American Dream advance the reflection and action needed now to support and defend the Constitution of the United States?

Saving the American Dream is a journey that goes where such questions lead. Its fundamental premise is that Americans moved to communal action by warned awareness and committed resistance are indispensable to meet challenges to the "general Welfare" that grow by the day.[1] Insights from American musicians and writers—philosophers, historians, novelists, poets, essayists, and religious thinkers—map the way.

Unpleasant Facts

Fighting to defend the Constitution, Paul Fussell, a gravely wounded combat veteran of World War II, became one of the leading literary scholars and cultural critics of his generation. His award-winning *The Great War and Modern Memory* drew on England's soldier-writers to show how the trenches of World War I shattered illusions about humanity's progress. Optimism depressed him.[2]

Fussell included a chapter on "A Power of Facing Unpleasant Facts" in his 1988 book *Thank God for the Atom Bomb and Other Essays*. His words help to ground what's ahead in the meditations that follow:

> Some exemplary unpleasant facts are these: that life is short and almost always ends messily; that if you live in the actual world you can't have your own way; that if you do get what you want, it turns out not to be the thing you wanted; that no one thinks as well of you as you do yourself; and that one or two generations from now you will be forgotten entirely and the world will go on as if you had never existed.[3]

One can argue with these judgments, but do they fit Donald Trump and minions such as JD Vance and Stephen Miller or Pam Bondi and Kristi Noem? If we cannot have our own way in the actual world, what should we want instead? How can we live so that life is not so messy? If we are remembered, perhaps only for a generation or two, what do we want to be remembered for? What if the world does not go on as though "We the People" never existed? What kind of world, what sort of country, will our American generations create and leave behind? "A more perfect Union" that promotes "the general Welfare" and secures "the Blessings of Liberty"? Or chaos and debris from a botched civilization?

Fussell's somber outlook leads to the serious perspectives of his contemporary, James Baldwin. In incisive novels such as *Go Tell It on the Mountain* and in piercing essays like those found in *Notes of a Native Son* and *The Fire Next Time*, Baldwin showed how deeply the legacy of slavery

1. For concurring views, see Greathouse, *Navigating Trumpworld*.
2. For an insightful interview with Fussell, see Fussell, "Last Curmudgeon."
3. Fussell, *Thank God*, 104.

and the persistence of racism scar American history and ought to focus what it means to save the American Dream. More than sixty years ago, he wrote an essay called "As Much Truth as One Can Bear." Arguing that "we are the generation that must throw everything into the endeavor to remake America into what we say we want it to be," Baldwin ended with a warning: "Not everything that is faced can be changed; but nothing can be changed until it is faced."[4]

We Americans need to bear the truths that American democracy is endangered by despotism, oligarchy, corruption, and division steeped in racism. Those unpleasant facts are entrenched in Donald Trump's second presidency. Its disrespect for the Constitution and the rule of law, its chaos-creating greed and incompetence, its contempt for ordinary Americans, and its abuse of migrants—all these assaults on the American Dream must be faced so that the Dream is not forsaken in a world that might go on as if it never existed.

In 2017, the *Washington Post* adopted the masthead slogan "Democracy Dies in Darkness." The keen political analyst William Kristol, a conservative but no longer a Republican, finds that view too optimistic. "Today, in the United States of America," he contends, "liberal democracy is being killed not in darkness but in broad daylight." Out in the open and unashamedly, "it's warfare by the government of the United States against the justice system, against the presentation of true facts, against free and fair elections. It's maximum warfare against the norms and institutions of a liberal democracy and republican self-government."[5] Kristol correctly sounded the alarm even more emphatically. Under Trump, he argued on August 25, 2025, the United States is in "a genuine, purposeful march toward despotism/dictatorship." He uses the terms interchangeably.[6] The next day, Trump asserted that he has "the right to do anything I want to do. I'm the president of the United States."[7] That's how dictators talk.

Kristol's point about free and fair elections is especially important. Americans who cherish democracy and who love the American Dream should have no illusions and make no mistakes: Knowing that fair and free elections now put them in jeopardy, Trump and his Make America Great Again (MAGA) crowd will be coming for the election process in 2026 and 2028. They can interfere in myriad ways: questioning census counts,

4. Baldwin, "As Much Truth." For a reliable assessment of Baldwin's authorship, see Glaude, *Begin Again*.

5. Kristol, "Democracy Dies in Daylight."

6. Kristol, "Bill Kristol: March."

7. Cameron, "Deploy National Guard."

gerrymandering to protect congressional seats, complicating voter registration and voting, delegitimizing mail balloting, protesting voting machines, and claiming voter fraud. By any means necessary, legal or illegal, Trump 2.0, as the current presidency and administration are often called, will do all it can to control, subvert, and, yes, rig the 2026 and 2028 elections to entrench destructive power. It should not be forgotten that on July 26, 2024, Trump told a gathering of Christian conservatives: "In four years, you don't have to vote again. We'll have it fixed so good, you're not going to have to vote." If Trump and his acolytes tried to rebut the antidemocratic, dictatorial vibe in that remark, they failed. Trump repeated the statement three days later.[8]

If Trump can find a way, he may violate the Constitution's two-term presidential limit, seize power in 2028, and stay in office until death. The distinguished American lawyer and jurist J. Michael Luttig has sounded the alarm:

> Donald Trump is clearly willing to subvert an election in order to hold on to the power he so craves, and he is now fully enabled to undermine national elections. No one can prevent him from remaining president of the United States for a constitutionally prohibited third term—except the American people, in whom ultimate power resides under the Constitution of the United States.[9]

Crucial problems are even closer than 2028. It can scarcely be assumed that the 2026 midterm elections will be fair and free. David A. Graham's "Donald Trump's Plan to Subvert the Midterms Is Already Under Way," an October 28, 2025, *Atlantic* analysis as ominous as it is prescient, draws conclusions that fit with Luttig's alarm:

> The midterm elections could be a . . . pivotal moment for American democracy. Defending the system in 2026 won't guarantee clean elections in 2028, but failing to do so would be catastrophic. Trump will exploit any weaknesses he can find; any damage to the system will encourage worse rigging in two years, and maybe even a quest for a third term. And if the president has two more years to act without any checks, there may not be much democracy left to save in 2028.[10]

Even if the threat of a third-term attempt by Trump is diminished as he ages and political circumstances weigh against it, forewarned must be forearmed.

8. Astor, "Trump Declines."
9. Luttig, "President for Life."
10. Graham, "Donald Trump's Plan."

We Americans often pridefully embrace the idea of American exceptionalism. Proponents believe that the United States is a "shining city on a hill," different from and superior to other nations because of its ideals of liberty, democracy, and individual rights, as well as because of its unique history of westward expansion and self-governance. Sometimes the American Dream is used to legitimate and advance such exceptionalism. As the literary critic Lionel Trilling once remarked, the United States of America is "the only nation that prides itself upon a dream and gives its name to one, 'the American dream.'"[11] American exceptionalism is partly truth and partly fiction, myth as much as reality. At best it denotes an aspiration. At worst it reflects ignorance and encourages arrogance.

Kristol rightly worries that American exceptionalism might be ominous and disastrous. "The dangers to our free political institutions are clear, present, and increasing in strength. The situation is grim. One fears that 'American exceptionalism' will culminate in an exceptional demonstration of a nation frittering away the privileges of freedom in as feckless a way as possible."[12] *Saving the American Dream* takes that threat seriously and shows how to resist it. Anticipating the crucial elections upcoming in 2026 and 2028, underscoring their importance and not taking for granted that they will be fair and free, these meditations for dark times concentrate primarily on the first seven months of Trump 2.0. The assessments cannot gauge the carnage unleashed by Trump 2.0 after the writing ended, except to say that the foul play will grow and the concerns, questions, and responses stressed in these pages will not be outdated.

Defending the Dream

The birthday of the American Dream is July 4, 1776, the day the Declaration of Independence was signed in Philadelphia. "We the People" of the United States take that date to be the birthday of our country too, although the Constitution of the United States was not signed until 1787 and was ratified only in 1789. But the Declaration's proclamation of equal and unalienable rights to life, liberty, and the pursuit of happiness encourages fundamental aspirations summarized by a concept—the American Dream—that now pervades the nation's history, culture, and politics. At its best, the idea of the American Dream encapsulates and advances the fundamental moral values and ethical aspirations that distinguish the United States. At its best, the

11. Trilling, *Liberal Imagination*, 251.

12. Kristol, "Toward Darkness or Dawn."

American Dream stands for what "We the People" ought to be and do to "secure the Blessings of Liberty to ourselves and our Posterity."

The American Dream, however, is not always the governing ideal it ought to be. The concept can be manipulated and abused, undermined and subverted, overridden, co-opted, and trumped so that its best meanings are squandered or lost. In these dark times, when the focus blurs, when ambiguity, distortion, and disillusionment lead to suspicion and skepticism about this normative ideal, efforts to save the American Dream at its best become paramount—especially as the nation's 250th birthday arrives on July 4, 2026.

Celebrations on July 4, 2025, were rightly muted—except when Trump 2.0 exalted the president's signing of the so-called One Big Beautiful Bill Act (OBBBA), passed by the slimmest of Republican majorities in Congress on July 3.[13] Stripping health care and food security from seventeen million poor and middle-class Americans, partly by making health insurance unaffordable for millions by failing to extend subsidies for insurance purchased through the Affordable Care Act's (ACA's) government-operated marketplaces, the bill brazenly rewards the richest Americans with huge tax cuts while reducing income levels for the poorest US households. The largest upward redistribution of income in American history also adds trillions to the national debt, which has surpassed $37 trillion.[14] Interest payments on the debt will soon exceed $1 trillion annually, more than the nation spends on Medicare or defense.[15] The megabill offers no relief. While destroying jobs, it pours $100 billion into Trump's anti-immigrant Immigration and Customs Enforcement (ICE) and Customs and Border Patrol (CBP), heralding ramped-up detention facilities and deportations without due process of law.

Republican Senator Mitch McConnell callously said that people worried about cuts to Medicaid will "get over it."[16] Vice President JD Vance cruelly called the cuts to Medicaid "minutiae" that are "immaterial compared to the ICE money and immigration enforcement provisions" in the megabill.[17] Far from accidental, the callousness and cruelty were the point. The Make America Great Again (MAGA) stalwart Senator Ted Cruz added to that sordid record by amending the megabill to ensure that it stripped millions of dollars from weather forecasting agencies and climate change research.

13. On OBBBA's contents and impacts, see Rattner, "How Bad Is This Bill?"; Bivens, "I'm an Economist"; *Time* staff, "'Big Beautiful Bill'"; Wolf and Luhby, "Trump's Megabill."

14. Whisnant, "US Debt."

15. Committee for a Responsible Federal Budget, "Interest on the Debt."

16. Sheth, "Mitch McConnell Says."

17. Wire, "Vance: Medicaid Cuts."

He vacationed in Greece while devastating Texas floods took the lives of hundreds of his constituents, most of them children.[18]

As of July 4, 2025, OBBBA was merely the latest act in a spectacle of antidemocratic authoritarianism that endangers all that Americans hold dear when we are at our best. Trump's boasting testified to that. "I can say very proudly that our country is more proud right now than it has been in many, many years. . . . The last two weeks, there's never been anything like it, as far as winning, winning, winning," he crowed on July 4, 2025, adding that "I just want you to know, if you see anything negative put out by Democrats, it's all a con job." The megabill, he claimed, is the "most popular bill ever signed."[19]

Trump's usual mixture of embellishments and lies attempted to cancel the fact that OBBBA is immensely unpopular and likely to become more so. A significant majority of Americans have judged the bill unacceptable. In addition, a June 2025 Gallup poll found that "a record-low 58% of U.S. adults say they are 'extremely' (41%) or 'very' (17%) proud to be an American, down nine percentage points from last year and five points below the prior low from 2020. . . . Additionally, Generation Z and millennials are much less proud of their country than their elders are."[20]

Ahead of OBBBA's passage, Democratic leader Hakeem Jeffries spoke for more than eight hours, the longest speech in the history of the House of Representatives, to protest the bill. "Budgets," he emphasized, "are moral documents. . . . Budgets should be designed to lift people up. . . . This reckless Republican budget that we are debating right now on the floor of the House of Representatives tears people down. . . . This reckless Republican budget is an immoral document."[21] Jefferies narrowly lost the vote to defeat the megabill but vowed repeatedly to press on for better times.

The retired US judge J. Michael Luttig also pressed on for better times when he published "The Self-Evident Truths of Freedom—and of Tyranny" in a July 2, 2025 Substack posting that went viral.[22] Luttig's essay recalled the "History of repeated Injuries and Usurpations, all having in direct Object the Establishment of an absolute Tyranny over these States" that led to the Declaration of Independence. He pressed Americans to see that Trump 2.0 is all too much like the eighteenth-century monarchy of England's King George III. Luttig stopped short of advocating rebellion, but he implied what I fervently believe: namely, that the midterm elections of 2026 and the

18. Milman, "Ted Cruz Ensured."
19. Moore et al., "Trump on Fourth of July."
20. Jones, "American Pride Slips."
21. Peller et al., "'Immoral.'"
22. Luttig, "Self-Evident Truths."

presidential election of 2028 will be decisive for the future of democracy in the United States. Defending the Declaration and the American Dream grounded in it are pivotal in that electoral struggle. It could be our last chance, at least in this generation, to thwart autocracy and oligarchy. That is why it is more than likely that Trump and his allies will do all they can to subvert if not steal these crucial elections.

A Democratic Republic No More?

Trump 2.0 shows that the Constitution alone cannot prevent the United States from becoming an oligarchic autocracy, but "We the People" can reverse that tide. This book encourages such effort, but nothing guarantees that result, because individually powerful though he is, Trump is the tip of a spear wielded by enablers who interact symbiotically with him. He needs them to advance his agenda; they need him to enhance theirs. As their goals and the steps toward them mix and mingle, the players in Trump 2.0 use one another.

Consider two examples. First, Donald Trump wants to deport undocumented migrants, but no one is more zealously invested in that nefarious project than Stephen Miller, Trump's deputy chief of staff. Miller cynically thinks that "we live in a world . . . that is governed by strength, that is governed by force, that is governed by power. These are the iron laws of the world since the beginning of time."[23] At its best, the American Dream rejects that cynical outlook, which Trump shares as he ramps up mass deportations in pursuit of a White America. Second, during his presidential debate with then–Vice President Kamala Harris on September 10, 2024, Trump claimed, "I have nothing to do with Project 2025. . . . I haven't read it."[24] But much of the early agenda of Trump 2.0 mirrors that nine-hundred-page plan, spearheaded by Christian nationalist Russell Vought, director of the powerful Office of Management and Budget, whose goal is to dismantle the federal government and to consolidate presidential power.[25] That project very much joins Trump and Vought at the hip.

The Millers and Voughts who serve and use Donald Trump will remain at play after the lame-duck president departs the White House. The country and the Dream can ill afford for the enablers of Trump 2.0 to retain power. Testifying to that are the events of June 12, 2025, which are emblematic of our dire straits.

23. Cameron, "Stephen Miller Asserts."
24. Contorno and Tolan, "Trump Said He Hadn't Read Project 2025."
25. See the text of Project 2025 in Dans and Groves, *Mandate for Leadership*.

On that Thursday, I felt that the United States had ceased to be a democratic republic when federal agents manhandled Alex Padilla, the senior US senator from California. Padilla was assaulted when he insisted on questioning the secretary of homeland security, Kristi Noem, about ongoing anti-immigration raids in the Los Angeles area.[26] Trump's promise to "stop the invasion of illegals into our country"[27] had grown worse in late May, when Stephen Miller ordered ICE to meet a daily quota of three thousand arrests and to "just go out there and arrest illegal aliens."[28]

Turning cruelty into cash, Miller stands to reap a financial bonanza from this policy, owing to his large investment in the data analytics company Palantir, which has a no-bid $30 million contract from Trump 2.0 to develop an information system that would allow ICE to target and surveil migrants in real time.[29] Meanwhile, the result of Miller's draconian policy was detention of day laborers, garment district employees, and agricultural workers in the Los Angeles area, many of them tax-paying, legal residents who had been in the country for years. Protests ensued. Against the wishes of California's elected leaders, the Trump administration sent federalized National Guard units and even the US Marines to Los Angeles.[30] Trump 2.0 may be weaponizing immigration policy to establish a police state and a dictatorship that especially purges people who are poor and Spanish-speaking.[31]

Bringing US military force to bear on American citizens in this way had never happened before in the country's almost-250-year history, but none of these police-state policies will be temporary unless and until "We the People" resist and quash them. Trump 2.0 relished the confrontation and the humiliation of Senator Padilla, who is the brown-skinned son of Mexican immigrants. Trump 2.0 proceeded undaunted. Two days later, a dictator-worthy military parade rolled through Washington, DC, on Trump's seventy-ninth birthday.

On that same day, June 14, in Los Angeles, unidentified, masked ICE thugs viciously beat and detained Narciso Barranco, an undocumented landscaper who has lived in the United States for thirty years, has no criminal record, and is the father of three US Marines. One of them, Alejandro

26. Hubler et al., "Calif. Senator Forcibly Removed."

27. Trump, "PROMISES MADE, PROMISES KEPT."

28. Findell et al., "White House Marching Orders."

29. Psaki, "Architect."

30. For documentation and details on these matters, see Trump, "PROMISES MADE, PROMISES KEPT"; and Fiallo, "Stephen Miller Explicitly Ordered."

31. Zagano, "Immigration Policy."

Barranco, said of the assault on his father, "It's hard for us. We feel hurt, we feel betrayed."[32]

Despotism flexes its muscle by demonizing people and by bringing military force to bear on its own people to quell opposition and cow people into obedience. The wanton attacks on Senator Padilla and Narciso Barranco, augmented by the Washington parade, showed that autocracy had arrived in the United States, despite nearly two thousand protests and rallies across the country on that fateful Saturday, which was dubbed "No Kings Day."

Trump's irrational but dangerous tyranny continues unabated. He disliked the weak job creation statistics reported on August 1, 2025, by Erika McEntarfer, the impeccable, Senate-confirmed head of the Bureau of Labor Statistics (BLS).[33] Underscoring his disdain for facts and truth and undermining economic confidence at home and abroad, Trump fired her. His nominee to succeed McEntarfer was E. J. Antoni, chief economist at the conservative Heritage Foundation.[34] A contributor to Project 2025, Antoni, a young economist with modest qualifications and known for distorting data to support partisan views, would have done Trump's bidding, but the resounding outcry against Antoni forced Trump to pull the nomination on September 30.

On August 11, 2025, the day before announcing Antoni's nomination, Trump took a far more drastic decision when his executive order declared a crime emergency in the District of Columbia.[35] Trump placed the District's police under federal control and put National Guard boots on the ground as well. Fabricating a crisis and rescue from it, a familiar scheme, Trump's authoritarian overreach is as chilling as it is inept. More American cities, especially those led by Democrats, are likely to join Los Angeles and Washington, DC, in facing Trump decrees that bring military power to bear on American civilians. The political analysts Peter Wehner and Robert P. Beschel Jr. are correct when they emphasize that "Trump is smashing up things on a scale that is almost unimaginable, and he seems completely untroubled by the daily hardships and widespread suffering he is leaving behind." It should be hoped that they are also correct when they add that "a little more than half a year into Trump's second term, the public's confidence in his skill as a chief executive is shattering."[36]

32. Sottile, "Marine Corps Veteran."

33. Casselman, "Trump Fired America's Economic Data Collector."

34. Casselman et al., "Trump's Pick."

35. Trump, Exec. Order No. 14333 (2025).

36. Wehner and Beschel, "Trump's Unforgivable Sin."

Elections in 2026 and 2028—as well as concerns about the affordability of day-to-day living, including health care, and resistance against Trump's hostility to democracy—could slow and derail the descent into dictatorship, but that hope assumes the elections will be free and fair. That assumption may not withstand the assaults of Trump 2.0, which could include the declaration of an election-crippling "national emergency" and martial law to manage it. In such circumstances, resistance to defend and protect the Constitution of the United States is as important as it has ever been.

Saving Dreams

Saving the American Dream is indispensable for the necessary resistance. But what is the American Dream? What are its saving strengths? Those questions are definitive and decisive because the American Dream is an idea and an ideal. The *Merriam-Webster* dictionary defines the Dream as "an American social ideal that stresses egalitarianism and especially material prosperity,"[37] and as "a happy way of living that is thought of by many Americans as something that can be achieved by anyone in the U.S. especially by working hard and becoming successful."[38] *The Oxford English Dictionary* identifies the Dream as "the ideal that every citizen of the United States should have an equal opportunity to achieve success and prosperity through hard work, determination, and initiative."[39]

Such definitions omit more than they admit. They downplay that the American Dream comprises a variety of ideas and ideals. Sometimes they fit together; sometimes they collide and clash. Always they are drenched in history, which gives the American Dream a history too. That history includes popular culture. Some recollections and artifacts illustrate the Dream's shifting complexity.

If you look for "the American Dream," that phrase appears anywhere, everywhere, and all the time. Some years ago, for instance, I was in a Japanese bar atop one of Tokyo's largest hotels. Potent with Kentucky bourbon, the featured drink that evening was called the American Dream. My home's freezer once contained American Dream ice cream. It could be purchased in nine flavors—none of them laced with Kentucky bourbon. It was healthier

37. *Merriam-Webster*, s.v. "American dream" (*n.*), https://www.merriam-webster.com/dictionary/American%20dream.

38. *Merriam-Webster*, s.v. "the American dream" (*n.*), https://www.merriam-webster.com/dictionary/the%20American%20dream.

39. *Oxford English Dictionary*, s.v. "American dream (*n.*)," https://www.oed.com/dictionary/american-dream_n?tab=meaning_and_use#5337887100 (dead link).

than the drink at the Tokyo hotel: The ice cream promotion claimed that "Dreams Do Come True!" because this ice cream—if it could be called that—was 99 percent fat-free.

Why would a potent alcoholic drink and fat-free ice cream get linked with the American Dream? That question points toward more food for thought. The American Dream Kitchen in Pittsburgh, Pennsylvania, delivers lots of mac and cheese, southern dishes, and pie (especially sweet potato and apple). Meanwhile, a grocery store chain in Southern California designed its paper bags with an anniversary proclamation that said, "Celebrating 50 Years of the American Dream." Nostalgia trips and anniversary celebrations, particularly one involving a grocery bag that can be empty as well as full—could such cultural notes say something more significant about Americans and their dreams than first meets the eye or than dictionary definitions grasp?

Consider some other items from my American Dream collection. Popular music produced many of them. Bruce Springsteen's classic "Born to Run" notes "a runaway American Dream." Jackson Browne's "For America" recalls the nation's "shining dream" as the song calls for waking "her up this time." For Crosby, Stills, Nash, and Young, one song was not enough. They produced a 1988 album called *American Dream*. Its title track repeats the chorus: "American Dream, American Dream. Don't know where things went wrong. Might have been when you were young and strong." Tracy Chapman echoed that sentiment in "Across the Lines," which bemoans race riots that "kill the Dream of America." The Oak Ridge Boys were more upbeat. The jacket notes for their 1989 *American Dream* album expressed gratitude to "a country where if you follow your dreams and work hard, the opportunities to succeed in life are there for you, no matter who you are." Their rendition of "The American Dream" starts back in 1952 when "you could take a walk downtown without being afraid." The song acknowledged "trouble on the other side of town," because everybody wants their share of the American Dream. But then the chorus urges optimistically, "Dream on, children, dream on. Don't let anybody tell you the Dream is gone."

Adding to the array of themes sounded in popular music, book titles often include "the American Dream." To name just a few examples, those titles include *Pursuing the American Dream*, *Cashing in on the American Dream*, *Waking Up Screaming from the American Dream*, and *Requiem for the American Dream*. The largest print size in which I have ever seen "The American Dream" was provided by the *Wall Street Journal* in 1985 when that newspaper contended "If the American Dream Has a Diary, This Is It."

During the 1980s, Prudential-Bache Securities proclaimed that "the American Dream can happen for you." Just let them plan and handle your finances, their gold-paper advertising advised. A decade on, their investors were defrauded of close to $8 billion. About the same time, a *Newsweek* cover juxtaposed American Dream/American Nightmare, alluding to the gap between an idealized vision and lived experience and to the fact that some versions of the Dream feed American carnage and vice versa. Forty years later, multiple lawsuits ensnared the American Dream megamall in New Jersey, whose DreamWorks Water Park, billed as the largest indoor water park in North America, was forced to close for several days in February 2025 when its centerpiece, a decorative helicopter, crashed down, injured four people, and cost the mall more than $20 million.[40]

Advertisements, foods, places, songs, books, newspapers, to say nothing of political speeches that invoke the American Dream almost as often as "God bless America"—all these cultural expressions use "the American Dream" in ways that should make us wonder why and think about the diverse meanings and enticements that are at play. But no item in my American Dream artifact collection is more intriguing in that way than *The American Dream Game.*

The American Dream as a game—that is an idea worth pondering, although Milton-Bradley's 1979 version is dated in more ways than one. The board game's goal, for example, is too modest. Becoming a millionaire would not be sufficient to win *The American Dream Game* today. Becoming a technocratic billionaire would be more like it. To get there, a different game board would be needed as well. The old game's strategies of investing in American Express, United States Steel, Ford Motor Company, and Kentucky Fried Chicken would not be an adequate portfolio. Amazon, Meta, Nvidia, Palantir, and a variety of cryptocurrencies would need to be in the mix, along with ample opportunities for corruption and grift.

The world has changed immensely since *The American Dream Game* appeared. In 1979, for example, Americans could scarcely imagine that a deceptive New York real estate dealer named Donald Trump would lie and cheat his way to a pernicious and destructive victory in the American Dream Game by becoming president and wannabe dictator of the United States.

As its accompanying "Success Book" claimed back in the day, *The American Dream Game* saluted "our American Free Enterprise System which affords us all the opportunity." Apparently, however, the salute was received less well than Milton-Bradley hoped. Almost as soon as it appeared, the game disappeared from the market. I own one of the few surviving copies. If a better fate lies in store for the American economy, which is so important to the Dream, Americans in the mid-2020s have plenty of reasons to be

40. Attrino, "American Dream Says Decorative Helicopter Crash."

concerned because Trump and his tariff terror may mean that players "lose their next turn," which is what happens in *The American Dream Game* when a roll of the dice makes you land on squares marked Worry, Doubt, or Fear.

One more item from my American Dream collection seems especially important during the anti-immigrant times of Trump 2.0. It is a photograph that my wife, Lyn, an elementary school teacher at the time, took for me. One day in the 1990s, a student of hers, a six-year-old boy, came to class in a new jacket. Shiny white, it had the word "Corvette" emblazoned across the front. On the left sleeve, just below two checkered racing flags signifying victory, were the words "American Dream." Obviously proud of his handsome jacket, the boy in the picture is smiling. He is the son of Vietnamese refugees.

A new white jacket, an American sportscar, checkered victory flags, a refugee-immigrant family, a smiling child—the American Dream. What has happened to the immigrant friendly American Dream that encouraged the child's parents to enter the United States? What has happened to that boy, who would be fortysomething today? Does he have American Dream aspirations? Is a Corvette among them? Does he vote in American elections? Is he for, against, or indifferent to Donald Trump and his deportation of undocumented immigrants?

My American Dream artifacts are full of penetrating, insistent questions. Furthermore, if you watch for more examples of the sort I have been sharing, you will likely find what my illustrations indicate: namely, that few terms are used more ambiguously and teasingly, few terms are bandied about more loosely—defined or undefined in so many ways—than "the American Dream."

To some people, the term is part of an ideology that snares and deludes, deceptively tantalizing the have-nots with hope while legitimating the haves with self-congratulation for their diligent, self-reliant initiative. On this view, the Dream, riddled with irony, becomes, if not a joke, an object of criticism, satire, derision, or contempt as a made-in-America label for a congeries of chauvinistic cliches mouthed by jingoists like the orator in a 1926 poem by E. E. Cummings: "next to of course god america i / love you land of the pilgrims and so forth."[41] To others, the American Dream merely signifies self-determined success, wealth, consumption of "the latest things," and acquisition of power. To still others, the American Dream at its best denotes a distinctive set of social and moral ideals, something profound and good, something deserving more than ironic criticism, let alone equation with material pursuits and power-seeking achievements. No doubt the concept of the American Dream invites all those meanings, but rather than

41. Cummings, "'next to of course god america i.'"

being indifferent to their unavoidable clashes and collisions, it is crucial to drive inquiry deeper, to be warned that the American Dream at its best is especially under assault and severely endangered during the dark times of Trump 2.0.

In the context of the American Dream at its best, dreams are aspirational. They indicate what we are for and what we can be. Saving dreams—aspirations that deserve saving because they can save our country—are much needed today. As my American Dream artifacts from popular culture indicate, the Dream is not a static concept, a one-size-fits-all-times-and-places idea. So, the question is not only "What is the American Dream?" which keeps attention focused on what is importantly constant about it. The question is also "What should be our version of the American Dream today?"

Dynamic and Potent

Evolving in difference-making ways, the American Dream is dynamic and potent. No scholar has done more to help unearth that story than the historian Sarah Churchwell, whose discerning book *Behold, America* provides what she calls "a genealogy"—an account of the origin and historical development—of the American Dream.[42] Published midway through Donald Trump's first presidential term, the book compares and contrasts the American Dream—Trump often called it dead—to the slogan "America First." Trump favors the latter theme, whose historical development parallels but opposes the American Dream. Churchwell's key points inform mine. Here are six clusters of them.

1. The American Dream would not exist without its founding forerunners, the Declaration of Independence and the Constitution of the United States. The phrases "American Dream" and "the American Dream" are not found in either of those essential eighteenth-century documents. Indeed, until about a century ago, those terms only appeared sporadically.
2. Early uses emphasized justice and equality, often criticizing overemphasis on individual aspiration and personal success, especially when those aims were pursued in ways that overrode the well-being and rights of other Americans. Often, says Churchwell, these phrases—"American Dream" and "the American Dream"—denoted "not the

42. Churchwell, *Behold, America*, 5. See also Churchwell, "Brief History." Additional useful studies of the American Dream include Delbanco, *Real American Dream*; Cullen, *American Dream*; Samuel, *American Dream*; Putnam, *Our Kids*; Leonhart, *Ours Was the Shining Future*; and Hauhart and Sardoč, *Handbook on the American Dream*.

accumulation of riches, but the risk posed to ideals of justice and equality by such accumulation."[43]

3. One reason for the growing use of "the American Dream" was that the term's meanings were not static. As the country moved beyond World War I and into the 1920s, the content of "the American Dream" gravitated toward individual liberty, personal success, and accumulation of wealth and power.

4. The Great Depression called the individualistic and materialistic interpretations of the Dream into question. When the historian James Truslow Adams published *The Epic of America* in October 1931, his bestseller made "the American Dream" ubiquitous in American culture. Adams called Americans to recover and update the Dream's earlier emphasis on justice and equality, but he recognized that the struggle for dominance—or at least the best mixture—between the Dream's idealistic emphasis on equality and social justice and its focus on material personal success rooted in money-making and power-building would be ongoing and decisive for the nation's future.

5. Franklin D. Roosevelt delivered his 1941 State of the Union address on January 6, eleven months before the Japanese attack on Pearl Harbor plunged the United States into World War II. The "Four Freedoms Speech," as it came to be known, emphasized freedom of speech and expression, freedom for all persons to worship in their own way, freedom from want, and freedom from fear. In a postwar 1947 speech, Harry S. Truman retained Roosevelt's emphasis on freedom of speech and religion, but substituted "freedom of enterprise" for freedom from want and fear. The changed emphasis epitomized the retooling of the postwar American Dream "as shiny middle-class comfort and ease, a tale of upward social mobility and infinite generational progress."[44] Eighty years on, the weakness of and lack of credibility behind this version of the Dream—it dominated for decades—becomes ever clearer amid the chaos of Trump 2.0, which unleashes fear and want in the land. The American Dream may still save us from Trump's disorder, but only if "We the People" reaffirm its anchoring in social justice, ethics, and good character.

6. Meanwhile, the slogan "America First" and its connotations have kept—and keep—affecting the American Dream, either by infiltrating or opposing it. On June 14, 2025, Donald Trump ignorantly boasted

43. Churchwell, *Behold, America*, 29.

44. Churchwell, *Behold, America*, 285.

that "I'm the one that developed 'America First,' and considering that the term wasn't used until I came along, I think I'm the one that decides [what the term means]."[45] In fact, the term and its meaning, Trump's included, have long been at play concurrently with the American Dream. Historically, America First policy has been isolationist, protectionist (think tariffs), anti-immigration ("100 percent American" is one of its slogans), and racist. Although Trump's June 2025 bombing of Iran is anything but isolationist, the America First profile nevertheless fits Trump to a T. Advocates of America First want to equate that outlook with the American Dream, but such nationalism contradicts the American Dream's emphases on justice, equality, and liberty, which have usually been understood to entail international cooperation, advancing human rights in the world, and free trade.

A Complex Fate

On February 4, 1872, a century and a half before the United States tipped into autocracy, the masterful novelist Henry James wrote a letter to his friend Charles Eliot Norton. The letter is remembered for this shrewd observation: "It's a complex fate, being an American." Often cited, James's appraisal is echoed in "We Americans," the 2019 popular song by the North Carolina folk-rock Avett Brothers.[46] It portrays Americans as children of Uncle Sam, a stern personification of the United States who has often appeared on military recruitment posters saying "I Want You."

Not so fast, the Avett Brothers resist. The American story is complicated and scarcely easy to read. Illustrating that fact, the dour visage of Uncle Sam has been co-opted by Trump 2.0. Updated for Trump's America, the 1940s Army recruitment poster now urges Americans to become deportation agents. Working for ICE, which received nearly $30 billion in July 2025 to bolster its ranks, Uncle Sam has a new tagline in Trump 2.0: "America has been invaded by criminals and predators. We need YOU to get them out."[47]

My country is scarred by greed and violence, disfigured by xenophobia and misogyny, haunted by racism and genocide against Indigenous peoples. Nothing can turn the clock back or completely atone for those sins. And yet the United States contains possibility and hope, commitment and promise that may yet create what the Constitution calls "a more perfect Union," one that moves toward pluralism and inclusiveness, stronger respect for persons

45. Scherer, "Trump Says He Decides."
46. Avett, and Avett Brothers, "We Americans."
47. Villagran, "Over 40 and Eager to Join ICE?"

and human rights, better liberty, sounder democracy, and firmer justice. Pulled and tugged between the right and wrong, the good and evil of my country's history, I am challenged by unresolvable moral tension, but I stand by my country because it can be better. Such critical hope informs my commitment to the American Dream.

Understanding the fate of being an American requires struggling with right and wrong, good and evil. I feel the tug and pull of the complex fate that is mine because I am an American Christian philosopher who has studied and written and taught about the Holocaust—Nazi Germany's genocide against the European Jews—for more than fifty years. The Holocaust and the American Dream collide and clash. That conflict governs my philosophical work. It concentrates on ethics, which emphasizes careful deliberation about the difference between right and wrong, encouragement not to be indifferent toward that difference, cultivation of virtuous character, and action that defends what is right and resists what is wrong. The Holocaust was wrong, or nothing could be. It is the antithesis of the American Dream, which, at its best, advances and defends democracy, inclusive human rights, and equal justice under the law and rejects and resists antisemitism, racism, and antidemocratic authoritarianism. Dedication to the Dream underscores why every condition that led to the Holocaust should be resisted. In turn, the Holocaust provides a lens that sharpens insight about the Dream's importance.

For longer than I have studied the Holocaust, I have taught and written about the American Dream.[48] Often ambiguous and problematic but also principled and insistent, that concept especially riveted my attention in 1973, when a Fulbright fellowship took me to the University of Innsbruck, Austria. The Fulbright Program has long been the flagship international educational exchange program sponsored by the US government, but attacks against it by Trump 2.0 mindlessly jeopardize its future. Back in the day, my Fulbright responsibilities included teaching Austrian students about American philosophy, literature, and religion. The American Dream became the organizing theme for my lectures.

Now in my eighties, having lived a personal version of the American Dream that I value and treasure, I keep trying—like the Avett Brothers—to do the best I can to grasp what it means, what it ought to mean, to be a citizen of the United States, especially after Donald Trump's election to a second presidential term on November 5, 2024. I may not live long enough

48. My publications about the American Dream include Sontag and Roth, *American Religious Experience*; Roth, *American Dreams*; Fossum and Roth, *American Dream*; Fossum and Roth, *American Ground*; Roth, *American Dream*; Roth, *Private Needs, Public Selves*; Roth, *Holocaust Politics*; and Grob and Roth, *Warnings*.

on American ground to see my country rid of Trump, but I intend to try. The roots of that determination go far back to my Christian forebears—Scots-Irish Quakers and German Pietist pacifists from Alsace-Lorraine who immigrated across the Atlantic to the United States in the mid-nineteenth century.[49] Like so many Americans, I am an immigrant child.

I was born in Grand Haven, Michigan on September 3, 1940. My father, Josiah, was a Presbyterian minister. My mother, Doris, and older sister, Muriel, were accomplished musicians. On my birthday, a Tuesday, the *New York Times* headlined two events. First, large formations of Nazi planes continued to bomb England as air-raid sirens wailed in London during the Blitz, the Battle of Britain. By that time in 1940, Nazi Germany occupied most of the western European continent, and Adolf Hitler aimed to conquer the United Kingdom as well. The United States helped British resistance to the Nazi onslaught but did not enter the war completely until the Japanese attacked Pearl Harbor on December 7, 1941.

The second story the *Times* featured on September 3, 1940, focused on the speech that President Franklin D. Roosevelt delivered the day before at the Labor Day dedication of the Great Smoky Mountains National Park.[50] Speaking at Newfound Gap, the mountain boundary between Tennessee and North Carolina, FDR called for national unity against Nazism, which had mounted, he said, "the greatest attack that has ever been launched against freedom of the individual." He also warned about an "enemy at home." He condemned "the mean and petty spirit that mocks at ideals, sneers at sacrifice and pretends that the American people can live by bread alone." Defense of democracy was on Roosevelt's mind as his speech echoed the oath that all Americans need to take and fulfill: namely, to "support and defend the Constitution of the United States against all enemies, foreign and domestic."

Born in the late Michigan summer of 1940, I have few firsthand recollections of World War II and none of the Holocaust. I can remember the ration books that my musical mother needed to buy sugar and shoes. My father grew vegetables in a "victory garden." I recall that the family car had a windshield sticker required for regulated gasoline purchases. My mind's eye retains dim visions of strangely clothed men working in the countryside. My father told me they were German prisoners of war. A radio broadcast in August 1945 stands out because my parents listened to it so intently. It announced the August 6 dropping of an atomic bomb on Hiroshima, Japan.

At the age of five, I knew no living Jews, but biblical people—Abraham and Moses, Rachel and Ruth, David and Jonathan, Joseph and Mary, Jesus

49. My biographical sketch is drawn from Grob and Roth, *Warnings*, 25–27.

50. Roosevelt, Address at Dedication.

and his followers—were vivid in the stories my parents read to me each wartime night before I fell asleep. I knew about the Ten Commandments and the idea that we should love our neighbors as ourselves long before I had heard of Treblinka or Auschwitz, crimes against humanity and genocide. Those biblical narratives—the people and teachings they contain—made deep and lasting impressions upon me.

Educated in good public schools in Michigan, Indiana, and California, I graduated from Pomona College in 1962, and then spent a year at Yale Divinity School, where I considered following in my father's footsteps by entering the ministry. But instead, my complex American fate led me into an academic career in philosophy, and after taking my PhD in that discipline at Yale University in 1966, I taught at Claremont McKenna College (CMC) for more than forty years.

When I was a young professor, my philosophical work was deeply influenced by American thinkers such as Josiah Royce, John Dewey, and especially William James, the elder brother of Henry James, whose lifelong conviction held that "philosophical study means the habit of always seeing an alternative, of not taking the usual for granted, of making conventionalities fluid again, of imagining foreign states of mind."[51] I share that outlook. Its insight serves democracy; its challenges keep me going.

After my 1972–73 Fulbright year at the University of Innsbruck, those challenges led me to teach an annual CMC course called Perspectives on the American Dream. Black voices nudged me in that work, especially what I heard in the poetry of Langston Hughes, who sounded themes Americans always need to hear and heed. In his 1951 *Montage of a Dream Deferred*, for example, Hughes used jazz rhythms and blues moods to resound his insistent, rebellious question, "What happens to a dream deferred?"[52] That question is as timely in the late 2020s as it was in the early 1950s. Hughes keeps inspiring me to resist Trump's assaults on the ideas and ideals that ought to guide American hearts and minds.

Postconstitutional Times?

With two-thirds of its people feeling that the United States was headed in the wrong direction, Americans—motivated by anger, fear, grievance, and insistence on lower prices no matter the cost—went to the polls on November 5, 2024. Less than a majority of a deeply divided "We the People" elected the despotic, Supreme Court–immunized Donald Trump—twice

51. James, "Teaching."
52. Hughes, "Harlem."

-impeached, liable for sexual abuse, convicted of multiple felonies, and indicted for more—whose aging, misogynistic, criminal face is reflected when the American people look in the mirror. Too many Americans are not better than that. The astute political analyst Trygve Olson put the point sharply:

> Trump isn't a fluke. He's not some weird one-off or a break from our political tradition. He's a mirror. He reflects something deeper—a shift in our culture, our institutions, our attention spans, and our tolerance for lies. . . . He reveals: That many Americans would trade freedom for certainty. That many institutions weren't as strong as we believed. That democracy, when left unattended, will rot from within. . . . Authoritarianism doesn't start with tanks in the street. It starts with excuses. With exceptions. With a little more power here, a little less accountability there. . . . I don't know if we win this fight. But I know how we lose it: By pretending this is normal. By wishing it away. By telling ourselves that America is different. The truth is, we are only different if we act different.[53]

Trump did not come close to winning the "mandate" he arrogantly claimed. With about 77.2 million votes in his favor, Trump received 49.9 percent of the popular vote in 2024. He won 312 votes in the Electoral College—270 votes were required for victory—thanks to 233,000 combined votes in Pennsylvania, Michigan, and Wisconsin. Absent that relative handful, Trump would have lost the election.[54] But Trump's election nonetheless calls into question whether we have a government of laws, not men. It shows "We the People" to be far less exceptional than American mythology presumes. The country's election of Donald Trump drubs the American Dream of "a more perfect Union," one grounded in the rule of law, inclusively pluralistic, and expansively democratic. Assessing the election's outcome, two people told me that "my faith in our fellow Americans is now at an all-time low," and "as a woman, right now it feels like I don't have a whole lot of power or influence."

Russell Vought is one of Donald Trump's most serious enablers. More than a henchman, this ideologue has visionary aims that are embedded in Project 2025, the tyrannical playbook that he orchestrated in Trump's service. Vought thinks that "woke," left-wing, "deep state" bureaucrats seized control of the United States in the twenty-first century, if not before, plunging the country into a "post-constitutional" crisis. According to Vought, lip service is paid to the Constitution in postconstitutional times, but the

53. Olson, "Trump Isn't an Anomaly."
54. Bump, "Trump's 2024 'Mandate.'"

threat is existential, consisting of anti-American, leftist, "globalist" forces that will destroy the nation's moral fabric unless they are stopped. The corrective—with Trump in the vanguard as "a gift of God"—must be a counter-revolutionary "radical constitutionalism." The issue, Vought insists, is not "just about winning an election to shift the see saw toward our agenda. It's about demanding that our leaders destroy this threat at every level with every tool."[55]

Even before his inauguration on January 20, 2025, Trump started to enact Vought's "radical constitutionalism," which will override the US Constitution, by nominating unqualified or disqualified loyalists to hold important offices. With the discredited Elon Musk atop the pack, at least for a time, a rogue's gallery of incompetent, corrupt Trumpists—Pete Hegseth and Kash Patel, for example; Tulsi Gabbard and Pam Bondi; Linda E. McMahon and Robert F. Kennedy Jr.—control much of American life and to no good end. They and their policies will hollow out American government and national security, encourage oligarchic kleptocracy, and take revenge on "enemies within," while rewarding billionaires with influence, tax cuts, and grifting opportunities that gut the middle class and further impoverish the poor.

The institutions and procedures of democracy are only as good as the people who create, inhabit, use, and change them. Character counts. Ethics matters. For democracy and the Dream to flourish, people must respect one another. They need to seek and tell the truth. They need to listen and learn from each other. They need to reject exclusion—racism, antisemitism, every form of supremacy—and embrace inclusive pluralism instead. They need to be courageous and just, as far as that is humanly possible.

These insights mean understanding that key conditions necessary for democracy and for the American Dream we need today cannot be codified into laws and rules, at least not completely. They depend upon, indeed they are, a culture that fosters and is informed by good habits of conduct in our personal and communal lives, by sound social norms—be honest, for example, and helpful to those in need—that are not necessarily laws but important standards that govern how people act. When such qualities grow, democracy changes for the better, and so does the American Dream. When such qualities wither, democracy changes for the worse, and the Dream is eclipsed by nightmares. Advancing democracy and the Dream takes determination because they are never fixed and secure. The American Dream, inseparable from democracy, does not exist apart from change, but how it

55. Zimmer, "Meet the Ideologue." See also Vought, "Renewing American Purpose." For Project 2025, see Dans and Groves, *Mandate for Leadership.*

changes is the difference between its ascent or demise. We are the ones who determine how that process unfolds and where it should be going.

We are the ones—that pronoun is fraught and fickle, but in the context of the American Dream, *we* are "We the People." That American *we* includes every citizen of the United States. It confers responsibility, especially on those of voting age, to care about and look after the good of all Americans, including the affordability of living day to day. If we fail to do that in the elections of 2026 and 2028, the American Dream and our democracy could be gone.

Music Lessons

When I write about the American Dream, I like to listen to American music. Often, I turn to classical composers such as Leonard Bernstein and George Gershwin, Amy Beach and Florence Price. When I hear orchestral performances of their music, I am reminded of music lessons that American citizens need to remember and practice. Music and truth, for example, have close relations. Interpretation and varied styles of playing are key parts of musical performance, but good orchestral musicians know that they must play together, that playing in tune is crucial, that a difference exists between right and wrong when notes and phrasing are at play. Ignorance or indifference about those matters results in dissonance and chaos. Good citizenship has much in common with good musicianship.

While writing and rewriting this preamble as changing events required, I listened not only to newscasts about the darkness of "Trump time" but also to music by Aaron Copland, that well-loved American composer who died at the age of ninety in 1990. The son of Russian Jewish immigrants who fled antisemitic pogroms, Copland took musical training in France, but it was American song and story that inspired him best. His well-known *Fanfare* was for the Common Man, His *Appalachian Spring*, a hallmark of American classical music, drew from folk songs and a poignant Shaker hymn, "The Gift to Be Simple." Those tunes and words, the memories and hopes they contain, keep moving us because of Copland's distinctive ways of evoking them.

I especially love Copland's 1942 *Lincoln Portrait*. Among its rich echoes of American melodies are some of Abraham Lincoln's words. Copland's score takes many of its quotations from Lincoln's Second Annual Message to Congress, which was delivered on December 1, 1862, just a month before his Emancipation Proclamation declared freedom for all slaves in the areas still in rebellion to federal authority. Copland's *Portrait* paints Lincoln as a "quiet and melancholy man," and yet it stresses that "*this* is what Abe Lincoln said":

> The dogmas of the quiet past are inadequate to the stormy present. The occasion is piled high with difficulty, and we must rise to the occasion. As our case is new, so we must think anew, and act anew. We must disenthrall our selves, and then we shall save our country.
>
> Fellow citizens, we cannot escape history. We of this Congress and this administration, will be remembered in spite of ourselves. No personal significance, or insignificance, can spare one or another of us. The fiery trial through which we pass, will light us down, in honor or dishonor, to the latest generation. We—even we here—hold the power, and bear the responsibility. In giving freedom to the *slave*, we *assure* freedom to the *free*—honorable alike in what we give, and what we preserve, We shall nobly save, or meanly lose, the last best, hope of earth.[56]

The office I occupied at the University of Innsbruck fifty years ago contained a large picture of Abraham Lincoln. It was strange to have that face looking at me amid baroque buildings and the Tyrolean Alps. But there it was as I did my daily preparation to teach Austrian students about the American Dream. Lincoln's presence in my life—as a boy, I often visited the Indiana homestead where he came of age—still helps me to understand how fundamental freedom is in the American Dream and the constitutional democracy it defends. So much depends on how "We the People" understand freedom's meanings, opportunities, limits, and responsibilities.

Freedom requires resisting autocracy, oligarchy, kleptocracy, corruption, incompetence, stupidity, and all the other vices that threaten to dominate American life amid Trumpworld darkness. Freedom entails seeking truth, respecting one another, honoring the differences between right and wrong, justice and injustice. Saving the American Dream is about all of that challenging work. To get it done, as the Avett Brothers remind us, "We the People" have to recognize that we are more than the sum of our parts, that we must love this land of ours together, sometimes in spite of but always because of the Constitution we have ordained to "establish Justice . . . and secure the Blessings of Liberty to ourselves and our Posterity."

56. Lincoln, Second Annual Message. See also Child, "Copland's 'Lincoln Portrait.'"

1

Times and Places

As Donald Trump began his second presidential term to destroy what is good and right, just and true about the American Dream, the bestselling novel *James* captivated readers who relished Percival Everett's masterful retelling of Mark Twain's 1885 classic, *Adventures of Huckleberry Finn*. Twain's book has often been challenged and banned because it raises so many discomforting questions about American life and the racism that afflicts it. As spring arrived in 2025, *James* had not yet become a banned book, but it might achieve that distinction because Everett, like Twain, makes Americans think long and hard about where we have been, where we are now, and where we should and should not be going.[1]

A runaway slave, Jim—he is and becomes James—has clandestinely learned to read and write, a crime that imperils him. Downriver on the Illinois shore of the Mississippi, Jim meets others fleeing enslavement. When his companions learn that Jim can read and write, one of them, Young George, says he will get Jim what he needs: a pencil. Two days pass before Young George returns with a stolen pencil. "Tell your story," he says to Jim. The price for that includes the whipping, probably whipping to death, which follows when a White slaver discovers the theft and blames it on Young George. "With my pencil," Jim says later, "I wrote myself into being. . . . My name is James . . . a man who can read and write, a man who will not let his story be self-related, but self-written."[2]

1. Kaloi, "Percival Everett Explains."
2. Everett, *James*, 84–93.

Writing the Constitution

Centuries before *James* and nearly a century before its prequel *Adventures of Huckleberry Finn*, the United States Constitution, the world's longest-surviving written charter of government, was authored and signed in the hot Philadelphia summer of 1787. Not with pencil but with pen and ink, the authors wrote a country into being, its name the United States of America. Originally, the Constitution scarcely recognized the forbears of Jim/James and his family, Sadie and Lizzie, who were called "other persons." It did not contain the words *slave* or *slavery*, but about half of the fifty-five delegates who signed the Constitution owned slaves, and the document dealt with—*whitewashed* is more accurate—the nation's "original sin" in ways that still haunt American life.

The original Constitution increased the power of slaveholding states. For the purposes of representation in Congress and taxation, the document provided that a slave—who had neither rights nor citizenship—would be counted as three-fifths of a person. In addition, Congress was prohibited from outlawing the international slave trade for a period of twenty years, allowing the importation of enslaved people until 1808. Enslaved people who escaped to other states had to be returned to their owners, even if those states were free states. Still further, the original Constitution helped to maintain the institution of slavery by empowering the federal government to suppress rebellions, including slave insurrections. After the Civil War, which nearly destroyed the United States, the Thirteenth, Fourteenth, and Fifteenth Amendments to the Constitution abolished slavery, granted citizenship to all people born in the United States, and affirmed that "the right of citizens of the United States to vote shall not be denied or abridged by the United States or by any State on account of race, color, or previous condition of servitude."

Saving the American Dream requires knowing key aspects of the history and provisions of the US Constitution. So, recall next that Article I, the Constitution's longest and most detailed, establishes the legislative branch of government, entrusting Congress, which consists of a House of Representatives and a Senate, to create the laws that are "necessary and proper" to carry out the responsibilities that the Constitution confers upon it. Those responsibilities include the power to lay and collect taxes, duties, imposts, excises—tariffs included. They also entail regulating commerce, declaring war, raising and supporting armies, and establishing post offices.

The Constitution puts Congress first among the three separate but equal branches of the federal government. Led by the president of the United States, the executive branch neither legislates nor stands above the law but implements and enforces the laws enacted by Congress. Comprised of the Supreme Court and other federal courts, the judicial branch interprets what the federal laws mean, determines their constitutionality, resolves legal disputes—including whether the legislative and executive branches have overreached their authority—and ensures fair and impartial application of the law. The judicial branch is checked and balanced by presidential nomination and the Senate's confirmation of federal judges and by constitutional legislative and executive acts that can limit or even overturn judicial rulings.

In theory, this eighteenth-century political invention by the Founding Fathers of the United States of America looks neat and nifty. Congress makes the laws, the president enforces them, and the judiciary decides whether congressional or executive actions are lawful and constitutional. Put into practice, however, the symmetry produces clashes and collisions. The checks and balances rarely work more than tolerably well. Power struggles rage.

Elections Matter

Rather than bemoaning the shortcomings of this complex and often cumbersome system of government, we Americans should be astounded that it has worked as well as it has since the Constitution's ratification on June 21, 1788. We Americans, moreover, should never take for granted that our constitutional order is secure, let alone guaranteed. That is true because the American constitution requires elections, which are essential for democracy but also fraught because elections have consequences. Their procedures and outcomes can be dangerous and even destructive of the very constitutional order that enshrines them. The character of the persons elected and of those who elect them does much to determine the fate of the American Dream.

Article I provides that state legislatures have the responsibility to establish the "times, places, and manner" for the election of citizens to hold the office of senator or representative. Article II prescribes a complex and indirect process for electing the American president to a four-year term. The so-called Electoral College system provides that the votes cast for president in each state go to a certain number of electors based on its population-determined representation in Congress. Selected according to each state's policy, the total of electors presently numbers 538. Each elector casts one vote following the general election, and the candidate who gets more than half (at least 270) wins. Usually, but not always, the national popular vote for president coincides with the tally in the Electoral College. In recent American history—in 2000 and 2016—the Electoral College winners, George W.

Bush and Donald J. Trump, respectively, did not receive the most votes in the general election.

Before the mid-nineteenth century, American election days were usually in the late autumn, but the specific date to which Americans are accustomed today was not determined until Congress passed an 1845 federal law declaring that presidential elections shall be held on the Tuesday following the first Monday in November.[3] So it was that on Tuesday, November 5, 2024, more than 150 million Americans went to the polls. Warnings were abundant but not persuasive enough.[4] In the times and places of Trump 2.0, the American Dream is badly dislocated. Whether needed reorientation takes place depends mightily on elections in 2026 and 2028.

Locating the Dream

In 1971, a countercultural writer named Hunter S. Thompson published a novel called *Fear and Loathing in Las Vegas.* It details the surrealistic romp of one Dr. Duke and his attorney. Blasting through the desert in a huge Chevy convertible, they eventually find themselves somewhere on the northeast outskirts of Las Vegas. Now in a Cadillac styled the White Whale, "zooming along Paradise Road," they stop at Terry's Taco Stand, USA, to find their way. "Let me explain it to you," Dr. Duke's attorney tells the waitress. "We're looking for the American Dream, and we were told it was somewhere in this area. . . . We were sent out here from San Francisco to look for the American Dream, by a magazine, to cover it."[5]

The directions they get from the taco stand's waitress and cook, whose name is Lou, are none too clear, but it seems that in one of its manifestations, the American Dream may once have been a discotheque known as the Old Psychiatrist's Club. Following those leads, Dr. Duke and his attorney finally locate what's left of the place: "A huge slab of cracked, scorched concrete in a vacant lot full of tall weeds," writes Thompson. "The owner of a gas station across the road said the place had 'burned down about three years ago.'"

Forty years earlier, amid the Great Depression that convulsed the United States and the world, James Truslow Adams (1878–1949) had a different vision, which, unfortunately did not preclude Thompson's. In 1931, Adams, who was largely self-taught but among the most successful American historians of his generation, published a widely read study called *The Epic of America.* The book sold half a million copies and was translated into

3. For further information on this point, see Levinson, "Presidential Election Day."

4. See, for example, Grob and Roth, *Warnings.*

5. Thompson, *Fear and Loathing,* 161, 164–65, 168.

a dozen languages. His publisher nixed Adams's plan to call it *The American Dream*, but the book—written mostly while Adams lived in England—championed and popularized that concept.[6] His expansive way of defining the American Dream helps to account for its persistent appeal.

The American Dream, said Adams, connotes "a land in which life should be better and richer and fuller for every [person], with opportunity for each according to his [or her] ability or achievement. . . . It is not a dream of motor cars and high wages merely, but a dream of a social order in which each man and each woman shall be able to attain to the fullest stature of which they are innately capable, and be recognized by others for what they are, regardless of the fortuitous circumstances of birth or position."[7] Adams underscored, moreover, that apart from the Dream, the glory of America's epic would be lost.[8] Indeed, he believed that this Dream was "the greatest contribution" the United States had "as yet made to the thought and welfare of the world."[9]

Before devoting himself full-time to historical research and writing, Adams had worked on Wall Street. Affected by the stock market's risky and fickle ways, especially as the Great Depression worsened, Adams believed in financial stability and deplored the burdens of national debt. At the same time, says his biographer Allan Nevins, Adams "supported progressive social legislation at home and internationalism abroad."[10] His fidelity to the Constitution went together with worry that Americans were overly optimistic. They needed to think more deeply and better about what the Constitution calls "the Blessings of Liberty."

As definitions of broad cultural concepts go, Adams's understanding of the American Dream has much to commend it. He was on target when his understanding of the American Dream emphasized equality of opportunity, respect for others, decent living standards, and cohesive social values that transcend materialism and wealth. He also knew that his account required questioning and reflection. Adams's summation invites awareness that the contents of the American Dream are not simply identified, let alone easily reconciled or smoothly put into practice. Instead, the contents and the actions they encourage are complex and contested. How, for instance, do Americans understand the words when the Dream is defined to mean a "better and richer and fuller" life for every American? Are such words

6. See the biography by Nevins, *James Truslow Adams*, 58–72, 89–96.

7. Adams, *Epic of America*, 415.

8. Adams, *Epic of America*, 423.

9. Adams, *Epic of America*, viii.

10. Nevins, *James Truslow Adams*, 90.

credible? When the issue is about having opportunity according to one's ability or achievement, to what extent can people "make it" on their own? And what about "circumstances of birth or position"? Is *fortuitous* the most accurate term to describe them? Is America, as sometimes proclaimed, another name for opportunity, or is that idea a leftover from a bygone myth?

Adams's account helps to show that the American Dream is appealing and elusive, tantalizing and ambiguous, challenging and mystifying, promising and deceitful, hopeful and frustrating. Thanks to him, the Dream keeps recurring in American culture. Advertising, books, music, and political rhetoric all show that the American Dream remains a vibrant concept. But for some people, the idea promises so much more than American life delivers. The concept seems "full of tall weeds" if it wasn't "burned down" years ago. But the Dream persists and deserves to do so when it is at its best, when the Dream, as Adams at his best saw, is primarily about democracy, human rights, and a social order that is pluralistic and inclusive. That version of the American Dream is the one worth saving especially during the dark times of Trump 2.0.

Waste, Fraud, and Abuse

Article I of the Constitution establishes conditions that must be met before a federal law exists in the United States. A bill, a proposed law, becomes a law only after both the House of Representatives and the Senate pass it, and the legislation is either signed into law by the president or not vetoed by the President within ten days while Congress is in session. Article I also gives Congress—the House of Representatives in particular—"the power of the purse," the ability to tax and spend public money for the national government. In addition, under Article I's "necessary and proper" clause, Congress has authority to create key governmental agencies, including the Department of the Treasury, the Department of Justice, the Department of Defense, and, much more recently, the Social Security Administration and Central Intelligence Agency (CIA). A department created by law can only be dissolved by another law.

Within hours of his presidential inauguration on January 20, 2025, Donald Trump signed Executive Order (EO) 14158, one of more than twenty he issued during his first day in office. During the first one hundred days of Trump 2.0, the president signed a record-setting 143 executive orders, the number rising to more than 160 by the end of June 2025. As controversial as it was malign, EO 14158 established the Department of Government Efficiency (DOGE). Despite its full name, DOGE never was an official government department, which can be established only by an act of Congress, but under Elon Musk and his ruthless allies, it nevertheless proceeded with vicious destructiveness deceptively masked in the stated purpose of "modernizing federal technology and software to maximize governmental efficiency and productivity."[11]

The Constitution does not contain the term *executive order*. The authorization for presidential executive orders, however, is in Article II of the Constitution, which makes the president responsible for ensuring that "the laws be faithfully executed." Typically, then, an executive order directs how officials and agencies are to carry out the provisions of federal law. Presidential power to issue executive orders, however, is not above reproach. It can be abused and abusive. Executive orders cannot contradict the Constitution or exceed the president's powers. They can also be reviewed by the judiciary and can be superseded by legislation. As those qualifications suggest, controversy and litigation often accompany presidential executive orders.

One of the most famous presidential executive orders is Abraham Lincoln's Emancipation Proclamation (January 1, 1863), which freed slaves in rebelling Confederate states and allowed Black men to join the Union army. Trump's EO 14158 was a far cry from the nobility of Lincoln's action during the Civil War. Lincoln sought to save the United States. With EO 14158 as his wrecking ball, Trump's unleashing of DOGE has contributed terribly to eroding the nation's economy, endangering the people's health, and putting the security of the United States at risk.

Not the abolition of slavery but an immensely destructive civil war focused on trumped up allegations of "waste, fraud, and abuse" drove DOGE, led by the unelected oligarch Elon Musk. Born in 1971 to a wealthy family in Pretoria, South Africa, Musk migrated to Canada in 1989, with citizenship there inherited through his mother. Ten years later, in 1999, he became a US citizen. Immensely wealthy owing to his key business roles in enterprises such as Tesla, SpaceX, and xAI and to lucrative contracts from the American government, Musk became the largest donor to Trump's 2024 presidential campaign. His reward was DOGE, which gave him outsized and highly problematic influence, sometimes bordering on control, in the Trump White House. He has supported neo-Nazi causes at home and abroad. During a Fox News interview on March 27, 2025, he doubled down on his treacherous claim that Senator Mark Kelly, a decorated veteran and astronaut, is a traitor—Musk's word—because Kelly backed American

11. Trump, Exec. Order No. 14168 (2025).

support for Ukraine's struggle against Vladimir Putin and Russia's ruthless invasion of that important ally.[12]

Musk is scarcely an American patriot. Staffed by his cadre of callow "tech bros," DOGE promised repeatedly to eliminate what it contended was massive "waste, fraud, and abuse." Relentlessly attacking pre-Trump government for committing those sins, Musk and DOGE ripped their way through the human infrastructure of the federal workforce by thoughtlessly firing thousands of essential employees and cruelly wiping away funding for education, scientific research, and foreign aid, which strengthens the United States abroad and supports the economy at home. Musk, allegedly the richest man in the world, is responsible for starving the world's poorest children, and the Trump administration is fully complicit in that crime.[13] In countless yet-to-be-felt ways, DOGE has threatened the American Dream, except when it comes to the rich and powerful few who stand to enhance their corrupt gain and dubious fame through massive tax cuts that Trump will finance by huge cuts in federal spending, whipped on the backs of ordinary Americans.

Average citizens will bear the brunt of slashes such as the March 2025 cancellation of $12 billion in federal grants that were being used by states to track infectious diseases and to support mental health services and addiction treatments.[14] That example, unfortunately, is scarcely more than a drop in the bucket, at least by DOGE's fluctuating standards, which, at least for a time, projected plans to cut $2 trillion from the $6.1 trillion federal budget and to reduce the 5.1 million-person federal workforce by 75 percent.[15] The DOGE website (doge.gov) claimed that as of March 24, 2025, the agency—its tagline was "the people voted for major reform"—saved American taxpayers $130 billion. That was barely a start if the goal was trillion-dollar reductions, but Musk and his minions were not stopped for lack of trying. The Brookings Institution identified representative examples of the impact these cuts will have: devastating disruption of distribution of Social Security and veterans' benefits; increased tax evasion and decreased government revenue; declining health and increasing death; impairment of agricultural productivity and increased food insecurity; decreasing intelligence services and increasing domestic terrorism; weakening national security and greater likelihood of international conflict.[16]

12. Hansen, "Elon Musk Doubles-down."
13. Kristof, "Waste Musk Created."
14. Mandavilli et al. "Trump Administration Abruptly Cuts."
15. Schwabish, "Implications of Shrinking."
16. Kamarck, "How DOGE Cutbacks."

Waste, fraud, and abuse—Trump, Musk, and DOGE found far less than they promised because those shortcomings did not exist to the extent and degree that they wanted the American people to believe. Waste, fraud, and abuse—far from eliminating them, Trump, Musk, and DOGE are the vandals who have inflicted them on the American people and the American Dream. Musk departed DOGE in late May 2025. Although officially disbanded in late November 2025, DOGE and its actions still impoverish American life, squashing hopes of upward mobility. Before he left, Musk trashed programs that support education, which has been a key path for pursuing the American Dream. Trump lies and cheats, undermining a belief that is foundational for democracy and for the Dream, namely, that honest effort works and persistent truthfulness prevails.

Voting Rights

Trump 2.0 is a wasteful and abusive fraud because its foundation is the "Big Lie" that Trump keeps telling and his acolytes keep repeating: The 2020 election was stolen from Donald Trump. *It was not.* Joe Biden decisively and honestly defeated Trump in that election, but Trump mounted an insurrection on January 6, 2021, to overturn that result. He dispatched no federal troops or police to stop the murderous and destructive coup attempt. Trump's plot failed, but his failure intensified his anger and rage. His enduring commitment to vengeance and retribution includes hatred for the United States, which, in his view, did him wrong. His disrespect for the American Dream runs deep, revealed in his nihilistic might-makes-right outlook and his transactional means-justify-the-end mentality. Trump's "flooding the zone" with Executive Orders bears witness to that assessment, and nowhere more than EO 14248, called Preserving and Protecting the Integrity of American Elections, which Trump issued on March 25, 2025.[17]

An April 24, 2025, preliminary injunction stalled this order, but the legal challenges were ongoing in August 2025. If allowed to stand in whole or in part, this far-reaching Executive Order would severely tighten and restrict voting rights. It reflects Trump's belief that the 2020 election was stolen from him, and it expands his power. Holding that "free, fair, and honest elections unmarred by fraud, errors, or suspicion are fundamental to maintaining our constitutional Republic," but claiming that "the United States now fails to enforce basic and necessary election protections," Trump's EO endangers American democracy and undercuts the American Dream by stratagems that restrain and diminish the right to vote.

17. Trump, Exec. Order No. 14248 (2025).

The problems begin with the fact that Article I of the Constitution specifies that only states and Congress can make or change the "time, place, and manner" of holding federal elections. The president has no such power. The order implies that fraud is widespread in American elections. Credible evidence does not support that claim.[18] In fact, reliable studies of American elections indicate that inaccuracies, let alone fraud, are minimal, and state and federal laws already make it illegal for unqualified persons to vote. Trump's EO is a classic case of fraud, waste, and abuse because it is a "solution" in search of a problem. Furthermore, the EO would disenfranchise millions of American citizens, mostly from minority and economically stressed groups, because it requires in-person proof of citizenship, with a valid US passport all but necessary to provide it, even though fewer than half of Americans possess one. The order also seeks to prevent states from accepting mail-in ballots after Election Day. Still further, states that fail to comply with the Executive Order will be subject to cuts in funding from federal agencies. The endgame is to shrink the electorate, make it Whiter and more MAGA, and to hang on to power in 2026, 2028, and beyond, including paving the way for Trump to hold lifetime control.

The right to vote anchors the American Dream. That right was strengthened by the 1965 Voting Rights Act, which President Lyndon Johnson spearheaded. Enacted on August 6, 1965, the Act responded to the brutal "Bloody Sunday" attack by White police against Black civil rights protestors, including the legendary John Lewis, at the Edmund Pettis Bridge in Selma, Alabama, on March 7, 1965. Buttressing the Fifteenth Amendment, ratified ninety-five years earlier, in 1870, the Voting Rights Act outlawed discrimination that had denied or abridged the right to vote, especially for Black Americans. By the end of 1965, some 250,000 new Black voters had been registered. Especially in the American south, states were put on notice that they could no longer impede the franchise of Black voters by imposing poll taxes, literacy tests, and other pernicious bureaucratic obstacles. By the end of 1966, only four out of thirteen southern states had fewer than 50 percent of Black Americans registered to vote.

Although the Voting Rights Act was reaffirmed in the 1970s and 1980s, it has been undermined by court rulings. The most egregious ruling of that kind took place on June 25, 2013, in the Supreme Court's 5–4 decision in *Shelby County v. Holder*.[19] Current conservative justices John G. Roberts Jr., Clarence Thomas, and Samuel Alito were in the majority. It struck down the requirement that certain jurisdictions with a history of discrimination

18. See, for example, Lopez, "Voter Fraud Is Very Rare."

19. United States Supreme Court, *Shelby County v. Holder* (2013).

must submit proposed changes to voting procedures to the US Department of Justice or a federal district court in the District of Columbia to ensure the changes would not harm minority voters. Restrictions on voting rights, especially in what became stronghold states for Trump, followed soon thereafter. Trump's EO 14248 extends the injustice of the Supreme Court's decision, laying waste to the American Dream in the process.

War Powers

On June 18, 2025, the reliable journalist John Harwood published a widely noted essay called "Trump Is Objectively Bad for America. Why Won't More Journalists Say So?"[20] Scrutinizing Trump through an ethical lens, Harwood based his judgment on fact. Trump violates the rule of law, enriches himself through corrupt transactions, destabilizes the economy with chaotic tariffs, disrespects democracy, and weakens the nation's security and reputation in the world.

Three days later, Harwood's appraisal was tested and affirmed when Trump gave the nation a terse, angry announcement. "A short time ago," he said, "the US military carried out massive precision strikes on the three key nuclear facilities in the Iranian regime: Fordo, Natanz and Isfahan. . . . Tonight, I can report to the world that the strikes were a spectacular military success. Iran's key nuclear enrichment facilities have been completely and totally obliterated."[21] Trump had no way of knowing if the massive raid—audaciously called Operation Midnight Hammer—had "completely and totally obliterated" Iran's nuclear capacity. So often he makes up his own reality, arrogantly presuming that his assertions establish truth. Especially in wartime, that disposition is irresponsible and dangerous. Trump was infuriated and petulant when eminent American journalists discredited his fanciful claims, reporting that "a preliminary classified US report says the American bombing of three nuclear sites in Iran set back the country's nuclear program by only a few months."[22]

Betraying Trump's vows to be a peacemaker and unifier, making a mockery of his egotistical boasts that he deserves a Nobel Peace Prize, Trump's war on Iran demonstrated his power but also called it into question.[23] Time will tell how much damage Trump did to the United States as well as to Iran. But the costs of ordering B-2 stealth bombers to drop

20. Harwood, "Objectively Bad."

21. Trump, "US Strikes on Iran."

22. Barnes et al., "Iran's Nuclear Program."

23. Hutzler, "Trump Vowed."

fourteen 30,000-pound bunker-busting bombs on Iranian nuclear sites are unknown, partly because JD Vance's *Meet the Press* spin the next day was nonsensical: "We're not at war with Iran," the US vice president said. "We're at war with Iran's nuclear program."[24]

Vance's deception was not persuasive. The US warred with Iran, the June 21 attack unprovoked and arguably illegal. Furthermore, while nuclear facilities can be destroyed, nuclear knowledge and determination cannot. Our bombing raid, ironically, may have the unintended consequence of ensuring that Iran becomes a nuclear-armed nation in the not-too-distant future. In the shorter term, the United States remains problematically embroiled in the Middle East, a region littered with the wreckage and upheaval caused over decades by Western powers, including American interventions, that mistakenly and arrogantly thought "we know best" about what is right for that turbulent part of the world. Adding fuel to the fire, since early September 2025, Trump 2.0 has conducted more than thirty lethal, and likely illegal, strikes on small boats in or near Venezuelan waters, resulting in more than 120 deaths.[25]

Article I of the US Constitution reserves to Congress the power "to declare war." Article II designates the president to be "Commander in Chief of the Army and Navy of the United States." The contested authority and responsibility between those two constitutional provisions create a fraught gray zone of debate, dissent, and disorder.[26] Trump's assault on Iran, for instance, took us into conflict-ridden territory that is both familiar and unmapped. Back in 1973, Congress passed the War Powers Resolution. This Vietnam-era legislation aimed to balance power between the legislative and executive branches in matters of war. It specified that a president could launch military attacks only in three circumstances: a "declaration of war," a "specific statutory authorization" from Congress, or "a national emergency created by an attack upon the United States, its territories or possessions, [or] its armed forces."[27] More specifically, the action sought to prevent the president from unilaterally ensnaring the United States in prolonged conflicts. It also required the president to notify Congress within forty-eight hours of deploying troops into situations where hostilities are imminent or have already begun. But congressional resolve weakened over the ensuing years, ceding significant war powers to presidents of both parties. Ongoing

24. Lebowitz, "Vance Says."
25. Gamio et al., "Tracking U.S. Military Killings."
26. Savage, "Iran Attack Illegal?"
27. United States Congress, War Powers Resolution.

questions, including definition disputes, persist regarding presidential orders for preemptive strikes against imminent national security threats.

Days before Trump bombed Iran, a 2025 War Powers Resolution was put before Congress by bipartisan lawmakers. It directed "the President to terminate the use of United States Armed Forces from hostilities against the Islamic Republic of Iran or any part of its government or military, unless explicitly authorized by a declaration of war or specific authorization for use of military force against Iran."[28] That step did not work. Trump's war hand is not likely to be stayed, leaving the country to contend with more of his despotism. Meanwhile, Trump's bombing of Iran or of alleged drug-smuggling boats off the coast of Venezuela has done nothing to save the American Dream. On the contrary, saving the American Dream entails resisting Trump's war powers.

Elizabeth Powel's Question

What is the Dream in the times and places of our Donald Trump–scorched American ground? Democracy and the rule of law are endangered in the United States. Authoritarianism dismantles governmental guardrails and moral constraints. Orwellian bans erase words. Freedom of speech can no longer be taken for granted. Evidence and truth are disrespected. Colleges and universities are besieged. Where and how is the American Dream to be found amid that great depression? Reflection on the nation's founding helps to provide perspective.

No one did more than Benjamin Franklin to give birth to the United States of America and its democracy. Diplomat, scientist, inventor, philosopher, humanitarian, slaveholder-turned-abolitionist, prolific and brilliant writer (his papers fill more than forty volumes), and ever the astute politician, Franklin traveled far and wide, knew the American colonies better than anyone, and envisioned what they could become if they united. He helped Thomas Jefferson write the Declaration of Independence, secured French funding and military support essential for liberation from the British, and presided over the 1787 constitutional convention in Philadelphia. His life contained shortcomings and contradictions, but he kept trying to honor his conviction that a person's highest calling is to do what is good and right.

In his eighties when he signed the US Constitution, Franklin had experienced personal vicissitudes and social upheavals before the nation was born. Stories about him abound. None is more significant for his legacy and

28. United States House of Representatives, Directing the President pursuant to section 5(c) of the War Powers Resolution.

our current situation than the report about an exchange he had with Elizabeth Willing Powel, an influential Philadelphian, shortly after the delegates to the 1787 convention had voted in favor of Franklin's motion to accept the Constitution. "What have we got," Powel asked Franklin, "a republic or a monarchy?" In words as circumspect as they were pithy and hopeful, Franklin not-so-simply said: "A republic, if you can keep it."[29]

A resolution adopted by the American Continental Congress on June 14, 1777, specified that the United States should have a flag. Its thirteen stars and stripes represented the uniting colonies. The flag still symbolizes national unity. But on January 6, 2021, it was desecrated when poles flying the Stars and Stripes were used to bludgeon police who stood against the violent, flag-waving American mob urged on by Donald Trump to storm the US Capitol and to obstruct the certification of Joe Biden's fair and free election as president. Most Americans, including members of that mob and perhaps even Donald Trump himself, know by heart the words of the Pledge of Allegiance that Americans often recite together: "I pledge allegiance to the flag of the United States of America and to the Republic for which it stands, one nation under God, indivisible, with liberty and justice for all." The January 6 insurrection, including Trump and his seditious followers who planned and unleashed it, disrespected those words and broke their promise.

According to the pledge, the country we Americans inhabit together has a flag that stands for a *republic*. Most Americans know something about the Republican Party, but it would be difficult even for most Republicans to specify what the word *republic* means. In fact, if the Pledge of Allegiance disappeared, most of us Americans would not have *republic* in our vocabularies. Even when the word is pronounced in that context, *republic* remains one of those words that gets recited thoughtlessly. American democracy flails because having a *republic* does not mean enough to us nowadays. But there are certain words that we need to hear, care about, and look after. *Republic* is one of them.

In American political history, as Benjamin Franklin understood and shows, the term *republic* refers primarily to a form of government. Such usage is embedded in the Constitution itself, whose Fourth Article guarantees "to every State in the Union a Republican Form of Government." That form places a premium on ingredients such as (1) a government of laws, not rulers, to secure liberty and justice; (2) the sovereignty of a people who are free and by whose consent government derives its power; (3) representative democracy; (4) defense of fair and free elections; (5) peaceful transfer of

29. For further information about Powel and the importance of women in the American founding, see Anishanslin, "What We Get Wrong."

power; and (6) a mixed political structure that checks and balances legislative, executive, and judicial authority.

Those elements stress process. They map *how* a republic should work. Granted, such forms are more than the means to an end, for these elements are to some extent ends in themselves. But only to some extent if they are taken by themselves, for American history also draws deeply on traditions that add other key elements to the formal republican vision. Two of those elements are especially important.

To discern them, recall that the word *republic* derives from the Latin *res publica*, meaning "the public thing." By themselves neither the Latin phrase nor its English translation clarifies much, but both do point in key directions: first, "the public" and second, "the thing" that is public.

In Latin, *publica*, from which we derive *public*, means "of the people." It does not refer to generic, unidentified people but to *the* people. *Particularity, identity, unity*—terms such as these help to specify the meaning. Each individual belongs to "the people." In republican tradition, moreover, the people *inhabit* a place. Inhabitation means that they do more than live there. The people establish a way of life in the territory of their dwelling. Their practices bestow history and tradition. But the relationship goes the other way as well. The place inhabits the people. Its horizons define what is possible and what is not, what is permitted and what is not. Membership in "the people," participation in its traditions, and recognition of its shared memories, values, and hopes entail responsibilities as well as privileges.

At least on American soil, a republican people is one whose inhabitation commits them to value and practice government by law, popular sovereignty, representative democracy, and the separation of governmental powers. But political philosophers, including Benjamin Franklin and other founders of the United States, have always added a fundamental warning: A republican way of life depends immensely on the *virtue* of the people. Self-discipline, compassion, responsibility, friendship, work, courage, perseverance, honesty, loyalty, and faith—those virtues are ones that Americans need to recover and revive. Paul's New Testament letter to the Philippians (4:8) points in that direction when he says, "Whatever is true, whatever is honorable, whatever is right, whatever is pure, whatever is lovely, whatever is of good repute, if there is any excellence and anything worthy of praise, let your mind dwell on these things." If Americans do so, divisiveness can be reduced, and chasms between red and blue America can be bridged. Democracy will be stronger and better. It will be treasured as a blessing. If Americans come together and make that happen, those who have died to defend the Constitution will be honored as they deserve. The American

Dream will survive. Its survival, in turn, can help to save our country, even from abused war powers.

James's Pencil

The action in Percival Everett's novel *James* takes place in 1861, the year the American Civil War began. At the end of the story, James and his family, Sadie and Lizzie, have made their way to Iowa, a free state. The story ends. The future of James, Sadie, and Lizzie remains in suspense. It is not known whether any of them ever got to vote in a fair and free election. But if James's treasured pencil had anything to do with it, perhaps they did. Or at least James might have written about the struggle to do so.

Words matter. Elizabeth Powel's question and Benjamin Franklin's answer prove it. So do Everett's novel and James's pencil. Arguably, words matter most when freedom is at risk, when democracy is at stake, when hopes and dreams, including those of the American Dream, are threatened and endangered. As Trump 2.0 undermines what is best in the American tradition, it is important to remember that those pernicious efforts feature and require the deletion and disappearance of words that are irreplaceable to keep our history from being erased and the American Dream from being "disappeared." The Trump administration fraudulently claims that it champions freedom of speech. But it seeks to chill conversation about the long history of discrimination, racism, White supremacy, inequality, and injustice, which are still inescapable elements of American life.

At its best, the American Dream resists, transforms, and, at least to some extent, overcomes those flaws that so much need mending if the United States is to keep making progress toward "a more perfect Union." But that progress cannot and will not happen if words such as *all-inclusive*, *bias*, *discrimination*, *diversity*, *hate speech*, *oppression*, *privilege*, *racial inequality*, and *social justice* are censored and eliminated from American vocabularies. Yet actions of that kind dictate how language must be used in Trump's autocratic and democracy-hostile regime. Hundreds of words, including those italicized above, have been deleted from government websites, flagged as objectionable, or removed altogether from government documents.[30] Anything having to do with diversity, equity, and inclusion (DEI) is found to be especially repugnant on the grounds that such discourse is at odds with Trumpist understandings of "merit," a term abused and wasted in current presidential pronouncements because the appointments that Trump has made, and the man himself, are so obviously mediocre and fraudulent.

30. Yourish et al., "Words Are Disappearing."

To save our country and to redeem the Dream, as many Americans as possible need to treasure, value, and use their version of James's pencil to defend what is right and true, just and good, and to act in solidarity with those who do. That company especially needs to include an electorate determined in 2026, 2028, and beyond to ensure that too-often silent or compliant representatives and senators are replaced by persons of good judgment and character, who take seriously their Article I responsibility to "provide for the common Defense and general Welfare of the United States," and who will never bend the knee to a president who attempts to cripple and deny that duty.

2

The State of the Union

Three interdependent dimensions stand out in James Truslow Adams's insight that the American Dream envisions "a land in which life should be better and richer and fuller for every [person], with opportunity for each according to his [or her] ability or achievement."[1] Absent any of them, lacking interaction and support among them, the Dream cannot be credible, its promise cannot be true, and betrayal and deception produce the American Nightmare instead.

One dimension of the American Dream emphasizes individualism, economic success, property acquisition, and wealth accumulation. If Americans cannot afford food, shelter, education, and medical care, the American Dream is a mockery. Aspirations for wealth have an understandable place in the Dream, but if they are pursued at the expense of or without regard for the well-being of all American citizens, then the American Dream is immoral.

A second dimension of the American Dream emphasizes community, shared moral values such as equality and justice for all, democracy and the rule of law, and respect for critical inquiry and pluralism that embraces diversity. If Americans are lonely and alone, discriminated against, or denied fundamental rights, if their questions and concerns are stifled or their diversity is denied or erased, then the American Dream is a snare and delusion, scarcely worthy to be touted, let alone admired.

A third dimension of the American Dream emphasizes possibility, opportunity, and especially new beginnings. The belief in new beginnings exemplifies better than any other the hopefulness—some would call it the naivety—of Americans and one of the fundamental reasons why rhetoric

1. Adams, *Epic of America*, 415.

about the Dream caught on in the United States. From their inception, American self-images reflected the idea that the past did not bind one irrevocably. Fresh starts could be made, tomorrow promised to be better than today, and progress seemed always to be possible. To speak of the American Dream, therefore, became one appealing way to epitomize the many principles and experiences that reinforced those hopes in American life.

Hopes and warnings mix and mingle in this third dimension. Possibility, for instance, is a fickle friend. Things can go from bad to worse, and good things should not be taken for granted. They can be snatched away and destroyed sooner or later. But failure, loss, and shortcomings need not be the last judgments. Especially if Americans are resilient and resistant, if they refuse to give up or give in to threats to the Dream—despotism, corruption, oligarchy, lies and liars, undeserved pardons—new beginnings can be made. Good times can roll again.

At its best, the American Dream incorporates and depends upon the wisdom of a biblical proverb: "A threefold cord is not quickly broken" (Eccl 4:12 NRSV). If the power of three is remembered, honored, and extended (that is, if we Americans make the three dimensions of the American Dream—its economic, ethical, and hopeful aspects—work together), then saving the Dream can save our country. But much depends on how Americans cope with the fact that Article II of the US Constitution grants executive power to "a President of the United States of America."

Presidential Qualifications

Who qualifies to be president of the United States? Winning a national election is paramount, but otherwise the constitutional requirements stated in Article II are minimal.

> No Person except a natural born Citizen, or a Citizen of the United States, at the time of the Adoption of this Constitution, shall be eligible to the Office of President; neither shall any person be eligible to that Office who shall not have attained to the Age of thirty five Years, and been fourteen Years a Resident within the United States.

That's it—no educational, economic, ethical, religious, or law-abiding requirements need to be met for eligibility and election. I can be a convicted felon and still be president of the United States. Donald Trump is proof of that. I can make corrupt deals and befriend despicable people and still be president of the United States. Donald Trump is proof of that too.

The founders hoped and trusted that any president would have integrity and virtue far exceeding the low bar for presidential eligibility established by the Constitution. Overly optimistic, they did not see Trump coming. They did ensure that a president "shall be removed from Office on Impeachment for, and Conviction of, Treason, Bribery, or other high Crimes and Misdemeanors," but that measure did not deter Trump, who has now betrayed his country again, and especially his MAGA base, by covering up the Jeffrey Epstein files.

These files comprise millions of items compiled by federal prosecutors as they prepared their cases against the American financier Jeffrey Epstein and his partner, Ghislaine Maxwell, for years of predatory child sex trafficking crimes.[2] Awaiting trial, Epstein died by hanging in his jail cell on August 10, 2019. On June 28, 2022, Maxwell received a twenty-year prison sentence for her part in perpetrating sex crimes against children. Meanwhile, continuing his long history of using conspiracy theories for political gain, Trump joined Kash Patel and Dan Bongino, FBI leaders, to claim that the Deep State protected elites who were Epstein/Maxwell clients. Exposing the conspirators, they claimed, must be a Trump 2.0 priority.

In late February 2025, the release of the Epstein files seemed imminent. The tease, however, was fraudulent because the Trump-Epstein relationship was proving too hot to handle.[3] News cycles looped photos of Trump cavorting with Epstein. Trump's accolades for Epstein became ubiquitous: "I've known Jeff for 15 years. Terrific guy," Trump told *New York Magazine* in 2002. "He's a lot of fun to be with. It is even said that he likes beautiful women as much as I do, and many of them are on the younger side. No doubt about it—Jeffrey enjoys his social life."[4] In addition, Trump repeatedly said of Maxwell, the convicted pedophile, "I wish her well," but his silence about her victims spoke volumes.

As August 2025 unfolded, the Epstein files had not been released. It was known, however, that Trump's name had surfaced in them with regularity. That fact did not mean that Trump was implicated in Epstein/Maxwell crimes, but after Attorney General Pam Bondi shared the findings with the president in May 2025, Trump 2.0 did an about-face. "Nothing to see here" became the incredible byword. Nor did Trump help himself by dispatching Deputy Attorney General Todd Blanche, his defense attorney, to interview Maxwell on July 24–25, 2025. Less than a week later, on August 1, Maxwell was transferred to a minimum-security federal prison camp in Bryan,

2. Barrett and Cameron, "Epstein Files."
3. Khardori, "Epstein Files Timeline."
4. Blake, "5 Big Questions."

Texas, further fueling speculation that Trump will pardon her in exchange for a statement that Trump was in no way involved in nefarious activities with Epstein.[5]

Sensing betrayal, much of MAGA balked. Trump had long convinced his base that he would expose the evils of the Deep State, underscoring that every attack against him was further evidence of a Deep State conspiracy to "get him" and "bring him down." Trump's reneging on release of the Epstein files, however, coupled with his misguided lawsuit against the *Wall Street Journal* for documenting his long friendship with Epstein, left Trump exposed and more vulnerable with his base than he had ever been.[6] By August 2025, Trump personified a Deep State of his own, covering up scandal that dirtied him and his cronies as well. On July 28, the political analyst Bill Kristol was on target when he called Trump "personally such a moral monster," adding later that Trump is "a disgusting human being."[7]

During the summer of 2025, Trump lost control of the Epstein/Maxwell narrative, which took on a life of its own and will not go away, at least not before the crucial 2026 midterm elections. The full impact of the scandal's reverberations remains to be seen, but an August 9–11 Economist/YouGov poll showed that "a majority of Americans think Trump knew some (27%) or a lot (44%) about the sex crimes committed by Epstein against underage girls before investigations into Epstein began; only 8% say he knew nothing about them."[8] Trump falls far from meeting presidential qualifications that ought to be at play beyond the minimal constitutional requirements about citizenship, age, and residency. Traits of good character—respect for persons, honesty, integrity, good judgment—cannot be codified like age and birthplace, but if our presidents lack such prerequisites, as Trump so clearly does, our country and its Dream may die.

Days and Years

Article II specifies that the American president holds that office for a term of four years, which equals 1,460 days. The Twentieth Amendment, ratified in 1933, decrees that a new presidential term begins at noon on January 20. At that time, the newly elected president takes the oath of office, as prescribed

5. Berman et al., "Two Days of Interviews." See also Turley, "Mystery of Ghislaine Maxwell."

6. Safdar and Palazzolo, "Jeffrey Epstein's Friends."

7. Kristol, "Bill Kristol: Trump Is a Moral Monster"; Kristol, " Bill Kristol: A Weekend of Tragedy."

8. Orth and Montgomery, "Trump Approval."

in Article II: "I do solemnly swear (or affirm) that I will faithfully execute the Office of President of the United States, and will to the best of my Ability, preserve, protect and defend the Constitution of the United States." The inaugural address that follows is often the occasion for proclaiming a new beginning for the nation and its citizens. Donald Trump's speech on January 20, 2025, was no exception to that rule. "I return to the presidency confident and optimistic that we are at the start of a thrilling new era of national success," Trump intoned.

> A tide of change is sweeping the country, sunlight is pouring over the entire world, and America has the chance to seize this opportunity like never before. . . . For American citizens, January 20th, 2025, is Liberation Day. . . . The American dream will soon be back and thriving like never before. . . . We stand on the verge of the four greatest years in American history. . . . The future is ours, and our golden age has just begun.[9]

New beginnings can be made, but Trump's are far from starting a golden age.

Article II states that the president "shall take care that the laws be faithfully executed," which requires the president to ensure that federal laws are enforced. Presidents have agendas of their own as well. They cannot legislate directly, but they can propose legislation, send a message to Congress urging its enactment, and provide draft legislation with explanatory material. Wanting to get things done before political honeymoons are over, inertia sets in, and it becomes too late, presidents, though not the Constitution itself, often underscore the importance of the first one hundred days of their term.

President Franklin D. Roosevelt gets credit for focusing attention on that time frame. Inaugurated on March 4, 1933, he used radio to speak to the nation. His "fireside chat" on July 25, 1933, referred to "the hundred days which had been devoted to the starting of the wheels of the New Deal." During that time, Roosevelt speedily got Congress to pass more than a dozen landmark bills, over seventy laws in all, and he issued scores of executive orders in a determined effort to spark the country's recovery from the Great Depression.[10] Ever since, the 100-day benchmark has energized American presidents to advance as much of their agenda as quickly as possible. Unfortunately, an accounting of the first hundred days of Donald Trump's second presidential term shows that far from putting the United States on the way to restoring confidence in the American Dream, making it thrive "like never before," his actions undermined the Dream, as they have continued

9. Trump, Inaugural Address.

10. Franklin D. Roosevelt Presidential Library, "'Action.'"

to do well beyond the opening months of 2025. Analyses by two perceptive American writers testified to that.

Writing in the *Atlantic* on February 24, 2025, Jonathan Rauch cogently contended that the early days of Trump's second term showed that his administration is and will be rife with corruption. (Six months later, the *New Yorker*'s David D. Kirkpatrick released the results of his diligent study, which showed that "some three and a half billion dollars in Presidential profits" have thus far lined the pockets of Trump and his family.[11]) Meanwhile, Rauch's assessment pivoted on his sound argument that Trump's presidential style can best be called *patrimonialism*, which is "less a form of government than a style of governing."[12] Rauch continued:

> [Patrimonialism] is not defined by institutions or rules; rather, it can infect all forms of government by replacing impersonal, formal lines of authority with personalized, informal ones. Based on individual loyalty and connections, and on rewarding friends and punishing enemies (real or perceived), it can be found not just in states but also among tribes, street gangs, and criminal organizations. . . . Patrimonialism is suspicious of bureaucracies; after all, to exactly whom are they loyal? They might acquire powers of their own, and their rules and processes might prove obstructive. People with expertise, experience, and distinguished résumés are likewise suspect because they bring independent standing and authority. So patrimonialism stocks the government with nonentities and hacks, or, when possible, it bypasses bureaucratic procedures altogether.

For a time, Rauch indicated, Trump's patrimonialism can coexist with democracy. It will even cloak itself in democratic disguises. But its impact is lethal to democracy, the rule of law, and the American Dream. Fortunately, patrimonialism has two inherent flaws that can be its undoing.

Incompetence is the first of patrimonialism's flaws. Trump 2.0 reeks of it. The administration's massive layoffs and firings of competent, essential people to manage public affairs—think experts who manage nuclear weapons or who can manage bird flu—are but one telling example. Incompetence will reveal itself. Its wrack and ruin may ignite needed resistance.

Corruption is the second flaw. "Patrimonialism is corrupt by definition," Rauch said, "because its reason for being is to exploit the state for gain—political, personal, and financial. At every turn, it is at war with the rules and institutions that impede rigging, robbing, and gutting the state."

11. Kirkpatrick, "How Much Is Trump Pocketing?"

12. Rauch, "One Word."

Corruption can undo Trump and his patrimonialism because, Rauch rightly contended, the public can come to understand and rebel against the fact that "the government is being run for *them*, not for *you*."

Rauch acknowledged that Trump's corruption is not new. In fact, Americans may be numb to it by now. But Americans do not have to settle for that. Possibility reminds us that things can change, that corruption does not have to prevail. The chance for new beginnings is real. Resistance to Trump can be intensified by persistently "hammering home the message that he is corrupt." Rauch shows that such action has ousted leaders before, and he believes that Trump's corruption can lead to the same result.

Complementing Rauch, the astute political observer Anne Appelbaum warns that permanent damage to the American Dream would turn the United States into Hungary. That county, said Appelbaum, "is a poor country, possibly *the* poorest, in the European Union."[13] But Trump and his MAGA acolytes love Hungary's dictator, Viktor Orbán, precisely because he has made his country corrupt, stagnant, and impoverished. Orbán provides their model for making the future not ours but theirs. Appelbaum depicts the model:

> Orbán slowly replaced civil servants with loyalists; used economic pressure and regulation to destroy the free press; robbed universities of their independence, and shut one of them down; politicized the court system; and repeatedly changed the constitution to give himself electoral advantages.

Trump's name could replace Orbán's, and Appelbaum's description would fit the wannabe American dictator.

Appelbaum's analysis echoes Rauch's because the corruption that keeps Orbán and his gang in power is all too much like the corruption that infests Trump 2.0, infects the country, and imperils the American Dream. "In many ways," Appelbaum concludes,

> Hungary is about as different from the US as it is possible to be: small, poor, homogeneous. But . . . as Elon Musk . . . sets fire to our civil service and makes decisions about the departments that regulate him; as the FBI and the Justice Department are captured by partisans who will never prosecute their colleagues for corruption; as inspectors general are fired and rules about conflicts of interest are ignored, America is spinning quickly in the direction of Hungarian populism, Hungarian politics, and Hungarian justice. But that means Hungarian stagnation, Hungarian corruption, and Hungarian poverty lie in our future too.

13. Appelbaum, "America's Future."

The analyses of Rauch and Appelbaum are sober and somber warnings. They lead to a basic guideline for interpreting and resisting what is said and done in Trump 2.0. *Keep eyes and ears open, keenly focused, and critically attuned. Then trust them and act accordingly.* Such senses discern differences between boasting and integrity, grandiose forecasts and grim realities, claims about making America great again and actions that attack the American Dream at its best.

Until valid receipts and reliable evidence back up Trump's upbeat claims about what he has done or will accomplish, assume that what is said is more likely false than true, more likely harmful than helpful, more likely deceitful than honest, and more likely faithless than faithful to the American Dream. At the same time, take Trump seriously, which often requires taking him literally. Trump obfuscates, exaggerates, and lies, but he often says the quiet parts out loud. Those parts embrace autocracy and reject democracy. Whenever Trump sounds that way, he should be taken at his word and banked on to do what he says.

On August 25, 2025, Trump's defense of his military occupation of Washington, DC, included his pronouncing, "I'm not a dictator. I'm a man with great common sense and a smart person."[14] That beggars belief. Watch what Trump does and remember what he keeps doing. He consolidates power and advances oligarchy. He bullies businesses, universities, and law firms to bend the knee to him. He rewrites and falsifies American history. He concocts phony emergencies and sends masked agents and armed military units to spread fear on American streets in response. Los Angeles and Washington, DC, came first. Chicago, Minneapolis, and other cities with Democrat- and Black-majority populations are likely to be next. He deports people without due process. He grows an internal if not secret police force to carry out his wishes. He fires people who tell him what he does not want to hear. He covers up massive sexual abuse. He weaponizes intimidation and fear. Lies pack his words. Trump is trying to orchestrate a not-so-slow coup to control American life. His actions are not "distractions." That word does not do justice to Trump's harm-doing. He has become worse than a wannabe dictator. The antithesis of the American Dream at its best, despotic Trumpworld is a dystopian nightmare. The country is not beyond saving, but time runs short.

Trump promises retribution against his opponents and revenge against his adversaries. That fury drives him. Article II of the US Constitution, he contends, gives him the presidential right to do whatever he wants. He seeks to prosecute and punish burning of the American flag when that is "likely

14. Anderson, "'I'm Not a Dictator.'"

to incite imminent lawless action," his vague loophole to skirt the Supreme Court's 1989 ruling that flag burning is constitutionally protected speech.[15] Authoritarianism energizes Trump. He aims to curtail voting rights, claims entitlement to more congressional support that will do his bidding, and seeks one-party rule in the United States. He uses government power to enforce a rigid, exclusionary definition of what it means to be American.[16] Hostility to pluralistic democracy ignites him. Whenever Trump speaks and acts in antidemocratic ways, trust what you hear and see, and oppose him. Whenever he claims to be serving the American people, defending the Constitution, protecting the nation's security, and restoring the American Dream, do not believe him and resist instead. Doing so means ousting his minions from political power and neutering his authority.

From Time to Time

Article II provides that one of the president's specific duties is, "from time to time give to the Congress Information of the State of the Union." The fulfilment of that duty usually takes place during a joint session of Congress early in a calendar year. George Washington gave the first of these reports on January 8, 1790. Since 1981, it has been customary not to call a first-year speech of this kind a State of the Union Address but, more modestly, a Joint Address to Congress. What the speech is called makes little difference. Whether in a State of the Union speech or a Joint Address, Trump did address Congress and the nation on March 6, 2025.[17]

Ranting for an hour and forty minutes, Trump set a record for the longest speech of this kind. It was big on boasting and bluster, falsehoods and fabulations, but small on specific aims that would make life, in the words of James Truslow Adams, "better and richer and fuller" for all Americans.[18] Trump's obfuscation was evident in references to the American Dream that he read from teleprompter text that he could not have written himself and probably saw only shortly before he mindlessly recited it. "The American dream is surging bigger and better than ever before," Trump and his teleprompter claimed. "The American dream is unstoppable, and our country is on the verge of a comeback, the likes of which the world has never witnessed and perhaps will never witness again. There's never been anything like it."

15. Savage and Broadwater, "Trump's Order." See also Quinn, "Trump Wants to Punish."

16. Axelrod and Basu, "Trump's Identity Project."

17. Trump, "Remarks by President Trump."

18. Adams, *Epic of America*, 415.

Beginning that way, Trump tried for a crescendo at the end, declaiming American exceptionalism in soaring cliches—"we will never let anything happen to our beloved country"—and affirming that we will "plant the American flag on the planet Mars and even far beyond. And through it all, we are going to rediscover the unstoppable power of the American spirit, and we are going to renew the unlimited promise of the American dream. . . . The golden age of America has only just begun. It will be like nothing that has ever been seen before." Rarely has presidential rhetoric so fraudulently blurred the lines between fact and fiction.

Three steps taken by Trump in his first one hundred days—discrediting the Smithsonian, allowing exposure of military plans on a commercial online platform, and instituting crippling tariffs—put that assessment in bold relief. They threaten truthful narratives about American history and culture, put national security at risk, and endanger the American economy.

Distorting American History and Culture

Titled Restoring Truth and Sanity to American History, Trump's Executive Order 14253, signed on March 27, 2025, targeted the Smithsonian Institution, a major guardian of American history and a repository for the culture of the United States.[19] With Vice President JD Vance as his right-hand man, Trump promised to "save" the Smithsonian. His salvation requires purging the Institution, its content and administration, allegedly to restore truth about American history, to combat "a divisive, race-centered ideology," and to celebrate "American greatness—igniting the imagination of young minds, honoring the richness of American history and innovation, and instilling pride in the hearts of all Americans."

Trump's intention is to discredit the Smithsonian's long-standing excellence, to install his confederates and right-wing scholars to preside over it, and to bend the world's largest museum complex to serve his jingoistic, antidemocratic autocracy. Much is at stake in this takeover. The Smithsonian comprises twenty-one museums, fourteen education and research centers, and the National Zoo. Eleven of the museums, including the National Museum of American History, the National Air and Space Museum, the National Museum of African American History and Culture, and the National Museum of the American Indian stand on the National Mall. Complemented by the Washington Monument at the center, the US Capitol and the Lincoln Memorial at its ends, the National Mall is a national park, specifically part of the National Mall and Memorial Parks unit of the

19. Trump, Exec. Order No. 14253 (2025).

National Park Service. Sometimes the Mall is called America's front yard. The Smithsonian's importance is underscored by the fact that its museums attract more than seventeen million visitors annually. Ten times that number consult the museums' websites every year.

James Smithsonian (1765–1829), a British scientist, donated his estate to the United States for the stated purpose of founding "at Washington, under the name of the Smithsonian Institution, an establishment for the increase and diffusion of knowledge." On August 10, 1846, the US Senate passed the act organizing the Smithsonian Institution, which was signed into law by President James K. Polk. From comparatively modest beginnings, the Smithsonian continues to grow. The Institution's magnificence and impact are immense, amplified by a well-trained and highly educated staff and by ongoing, cutting-edge research that supports museum exhibitions and the narratives that contextualize them. The Smithsonian does superbly what all good museums do. It informs the public accurately. It raises questions that arouse curiosity and inspire further critical inquiry. Its mission is not to glorify America but to encourage American aspirations toward "a more perfect Union." If Trump dominates the Smithsonian, the baleful consequences for the American Dream are considerable.

Ever the liar, Trump purports to ensure that American history is celebrated accurately, fairly, and with pride. Ever the hypocrite, he will combat "corrosive ideology," ignoring that his transactional tyranny is its prime contemporary example in the United States. Ever the boasting narcissist who inflames deep divisions among Americans to serve his ends, Trump preposterously asserts that his stewardship of our heritage and culture will foster "unity and a deeper understanding of our shared past." His Smithsonian-targeted word salad is pernicious nonsense.

In Executive Order 14253, Trump falsely described the Smithsonian as part of a conspiratorial "revisionist movement" that reconstructs "our Nation's unparalleled legacy of advancing liberty, individual rights, and human happiness . . . as inherently racist, sexist, oppressive, or otherwise irredeemably flawed." Predictably, Trump blamed Joe Biden and "the prior administration," for advancing "this corrosive ideology." Trump's whitewashed version of American history has no place for nuance and development, for criticism as well as celebration, for awareness that our "more perfect Union" is an aspiration not a fact, a challenge not an already-made accomplishment. Trump compromises and eviscerates the American Dream, which depends on change, the correction of shortfalls and shortcomings, the encouragement to right what is wrong, to create justice where injustice persists, and to honor and include the diversity that is undeniably a growing part of

American life. That diversity, much to Trump's dismay, will not be repressed let alone eliminated by Trump's dogmatism, racism, misogyny, and sexism.

Those flaws—dogmatism, racism, misogyny, and sexism—permeate Trump's distortions of American history and culture, which were amplified in another Executive Order (14168). Proclaimed on January 20, 2025, one of the first acts of Trump 2.0, this order has profound implications for interpretations of American history and culture and how narratives in the Smithsonian reflect them.

Purportedly issued to defend women from gender ideology extremism, Trump's Executive Order 14168 stipulates dogmatically that gender "does not provide a meaningful basis for identification and cannot be recognized as a replacement for sex."[20] *Sex*, he further decreed, "shall refer to an individual's immutable biological classification as either male or female." According to Trump, there are "two sexes, male and female. These sexes are not changeable and are grounded in fundamental and incontrovertible reality." Immutable, incontrovertible?Trump seems to know a lot. If Trump says it, must it be so? He seems to think so. Distortions of American history and culture are magnified by Trump's ignorance of biology and evolution. Simply taking Trump's word for anything is usually a fool's errand.

Critical reactions to Trump's attack on the Smithsonian were prompt and robust. Soon after Executive Order 14168 appeared, the American Historical Association (AHA), supported by at least twenty-five other academic groups, vigorously defended the Smithsonian. Trump's attack, said the AHA, "egregiously misrepresents the work of the Smithsonian Institution. The Smithsonian is among the premier research institutions in the world, widely known for the integrity of its scholarship, which is careful and based on historical and scientific evidence." In addition, the AHA clarified what historical work—at its best, not as Trump's text misconstrues and perverts it—seeks to do:

> Historians explore the past to understand how our nation has evolved. We draw on a wide range of sources, which helps us to understand history from different angles of vision. Our goal is neither criticism nor celebration. It is to understand—to increase our knowledge of—the past in ways that can help Americans to shape the future. The stories that have shaped our past include not only elements that make us proud but also aspects that make us acutely aware of tragedies in our nation's history. No person, no nation, is perfect, and we should all—as individuals and as nations—learn from our imperfections.[21]

20. Trump, Exec. Order No. 14168 (2025).

21. American Historical Association, "Historians Defend the Smithsonian."

The AHA statement emphasizes attitudes, virtues, and commitments that are essential for saving the American Dream. Concurrently, the AHA indicts Donald Trump, whose lack of those qualities erodes the Dream. His disdain for historical accuracy and his inattention to historical detail go beyond rejecting sound scholarship and accurate analysis. That disdain disrespects the intelligence and integrity of the American people when we are at our best.

About four months later, on August 7, 2025, the eminent American historian David Blight upped the ante. Denouncing Trump's "political war on the historians' profession, our training and integrity," Blight more than decried the Trump 2.0 determination to entrench what Blight called "official triumphal narratives rooted in a brand of pickled patriotism designed to force the past to serve the present."[22]

Blight called out the Heritage Foundation and its president Kevin Roberts, a historian who championed the authoritarian playbook called Project 2025. Accurately dubbing them "Trump's history department," Blight has invited Roberts "to join a small group of historians in a series of discussions/debates. He can choose his companions, and we will choose our participants. I challenge him to a series of civil debates in major television or podcast outlets, or especially a public venue before the 2026 anniversary of American independence. What are and ought to be the big questions and answers about American history at this important marker in time?"

It remains to be seen whether Roberts and his Trumpist historians are up to such a challenge, but open discussion and public debate of exactly this kind are much needed, and not least because Trump has renewed his intention to dominate and control the Smithsonian. On August 12, 2025, a White House directive went to Lonnie Bunch III, who heads the Institution. It called for "a comprehensive internal review of selected Smithsonian museums and exhibitions . . . to ensure alignment with the President's directive to celebrate American exceptionalism, remove divisive or partisan narratives, and restore confidence in our shared cultural institutions."[23] Trump's ignorant assault against reliable scholarship is unrelenting. His Truth Social rant on August 19, 2025, spewed this irrationality: "The Smithsonian is OUT OF CONTROL, where everything discussed is how horrible our Country is, how bad Slavery was, and how unaccomplished the downtrodden have been—Nothing about Success, nothing about Brightness, nothing about the Future."[24]

22. Blight, "What if History Died?"

23. Halligan et al., "Internal Review." See also Bowley, "Historians Alarmed."

24. Kingsberry and Ables, "Trump Says."

Trump's judgment is profoundly wrong. The Smithsonian itself is a huge American success story, one that helps Americans to see how to make our country's future brighter and better. The Smithsonian rightly points Americans in those directions through its world-class scholarship, its art, and its sharing of knowledge and insight, which do not glorify the inglorious or sugarcoat the bitter but instead illuminate and inspire by showing how where we have been can help us to see better where we ought to be going.

Prominent among the eight museums singled out for review are the National Museum of American History, the National Museum of African American History and Culture, and the National Museum of the American Indian. If Trump and his "reviewers" have their way, American history, especially its chapters about slavery, about genocide against Indigenous peoples, and about disdain for women's rights, will be whitewashed and airbrushed in untruthful and unethical ways that violate not only the standards of reliable scholarship and historical accuracy but also the norms of respect and decency. American "exceptionalism" of that kind has nothing to do with the American Dream at its best and should be deplored. If it isn't, the risks include national security.

Risking National Security

On March 15, 2025, the United States bombed Houthi targets across Yemen. Backed by Iran and aligned with Hamas in the Israel-Hamas war that began on October 7, 2023, the Houthis had wreaked havoc on commercial shipping in the Red Sea. Since January 2025, Americans attacked their installations to protect shipping zones. These attacks required intelligence gathering, careful planning, and critical information sharing. Secrecy and secure communications among American leaders were necessary to maximize mission success, which included minimizing risk to American military personnel. March 15, 2025, a mission day for action against the Houthis, became a scandal called Signalgate. It revealed more of the incompetence, arrogance, ignorance, and immorality that are emblematic of Trump 2.0 and its disrespect for the American Dream.

Secretary of Defense Pete Hegseth, a man of dubious distinction, personified the debacle. His Princeton and Harvard educations largely lost on him, Hegseth became Trump's unqualified—no, disqualified—nominee to become Secretary of Defense, a massive job that entails overseeing the Department of Defense, about three million people, hundreds of military bases at home and abroad, and an annual budget of about $900 billion, almost 15 percent of the US budget.[25]

By the narrowest possible margin, 51–50 (a margin made possible by Vice President JD Vance's tie-breaking vote), the US Senate confirmed Hegseth's nomination and put him in Trump's cabinet. A decorated National Guard major who had seen combat in Iraq and Afghanistan, Hegseth nevertheless has a résumé that should have disqualified him. A former Fox News host who amplified Trump's lie that the 2020 election was stolen, Hegseth also mismanaged two not-for-profit organizations, abused women, and has had problems with alcohol. His chesty tattoo, Deus Vult (God wills it), ironically mocks him. So do his repeated claims that he stands for meritocracy and knows exactly what he is doing. His presiding over Signalgate would be a cruel joke, material for *Saturday Night Live*'s lampooning, if it were not such a lethal revealing of the risk to national security that this "Sec Def" shows himself to be.

The Signalgate timeline indicates that on March 11, 2025, National Security Advisor Michael Waltz, a former Army Special Services officer and multiterm member of Congress from Florida, organized an online texting conversation with seventeen additional Trump officials—including Vice President Vance, Secretary of State Marco Rubio, Director of National Intelligence Tulsi Gabbard, and CIA Director John Ratcliffe as well as Hegseth—to establish, in Waltz's words, "coordination on Houthis, particularly for over the next 72 hours."[26]

Waltz blundered. Compounding his incompetent judgment to hold the chat on Signal, a messaging platform that incorporates key security features but not enough security to protect highly sensitive communications, Waltz included on his invitation list the journalist Jeffrey Goldberg, the *Atlantic*'s editor in chief. Thinking at first that his inclusion might be an attempt to entrap him in a disinformation scheme, Goldberg nevertheless joined the group on March 15, soon realizing that he was receiving real information that should not be his: plans for attacks on Houthi positions two hours before the scheduled start of the bombing.[27]

Convinced that he had witnessed an egregious security breach, Goldberg reported his experience; his reports were met with typical Trumpist reactions to truthful journalism: repeated denials and attacks. No classified

25. Groves and Finley, "House Passes Defense Bill"; Groves and Mascaro, "Pete Hegseth Faces Deepening Scrutiny"; U.S. Government Accountability Office, "Defense Workforce."

26. Watson, "Trump Officials."

27. Goldberg and Harris, "Attack Plans." See also Goldberg, "Accidentally Texted Me."

information had been shared on Signal, the Trumpists insisted. Jeffrey Goldberg was an unreliable, lying member of the not-to-be-trusted press. After thinking carefully about what to do, Goldberg resisted the false denials and defaming attacks. He came forward with his screenshot-by-screenshot transcript of what had been said and by whom. Pete Hegseth was the key source of a highly significant security breach, which raised questions about him and the nation's security that went well beyond the March 15 texting session.

Improperly sharing war plans, Hegseth likely committed crimes, and certainly his recklessness needlessly endangered American military personnel, who now have little reason to trust him. Irresponsibly sharing anti-European views, shared by the like-minded JD Vance,[28] Hegseth risked national security leaks, not least by driving deeper existing wedges between the United States and our NATO allies. In addition, Signalgate was not likely a one-off event. Why would it be? Top-secret discussions and conferences take place all the time in American government. Why would Signalgate be the only one during the incompetence of Trump 2.0 that would risk national security in a dangerous world?

New York Times columnist David French, a savvy former Army lawyer, got it right when he said, with Pete Hegseth top of mind, "there is not an officer alive whose career would survive a security breach like this."[29] Demands for Hegseth to resign or be fired were ignored by Trump, further evidence that incompetence and corruption rot his administration. That evidence grew on April 3, 2025, when Trump purged highly competent national security officers, likely part of a cover-up to scalp them instead of Hegseth. First, on April 3, Timothy Haugh, a four-star Air Force general, was fired as head of the National Security Agency, which oversees wiretapping and cyberespionage services, along with his civilian deputy, Wendy Noble.[30] That same day, at least four proficient staff members of the National Security Council, which advises the president on the most important security challenges facing the country, were sacked by Trump: Thomas Boodry, who oversaw legislative affairs; Maggie Dougherty, who oversaw international organizations; David Feith, a senior director overseeing technology and national security; and Brian Walsh, a senior director overseeing intelligence matters.[31]

28. Smialek and Erlanger, "Now Europe Knows."
29. French, "Hegseth's Group Chat Debacle."
30. Nakashima et al., "National Security Chief Ousted."
31. Nakashima et al., "Trump Ousts Members."

These firings were urged by the far-right influencer Laura Loomer.[32] Speaking with Trump in the Oval Office the day before, she deemed this group disloyal to him. National Security Advisor Michael Waltz, who was also in the room, was unable or unwilling to defy Loomer and save his own staff. He suffered humiliation and resigned on May 1, 2025. His "reward" was to become Trump's nominee to serve as US ambassador to the United Nations. After months of delay, Waltz received the required Senate confirmation on September 19, 2025. Few Trump loyalists survive unscathed, because in Trump's world, loyalty runs only one way. Underlings must obey, but only if they keep bending the knee will Trump be loyal to them.

Loomer's biography is at least as problematic as Pete Hegseth's. She has frequently posted anti-Islam and anti-immigrant smears on social media, and she made racist and sexist attacks against former Vice President Kamala Harris, who ran against Trump in 2024. A conspiracy theorist, Loomer has called the 9/11 attack on New York and Washington, DC, "an inside job." No doubt she would approve Trump's attack on the Smithsonian, because she has called herself a "pro-white" nationalist who thinks that the United States "really was built as the white Judeo-Christian ethnostate" and that immigration and calls for diversity are "starting to destroy this country."[33]

Deceitful and corrupt, Trump and Loomer are made for each other. With Trump in the White House, Loomer in the Oval Office, and Pete Hegseth in charge at the Pentagon, the American Dream is weakened because the United States is becoming less and less secure. That judgment holds because Trump's vaunted National Security Strategy, published on December 4, 2025, undercuts its own claims. Trump called the document "a roadmap to ensure that America remains the greatest and most successful nation in human history, and the home of freedom on earth." Its aim, he added, is to "make America safer, richer, freer, greater, and more powerful than ever before."[34] On the contrary, Trump's roadmap encourages American aggression in the Western Hemisphere, supports divisive spheres of influence that carve up the world to enrich dictators, and disrespects alliances that have supported human rights and international law since World War II. Far from advancing the American Dream, Trump's National Security Strategy endangers it.

32. Swan et al., "Loomer's Role in the Firings."
33. Shuham, "Anti-Muslim Extremist." See also Allison, "Laura Loomer's Rise."
34. Trump, National Security Strategy.

Imposing Toxic Tariffs

April Fool's Day 2025 began a momentous week in American history. At 8:06 PM on that first day of April, Cory Booker ended his twenty-five-hour-and-four-minute filibuster on the floor of the US Senate. Breaking the previous record held by Strom Thurmond, the South Carolina senator who in 1957 had protested civil rights and defended racial segregation, Booker said, "We all must look in the mirror and say, 'We will do better.'"[35] That same Tuesday, voters in Wisconsin did so when they convincingly elected Susan Crawford to a state supreme court seat, a victory that defeated not only her opponent but also Elon Musk, who claimed that the future of civilization itself depended on Crawford's losing and poured more than $25 million into the campaign against her.[36]

The next day, April 2—number 73 of Trump's first one hundred days in office—was to be Liberation Day, again, according to Donald Trump, who hosted a Rose Garden announcement gathering at the White House. It began shortly after the stock market closed at four o'clock in the afternoon. Beginning with a rant as false and incoherent as it has been familiar, the carnival barker Trump said:

> Foreign cheaters have ransacked our factories, and foreign scavengers have torn apart our once beautiful American dream. We had an American dream that you don't hear so much about. You did 4 years ago and you are now, but you don't too often for many years and decades even, you didn't hear too much about. Our country and its taxpayers have been ripped off for more than 50 years, but it is not going to happen anymore. It's not going to happen. . . . My fellow Americans, this is Liberation Day, waiting for a long time. April 2nd, 2025, will forever be remembered as the day American industry was reborn, the day America's destiny was reclaimed, and the day that we began to make America wealthy again. Going to make it wealthy—good and wealthy.[37]

As revealed in his Truth Social decrees and tirades, Trump has an impoverished vocabulary. *Hoax* is his word for any criticism or indictment against him. *Rigged* is his term for any decision or election that does not go his way. *Ripped off* is his relentless grievance. But nothing denotes verbal vacuity more than his calling *tariffs* "the most beautiful word in the dictionary," a sign that he could scarcely be more wrong, arrogant, dogmatic, and

35. Elliott, "Cory Booker Reminds Democrats."
36. Ewing, "Musk Said Wisconsin Would Decide."
37. Trump, "Remarks on New Tariffs."

misinformed.[38] It can never be repeated enough—because Trump seems unable or unwilling to understand—that American tariffs are taxes paid to the American government by American importers of foreign goods or by American consumers who are charged higher prices to offset the costs to companies. Entailing the highest tax increase in more than sixty years, Trump's tariffs will cost a typical US. household $3,800 each year they are in place.[39]

Far from making Americans "wealthy—good and wealthy," Trump's tariffs—he falsely imagines that they "will give us growth like you haven't seen before"—are toxic. What happened before the end of the first week of April testifies to that. By week's end, Trump had single-handedly destroyed $6.4 trillion in wealth. The stock market plummeted, suffering its worst losses since June 2020 during the COVID-19 pandemic. Fears of recession, if not depression, rose at home and abroad, and chaos and uncertainty engulfed not only the business world but also the American Dream of countless individuals. None of the carnage was necessary. Trump is responsible, no one else, but he showed his bottomless irresponsibility by meeting Saudis at a golf tournament while his country rightly sensed that its future is very much at risk.

True, after the shocking downturn in early April 2025, a resilient American economy bounced back significantly, and Trump continues to insist that the long-term payoff of his tariffs will be worth any short-term pain. "The markets are going to boom," he said during that fateful first week of April 2025. "The stock is going to boom, the country is going to boom, and the rest of the world wants to see is there any way they can make a deal."[40] We trust such pronouncements at our peril. The full force of Trump's chaotic tariff scheme will not be felt until the second half of 2026 is far along, but no reliable economist thinks that Trump's rosy narrative is true, because his policies are so erratic, chaotic, and incoherent.

The purported purpose of the ever-changing tariffs and the "economic revolution" they are supposed to fuel is not only to leverage tariff reductions by other countries but also to stimulate more goods production in the United States and thus to create more high-paying jobs for American workers. That plan is not nonsense, but for at least two reasons, it will not make as much sense as Trump believes. First, existing production capacity within the United States is insufficient to support such hopes. It would take time and huge investment to move toward curbing the country's reliance on international trade. Second, these steps, if successful, would require paying

38. Treisman, "'Most Beautiful Word.'"

39. Wolfers, "Your Life." See also Wong and Epstein, "Trump's Tariffs."

40. Hutzler et al., "Tariffs Roil Markets."

increased American labor costs. Prices on the goods produced would go up accordingly. Trump's toxic tariffs will increase inflation and decrease the standard of living for most Americans. Neither Trump's economic theory, such as it is, nor his math add up.

Nor does the spin spewed by Trump's true believers and lackeys, skeptical though some have become.[41] "Short-term pain for long-term gain" is word salad without specificity and meaning. The market overreacted during the spring 2025 downturn. Who says, and by what authority? As inflation and interest on the huge national debt rise, do Trump's assurances mean that markets will not plummet again? Trump's tariffs are negotiating tools that he will use to show his mastery of "the art of the deal"—such deals, as Trump's personal history shows, often result in bankruptcy, moral as well as financial. "We'll see," Trump likes to say. Indeed, Americans will, and if their judgment is sound, it will find that Trump—malignantly narcissistic, functionally illiterate, cognitively declining—is a failed, criminal con man. He may be good at branding. His sales pitches can rake in cash. He knows how to amplify grievances. But he has no vision for the United States, no faith in the American Dream, except insofar as he reduces and diminishes it to self-interest and selfishness.

Trump and his unrelenting, lie-filled PR continue to take Americans on a long ride to ruin. Trump is no astounding magician or invincible mastermind. He is an old bully whose power inflicts cruel damage, but like all bullies, he lacks courage. What's more, Trump is a failure. His criminal activity is exposed. His addiction to flattery is obvious. The Russian dictator Vladmir Putin dupes and plays him repeatedly. Trump's incompetence grows as he ages. It is all there to see, if Americans trust their eyes and ears. Relief may be a long time coming, owing to Trump's mystifying presence and the foolish loyalty that so many Americans—ignominiously first and foremost Republicans in Congress—find hard to give up, no matter how bad things become. But facts are real and stubborn. They are not going away. If Americans attend to them, their resistance and rebellion against Trump and his toxic tariffs will grow.

Breaking Things

At the end of the first week of April 2025, while Donald Trump palled around with his Saudi friends at his Trump National Doral Golf Resort, hundreds of thousands of Americans—from all fifty states and in more than 1,200 locations, big cities and small towns—rallied in "Hands Off" protests

41. Casselman, "Trump Says."

against Trump, his tariffs, and his sidekick Elon Musk, whose damage to the United States immensely compounds Trump's.[42] The tariff-driven protests were worldwide as well, taking place, for example, in London, Paris, and Berlin.

As markets cratered earlier in the month, Trump toadies went on Sunday news shows to quell unrest, but their spin was as unconvincing as it was deceptive.[43] On April 6, NBC's *Meet the Press* audience was scarcely comforted, let alone amused, when Secretary of the Treasury Scott Bessent touted the previous Friday's "record volume" of stock market transactions, incredibly insisting that "everything is working very smoothly so the American people, they can take great comfort in that. . . . Americans who want to retire right now, Americans who have put away for years in their savings accounts—I think they don't look at the day-to-day fluctuations of what's happening."[44] Bessent is not in touch with reality, which is arguably a prerequisite for being in Trump's good graces.

On ABC's *This Week*, the fabulist Kevin Hassett, Trump's dubious National Economic Council director, claimed that he had a report showing that "more than fifty countries have reached out to the president to begin a negotiation" about tariffs. He did not produce the report or verification for the accuracy of what he was saying. According to Hassett, Trump is "not trying to tank the market. He's trying to deliver for American workers."[45] He gave no evidence to support the latter claim, let alone to demonstrate its truth.

On *Fox News Sunday*, Markwayne Mullin, the extremist MAGA senator from Oklahoma, who supports the claim that the 2020 election was stolen from Donald Trump and holds that abortion should be illegal in all circumstances, including in cases of rape, incest, and even if the mother's life is at risk, asserted that Trump's tariff policy "isn't a trade war. This is balancing our economy with countries that have taken advantage of us. There's countries for decades that have gotten rich over the backs of the workers here in America." But Mullin produced no evidence to verify the accuracy of his grievance-laden proposition that Trump is merely balancing our economy.

The nonsense will continue as Trump's toxic tariffs do their poisonous worst—and to what end? The *Atlantic* essayist Derek Thompson does not miss the mark when he argues that the tariffs are about nothing more or less than

42. For an insightful account of Musk's worldview, see Lepore, "Failed Ideas."

43. Romm and Swanson, "Trump Says Tariffs."

44. Bessent, Interview by Kristen Welker.

45. Hassett, Interview by George Stephanopoulos. (See the bibliography for either the link to the program from the ABC News YouTube channel or the transcript of program published by ABC News.)

Trump's craven, chaotic personality, which drives an endless and destructive cycle—"leverage, threat, concession, repeat"—across American life.[46]

Thompson has an ally in the great American novelist F. Scott Fitzgerald. A century ago, on April 10, 1925, he published his classic, *The Great Gatsby*. It does not contain the term *American Dream*, but few studies have offered a more penetrating critique and insightful perspective on what goes wrong when power-hungry, wealth-driven, corrupted versions of that ideal gain control. As Nick Carraway, the narrator of Fitzgerald's masterpiece, says, people who live like that—Donald Trump and Elon Musk would be primary among them—are "careless people." They smash "things and creatures" and then retreat "back into their money or their vast carelessness, or whatever it [is] that [keeps] them together." Other people, Carraway/Fitzgerald testify, will have to "clean up the mess."[47]

When the founders wrote Article II of the Constitution, establishing the office of President of the United States, they did not imagine that "We the People" would have to clean up a mess like the corrupt and inept one that Trump, Musk, and their gang are leaving us. But the American Dream of "a land in which life should be better and richer and fuller for every [person], with opportunity for each according to his [or her] ability or achievement" lives on.[48] As Cory Booker reminded Americans in his epic Senate speech on April 2, 2025, "the power of the people is greater than the people in power."[49]

46. Thompson, "Only One Way."

47. Fitzgerald, *Great Gatsby*, 109. See also Wehner and Beschel, "Trump's Unforgivable Sin."

48. Adams, *Epic of America*, 415.

49. 177 Cong. Rec. S2006 and S2018 (daily ed. March 31, 2025) (statements by Sen. Booker); see the record and video of the twenty-five-hour speech linked in an article called "Senator Booker's Speech" on his website (https://www.booker.senate.gov/senator-bookers-marathon-speech).

3

Good Judges

Best known for *The Scarlet Letter* (1850), a novel that explored themes of sin, guilt, and redemption in Puritan America, Nathaniel Hawthorne also wrote brilliant short stories that brought keen judgment to bear on his country's misguided ways. They still stand as insightful cautionary tales. "Earth's Holocaust" is a timely example. Set on "one of the broadest prairies of the West,"[1] the story depicts what could be forebears of contemporary Americans who seek to destroy the so-called Deep State, an alleged network of governmental, bureaucratic, and intellectual elites that want to block Trump 2.0 and the will of the people it claims to represent.

The folly depicted in Hawthorne's story includes "that all written constitutions, set forms of government, legislative acts, statute-books, and everything else on which human invention had endeavored to stamp its arbitrary laws, should at once be destroyed, leaving the consummated world as free as the man first created."[2] Hawthorne's story acknowledges that reform is always needed but warns that destruction of time-tested norms, traditions, and institutions will lead nowhere good.

Writing like a latter-day Hawthorne in the *Atlantic* on April 7, 2025, the conservative David Brooks echoed sentiments shared by many Americans when he called his insightful essay "I Should Have Seen This Coming." Increasingly, Americans find that Donald Trump is a quixotic autocrat who will sabotage the American Dream if left unchecked. Brooks rightly drove that apprehension deeper.

> If there is an underlying philosophy driving Trump, it is this: Morality is for suckers. The strong do what they want and the

1. Hawthorne, "Earth's Holocaust" (Project Gutenberg ebook).
2. Hawthorne, "Earth's Holocaust" (Project Gutenberg ebook).

> weak suffer what they must. This is the logic of bullies everywhere. And if there is a consistent strategy, it is this: Day after day, the administration works to create a world where ruthless people can thrive. That means destroying any institution or arrangement that might check the strongman's power. The rule of law, domestic or international, restrains power, so it must be eviscerated. . . . Trumpism has become a form of nihilism that is devouring everything in its path.[3]

The term *nihilism* is rooted in the Latin *nihil*, meaning "nothing." Scorning the tradition that ultimately some things are true, beautiful, and good and others are not, nihilism rejects that outlook as a sham and a scam. Instead, nihilism entails annihilation; it welcome chaos and thrives on destruction. It reduces truth to opinion or to "whatever I say it is." Nihilism holds that might makes the only credible form of right; seeks power to dominate and control others; puts self-interest over any higher value; regards lying and lies, big and small, as legitimating tools; believes that the end justifies the means; and pursues disorder as part of that plan. Donald Trump is one of nihilism's powerful personifications.

Trump's nihilism entailed that two days after Brooks's essay appeared, at midnight on April 9, the president was expected to ramp up his reign of tariff terror. He would unleash the most extensive regimen of import taxes since President Herbert Hoover worsened the Great Depression by signing the Smoot-Hawley Tariff Act into law on June 17, 1930. And then . . . Trump's nihilism led him to pause, to back off—at least for a time—from his problematic plans. Just hours after escalated levies against some sixty of the nation's trading partners were to go into effect, Trump put a ninety-day hold on the stiffest tariff increases but not for China.[4]

Stephen Miller, Trump's deputy chief of staff, who is friendly toward White supremacy, gaslighted Americans by claiming that "you have been watching the greatest economic master strategy from an American President in history."[5] But there was no plan, only a reaction when a collapsing treasury bond market spooked Trump. Long considered a financial haven for investors at home and abroad, treasury bond purchases are essential to generate federal revenue. Especially when foreign investors began dumping US treasury bonds, disaster threatened the American economy. Trump blinked and backed off. Nevertheless, most countries were still left to face

3. Brooks, "I Should Have Seen." See also Brooks, "Right-Wing Nihilism."
4. Farrell et al. "Trump Announces Sudden Reversal."
5. Collinson, "Trump's Tariff Mayhem."

tariffs of 10 percent, and by April 10, 2025, the tax on Chinese imports temporarily rose to a whopping 145 percent.[6]

Corruption compounded chaos. Hours before announcing the tariff pause, Trump used his Truth Social platform to alert his wealthy allies. "This is a great time to buy," he said, tipping them that his next steps on tariffs would manipulate the market. On the news of a tariff pause, the US stock market soared upward. Trump's in-the-know, well-off collaborators became better off, making billions by buying low before the market rocketed upward with historic gains. Not all was well, however, for those favored few or any American investors, because in the next day's trading, the market gave back much of the gain as senses of chaos and distrust, multiplied by market manipulation if not insider trading, took hold.

A few days earlier, questions had been asked and responses given as though a clear tariff strategy was at play. Was Trump leveraging negotiations, and, if so, would they help to "make American great again" by reducing if not eliminating trade imbalances that Trump finds objectionable and by putting in their place a global trading field tilted in favor of the United States? Or was the plan to set tariffs and leave them in place on the theory that industry and jobs, especially manufacturing ventures, would be "reshored," brought back to the United States to make the nation's economy thrive as never before?

As the saying goes, "two things can be true at once," but those propositions were never compatible. None of Trump's economic conjurors—wheather Secretary of Commerce Howard Lutnick, Secretary of the Treasury Scott Bessent, Director of the National Economic Council Kevin Hassett, or Director of the Office of Trade and Manufacturing Policy Peter Navarro—could square that vicious circle. Yet these discussions seemed not even remotely valid after Trump injected more chaos into the market with his unpredictable judgment and appeals to "instinct," as if his feelings about what to do were foolproof and even infallible. No amount of spin proclaiming that "this was the plan all along" could mend the self-inflicted rupture that Trump knew not how, or even cared, to repair. The wreckage testified that Trump and Trumpism have become, as David Brooks has said, "a form of nihilism that is devouring everything in its path."[7]

6. Collinson, "Trump's Tariff Mayhem."

7. Brooks, "I Should Have Seen."

Reclaiming the Dream

On April 2, 2025, a week before Trump's incoherent tariff policies reached new levels of chaotic nihilism, the Democrat Mallory McMorrow, a state senator in Michigan, announced her campaign to replace US Senator Gary Peters, who will not seek reelection in 2026. Looking back to 2008, McMorrow recalled that "I graduated right into the recession. I had a great internship that did not lead to a job. I had tens of thousands of dollars in student loans. I spent a couple of nights sleeping in the back seat of my car. And what I know is that there are so many people who simply do not believe that the American dream is possible for them anymore."[8] So, it bears watching that McMorrow's campaign theme emphasizes reclaiming the American Dream.

McMorrow does not think that morality is for suckers. She stresses aspirations and hard work to fulfill them. "Your aspiration," she argues, "is not, 'Well, I just want to pay the bills and put food on the table.' It's, 'I want to be able to work myself out of this situation to where I have a house in a great community and my kid is going to a great school.'" As though echoing James Truslow Adams, she aims higher and better than Trump and his minions. McMorrow says:

> The idea that if you work hard, you get a good education—which should be available no matter where you are—you will be able to have a good life, afford to buy a house and raise a family, and in a place like Michigan, maybe have a place up north and go on vacation. We've just lost that universal value. We're the first generation that did worse than our parents. And I think people just are so angry with the idea that, "I did everything right, and I still can't afford anything, and I am never going to get to where I want to be."[9]

McMorrow refuses to settle for that, especially in a Trump-inflicted downturn that did not have to take place and must not be the end of what we know is better, good, right, and true. "For a lot of people," she acknowledges with resisting regret, "the American dream is no longer an option, and we are fighting to make sure that you have good schools, you have enough housing, you have solid infrastructure so that you can realize the American dream again."[10] McMorrow's campaign defies Trump's nihilism.

8. King, "Democrat Mallory McMorrow."
9. Alter, "Mallory McMorrow."
10. Alter, "Mallory McMorrow."

SCOTUS Immunization

Article III of the US Constitution establishes "the judicial Power of the United States," especially with regard to "one supreme Court." What, if anything, does that provision have to do with (1) Trump's ruinous tariffs, which imperil the American Dream, making it seem unreachable if not impossible, and (2) the determination of a Mallory McMorrow to reclaim the Dream for her constituents? The best answer is: Almost everything. Recent events and some history about the Supreme Court of the United States (SCOTUS) clarify that judgment.

Why is Donald Trump in the White House for Trump 2.0? Multiple answers exist, but one of the most important goes back to August 1, 2023. That is when federal charges were brought against Trump for attempting to overturn the 2020 US presidential election—before, during, and after January 6, 2021.[11] On that fateful winter day, so immensely harmful to the American Dream, a Trump-inspired MAGA mob stormed and desecrated the US Capitol. It threatened the life of then–Vice President Mike Pence. It committed insurrection when a Trump-blessed, if not Trump-orchestrated, coup attempt took place by means of corrupting the presidential election certification in the US Congress. To this day, Trump maintains that the election was rigged and stolen from him. That Big Lie still enthralls his loyalists. Denial of it would cost them the perks of power and wealth that depend on Trump's favor and their fear of losing it.

On November 15, 2022, Donald Trump announced that he would run for president again in 2024. That announcement complicated matters three days later, on November 18, when the overly cautious, slow-to-act Attorney General Merrick Garland appointed a special counsel, Jack Smith, a veteran prosecutor from the Department of Justice and the International Criminal Court in The Hague, Netherlands, to oversee the criminal investigation against Trump.[12] Candidate Trump repeatedly denounced the investigation against him as election interference. Undaunted, Smith obtained a federal grand jury indictment against Trump some eight months later. It charged Trump on four counts, all of them pertaining to widespread efforts to overturn the 2020 election.

On August 3, 2023, Trump appeared in federal court in Washington, DC, where he pleaded not guilty on all charges. On his way from the court, Trump lamented, "This is a very sad day for America. This is a persecution

11. Smith, "Final Report of the Special Counsel's Investigations."

12. Barrett and Stein, "Garland Names Special Counsel."

of a political opponent. This was never supposed to happen in America."[13] August 28 was the date set for the first hearing before federal judge Tanya S. Chutkan. Unfortunately, Trump's trial never happened.

Eyeing a March 2024 trial date for the case labeled *Trump v. United States*, Chutkan started a jury selection process, but it stalled on October 5, 2023, when Trump's attorneys filed a motion to dismiss the case on the grounds that the actions by Trump noted in the indictment were "official duties" and thus Trump had immunity against the charges. Chutkan ruled against that motion on December 1. When Trump's lawyers indicated on December 7 that they would appeal the Chutkan decision, the federal prosecutor Jack Smith, realizing that Trump's strategy—delay, delay, delay—might run out the clock, petitioned SCOTUS to skip the appeals court and resolve the immunity dispute directly on an expedited basis. Promptly, SCOTUS said they would consider that petition, but the court favored Trump by following its own version of delay, delay, delay.

On December 22, SCOTUS rejected Smith's request, sending *Trump v. United States* back to the appeals court in the District of Columbia, which took up the case on January 9, 2024.[14] On February 6, the three appeals court judges unanimously upheld Chutkan's district court ruling against Trump and his contention that he had presidential immunity against the charges in *Trump v. United States*. On February 12, 2024, Trump appealed the case to SCOTUS. Two days later, special counsel Smith again petitioned SCOTUS to expedite the case. Two weeks passed before SCOTUS announced that it would hear the case but scarcely on an expedited basis because arguments were not to begin until April 25, almost two months later. When the deliberations were at last underway, it became clear that the conservative SCOTUS majority wanted to do much more than rule on the particulars of Trump's actions. Trump-appointed justices Neil Gorsuch and Brett Kavanaugh intoned, respectively, that "we're writing a rule for the ages" and "this case has huge implications for the presidency, for the future of the presidency."[15]

The deliberations hinged on two key questions: What constitutes an official act of a president as opposed to private conduct? Does a president have absolute or only limited immunity from prosecution for official acts? Justice Sonia Sotomayor raised a question that exemplified the thorny nature of the case: "If the president decides that his rival is a corrupt person

13. Thrush and Savage, "Trump, Arraigned."

14. For a thorough timeline of events, see Faulders, "Timeline: Special Counsel's Probe."

15. Bomboy, "Supreme Court Tackles."

and he orders the military or orders someone to assassinate him, is that within his official acts for which he can get immunity?"[16]

Not until July 1, 2024, did SCOTUS rule, determining in a 6–3 decision that presidents have absolute immunity for acts committed as president within their core constitutional purview, at least presumptive immunity for official acts within the outer perimeter of their official responsibility, and no immunity for unofficial acts.[17] But SCOTUS did not rule explicitly on the charges against the former president in *Trump v. United States*. Instead, SCOTUS sent the case back to Chutkan in the district court, leaving her to wrestle with the question of how to classify Trump's acts as identified in the indictment against him. If SCOTUS had ruled "for the ages," it had also dodged the Trump indictment. SCOTUS delayed his prosecution. It handed Trump not only release from trial but also immunity from prosecution in a second term. Clever lawyers could be expected to define any action taken by Trump as fitting within the parameters of official duties or "acts within the outer perimeter of . . . official responsibility."[18]

Trump ran out the clock. No trial would be possible until after the election, and with Trump's election on November 5, 2024, the Department of Justice tradition that no sitting president could be prosecuted saved Trump from further duress in the matter. On November 25, 2024, Jack Smith filed a motion to dismiss the case. When Judge Chutkan concurred, Trump was off the hook.

Had Trump stood trial, the chances were good that a jury of his peers would have convicted him. A guilty verdict would not have precluded his being elected and serving a second presidential term. Indeed, on Election Day 2024, Trump was already a proven criminal, convicted of thirty-four felonies in a New York court on May 30, 2024, for scheming to illegally influence the 2016 presidential election through a hush money payment to Stormy Daniels, an adult-film star.[19] Trump still won election, but *Trump v. United States* would have put Trump in the dock for much more serious charges. A trial and a guilty verdict might have led to his defeat, but we will never know. The reason is that SCOTUS prevented, perhaps intentionally, a preelection trial and verdict. Even worse, the 6–3 SCOTUS decision in *Trump v. United States* effectively immunized Trump from any second-term

16. Bomboy, "Supreme Court Tackles."

17. United States Supreme Court, *Trump v. United States* (2024). See also Sands, "Trump's Immunity."

18. United States Supreme Court, *Trump v. United States* (2024).

19. Sisak et al., "Guilty."

legal liability, gutting the fundamental proposition that no American, not even Donald Trump, is above the law.

With concurring opinions by Justices Elena Kagan and Ketanji Brown Jackson, Justice Sonia Sotomayor's dissent summed up the consequences of the majority's decision in *Trump v. United States*. To its sorrow and shame, the nation suffers from them throughout Trump 2.0. Sotomayor wrote:

> The Court effectively creates a law-free zone around the President, upsetting the status quo that has existed since the Founding. This new official-acts immunity now "lies about like a loaded weapon" for any President that wishes to place his own interests, his own political survival, or his own financial gain, above the interests of the Nation. *Korematsu v. United States*, 323 U. S. 214, 246 (1944) (Jackson, J., dissenting). The President of the United States is the most powerful person in the country, and possibly the world. When he uses his official powers in any way, under the majority's reasoning, he now will be insulated from criminal prosecution. Orders the Navy's Seal Team 6 to assassinate a political rival? Immune. Organizes a military coup to hold onto power? Immune. Takes a bribe in exchange for a pardon? Immune. Immune, immune, immune.
>
> Let the President violate the law, let him exploit the trappings of his office for personal gain, let him use his official power for evil ends. Because if he knew that he may one day face liability for breaking the law, he might not be as bold and fearless as we would like him to be. That is the majority's message today.
>
> Even if these nightmare scenarios never play out, and I pray they never do, the damage has been done. The relationship between the President and the people he serves has shifted irrevocably. In every use of official power, the President is now a king above the law.[20]

Saving the American Dream requires resistance to overturn immunity that makes Donald Trump or any American president "a king above the law."

Decisions Bad and Good

Article III of the US Constitution attempts to ensure that the United States will enjoy what the founder John Adams called "a government of laws, and not of men." In addition to establishing "one supreme Court," this article provides for the establishment of other courts "as the Congress may

20. United States Supreme Court, *Trump v. United States* (2024).

from time to time ordain and establish." Recognizing that the Constitution required work as soon as ratification took place on June 21, 1788, the new Congress passed the Judiciary Act of 1789, which President George Washington signed into law on September 24. In addition to defining the Supreme Court as having one chief justice and five associate justices, the Judiciary Act established thirteen district courts, one for each of the original states, and three circuit courts to handle appeals.[21]

As constituted in 2025, the federal judiciary system still has three levels as designated in 1789. Presently, federal cases go to trial first in a courtroom within one of the nation's ninety-four federal judicial districts. These districts are organized into twelve regional circuits, each with a Court of Appeals. The appellate courts review district court decisions to ensure that procedures have been fair and that the law has been rightly applied. SCOTUS is the final level of appeal. Appointed by the president and confirmed by the Senate, federal judges have no term limits and can be removed only by impeachment and conviction for a high crime or misdemeanor. *Trump v. United States* went through the steps from district to appellate court and then to SCOTUS.

The importance of district courts should not be underestimated. The federal district court is the starting point for any case arising under federal statutes, the Constitution, or treaties. Such cases can be civil or criminal. Civil cases involve disputes between persons or entities; criminal charges are not at play but alleged damages and remedies for them are. Criminal cases involve governmental prosecution of an individual or entity for violating a law. In a district court, civil cases originate with a complaint brought to the court by a plaintiff, who also serves a copy on the defendant (that is, alerts the defendant of the lawsuit). Criminal cases originate when the government, after proper legal investigation, formally charges an individual or entity with a crime.

In general, district court decisions do not bind the whole country, except when they have done so. Issuing injunctions, for example, is among the most important actions taken by a judge in a federal district court. An injunction orders that a party—it even could be the US president—must do or not do a specific act, at least until further deliberation takes place. Since the 1960s, district courts have sometimes issued nationwide or universal injunctions to prevent the federal government "from implementing a challenged law, regulation, or other policy against all relevant persons and entities, whether or not such persons or entities are parties participating in

21. United States National Archives, "Federal Judiciary Act (1789)."

the litigation."[22] In the early months of Trump 2.0, federal judges put more than forty restraints on his actions, the decisions grounded in evidence that illegal and unconstitutional steps were being taken.[23] Trump supporters pushed back by demanding impeachment of judges and legislation that would restrict federal judges' ability to declare nationwide injunctions.[24]

Nationwide injunctions from federal district court judges are imperfect tools. Halting government policies for everyone around the country, they may infringe too much on the government's ability to administer policies, problematically encourage plaintiffs to "shop" for "friendly" judges, hinder the rule of law by substituting hasty intervention for careful deliberation, and sow uncertainty and confusion when policies are prematurely blocked and then reinstated on appeal as cases progress through the courts. The counterarguments are that time can be of the essence, justice delayed is justice denied, and nationwide abuses of government power—especially when they are patently illegal and unconstitutional—require prompt nationwide relief.

An impending collision became real on January 20, 2025, the first day of Trump 2.0, when the president signed Executive Order 14160, Protecting the Meaning and Value of American Citizenship.[25] Rejecting birthright citizenship, it directed that "no department or agency of the United States government shall issue documents recognizing United States citizenship, or accept documents issued by State, local, or other governments or authorities purporting to recognize United States citizenship, to persons: (1) when that person's mother was unlawfully present in the United States and the person's father was not a United States citizen or lawful permanent resident at the time of said person's birth, or (2) when that person's mother's presence in the United States was lawful but temporary, and the person's father was not a United States citizen or lawful permanent resident at the time of said person's birth." Part of Trump's anti-immigrant policies, the order would result in thousands of stateless newborns—as many as 255,000 annually, according to reliable estimates—who could be subjected to the cruel deportation policies of Trump 2.0.[26]

The crisis produced by Executive Order 14160 was profoundly constitutional because the measure itself is so deeply unconstitutional. Trump intended to upend the Fourteenth Amendment and its guarantee of birthright

22. Lampe, "Nationwide Injunctions, January Through March."

23. Jouvenal et al., "GOP Lawmakers Take Aim."

24. Walker, "House Passes Bill."

25. Trump, Exec. Order No. 14160 (2025).

26. Van Hook et al., "Repealing Birthright Citizenship."

citizenship: "all persons born or naturalized in the United States and subject to the jurisdiction thereof, are citizens of the United States and of the State wherein they reside." SCOTUS affirmed birthright citizenship in *United States v. Wong Kim Ark* (1898), establishing that a person born in the US to Chinese immigrants was a citizen.[27] The ruling reaffirmed citizenship for virtually all individuals born in the US with exceptions for children of foreign diplomats or enemy occupiers. Subsequent congressional acts, such as the Nationality Act of 1940, have done likewise. Trump's Executive Order 14160 violates the Constitution and the law, blatantly and many times over. Among other things, the Constitution makes it unlawful for the president or Congress to take away the citizenship rights that are clearly stated in the Fourteenth Amendment. Only a further amendment to the Constitution could revise or reject the Fourteenth Amendment. Unless American democracy is completely destroyed, the chances of such action are slim to none.

Americans celebrate that we are a nation of immigrants, a story more complicated and painful than we like to admit. Indigenous people inhabited the land for centuries before the United States displaced and dispossessed them. Enslaved Africans had no choice as the harrowing Middle Passage brought its survivors to American ground, which became their children's home. The family histories of most Americans are not like those of Indigenous or Black people, but they are stories about women, children, and men who came here from afar. Hence, it is our time-honored tradition, enshrined in law, that American citizenship is bestowed not by any political officer but by one's birth. For at least three reasons, moreover, birthright citizenship is foundational for the American Dream: (1) It reinforces democracy by affirming that the nation's life is grounded in shared values, including equal opportunity, not on ethnicity or race, caste or class. (2) It ensures that all children born in the US are recognized as equal under the law, regardless of their background, a principle of inclusion that is a core element of the American Dream. (3) By advancing security for families in the United States, birthright citizenship promotes economic growth for them and for the United States.

Trump's signature on Executive Order 14160 was barely dry before twenty-two states and the District of Columbia, plus numerous immigrants' rights groups, joined lawsuits to challenge in federal district courts his order against birthright citizenship. Nationwide injunctions from federal district courts followed, prompting the Trump administration to appeal to the Supreme Court on the grounds that lower courts lacked the authority to issue such restraints. SCOTUS, the administration argued, should limit the effect

27. United States Supreme Court, *United States v. Wong Kim Ark* (1898).

of injunctions to the specific plaintiffs in each case, rather than applying them to everyone nationwide.[28]

Disguised as an attempt to overturn the Fourteenth Amendment, which even Trump 2.0 knew was a losing proposition, the real objective in Trump's appeal to SCOTUS was to damn the authority of federal district judges to issue nationwide injunctions. If Trump could prevail in that case, the floodgates would open. He could rule largely as he pleased. Neither the rule of law nor democracy itself would block his way, at least not much. The American Dream would be crippled if not dead.

Procedure Matters

SCOTUS took the bait or, more accurately, the opportunity not to adjudicate the "merits" of Trump's clearly unconstitutional destruction of birthright citizenship, but to rule on a procedural matter, the injunction issue. SCOTUS's hypocrisy was self-evident. The Trump-packed, conservative court had nothing to say about nationwide injunctions that were issued against the administration of Joe Biden, but when Trump's wishes were at stake, the conservative majority bent the knee and kissed the ring to bless a thinly disguised mandate for an imperial presidency.

Argued on May 15, 2025, and decided on June 27, 2025, *Trump v. CASA, Inc.* held by a predictable 6–3 majority that lower courts can only issue nationwide injunctions when necessary to provide complete relief to the plaintiff, not to universally block policies nationwide.[29] This decision meant that Executive Order 14160 remained at play, at least for a time, with results as destructive as they are chaotic. Children born in some states might not be citizens until and unless SCOTUS rules to defend birthright citizenship against Trump's executive order, an action that might not come, if it does, until months pass.[30] At least in the short run, SCOTUS created a chaotic, unworkable patchwork regarding birthright citizenship. Furthermore, the majority invited Trump to issue more tyrannical executive orders that only the Supreme Court could prevent from having the force of law unless those harmed are equipped to sue and wealthy enough to litigate for their rights.

Amy Coney Barrett wrote the decision for the majority, which included Justices Samuel Alito, Neil Gorsuch, Bret Kavanaugh, Chief Justice John

28. VanSickle, " Supreme Court Agrees to Review Trump Order."

29. For an early critical view of the decision, see Firestone, "Supreme Court's." For an early sympathetic view, see Bray, "Supreme Court." For a perceptive overview of the issues, see Cohn, "By Ruling Against Nationwide Injunctions."

30. On these points, see Jordan, "What the Supreme Court's Ruling."

Roberts, and Clarence Thomas.[31] Barrett's decision, grounded in an arcane "originalist" legal philosophy, can be summarized in her own words.[32]

> The issue the Court decides is whether, under the Judiciary Act of 1789, federal courts have equitable authority to issue universal injunctions. . . . Universal injunctions likely exceed the equitable authority that Congress has given to federal courts. . . . Universal injunctions were conspicuously nonexistent for most of the Nation's history. . . . The universal injunction lacks a historical pedigree. . . . Because universal injunctions lack a founding-era forebear, federal courts lack authority to issue them. . . . Nothing like a universal injunction was available at the founding, or for that matter, for more than a century thereafter. Thus, under the Judiciary Act, federal courts lack authority to issue them. . . . The Government here is likely to suffer irreparable harm from the District Courts' entry of injunctions. . . . When a court concludes that the Executive Branch has acted unlawfully, the answer is not for the court to exceed its power, too.

One of Barrett's distinguished SCOTUS predecessors, Oliver Wendell Holmes Jr. (1841–1935), served on the Supreme Court for thirty years. The law, he observed, has sometimes been called "the government of the living by the dead." But, he judiciously added, "the present has a right to govern itself so far as it can."[33] Barrett's slavish originalism enslaves the present and the future to the past in our especially dire times. "As a legal matter," Joanna R. Lampe astutely argues, "no federal statute explicitly authorizes the courts to issue nationwide injunctions, nor does any statute expressly limit the courts' ability to do so."[34]

Barrett's opinion left the door open for cumbersome class-action suits to gain relief from unlawful actions like Trump's. Her ruling stopped short of calling nationwide injunctions unconstitutional but severely limited them by inconclusively appealing to the dead to govern the living. In practice, nationwide injunctions are part of a persistent movement encouraged by Holmes's insistence that present circumstances and future well-being have a rightful place in legal decision-making, especially when tyranny and lawlessness immediately threaten. If they are relatively recent tools and "lack a founding-era forebear," that is scarcely a convincing, let alone sufficient,

31. United States Supreme Court, *Trump v. CASA, Inc.* (2025).

32. On originalism, see Dennie, *Originalism Trap*; Lepore, "Originalism Killed the Constitution."

33. Holmes, "Learning and Science" (1895).

34. Lampe, "Nationwide Injunctions: Law, History, Proposals."

reason to virtually ban them as SCOTUS has done. Even if nationwide injunctions are abused from time to time, that shortcoming calls only for their use to be sagacious. Barrett to the contrary notwithstanding, the nationwide injunctions against Trump's Executive Order 14160 were precisely of that kind and much needed.[35] As of July 2025, Congress had considered but not passed legislation to limit or prohibit nationwide injunctions, but the SCOTUS ruling has definitely and unfortunately curtailed them.

In a spirit that echoed Holmes, dissents from Ketanji Brown Jackson, Elena Kagan, and Sonia Sotomayor were as heated as they were on target. Sotomayor wrote:

> No right is safe in the new legal regime the Court creates. Today, the threat is to birthright citizenship. Tomorrow, a different administration may try to seize firearms from law-abiding citizens or prevent people of certain faiths from gathering to worship. The majority holds that, absent cumbersome class-action litigation, courts cannot completely enjoin even such plainly unlawful policies unless doing so is necessary to afford the formal parties complete relief. That holding renders constitutional guarantees meaningful in name only for any individuals who are not parties to a lawsuit. Because I will not be complicit in so grave an attack on our system of law, I dissent.[36]

Jackson said:

> The Court's decision to permit the Executive to violate the Constitution with respect to anyone who has not yet sued is an existential threat to the rule of law. . . . Make no mistake: Today's ruling allows the Executive to deny people rights that the Founders plainly wrote into our Constitution, so long as those individuals have not found a lawyer or asked a court in a particular manner to have their rights protected. This perverse burden shifting cannot coexist with the rule of law. In essence, the Court has now shoved lower court judges out of the way in cases where executive action is challenged, and has gifted the Executive with the prerogative of sometimes disregarding the law. As a result, the Judiciary—the one institution that is solely responsible for ensuring our Republic endures as a Nation of laws—has put both our legal system, and our system of government, in grave jeopardy. . . . By needlessly granting the Government's emergency application to prohibit universal injunctions, the Court has cleared a path for the Executive to choose law-free action

35. Trammell, "Constitutionality."

36. United States Supreme Court, *Trump v. CASA, Inc.* (2025).

> at this perilous moment for our Constitution—right when the Judiciary should be hunkering down to do all it can to preserve the law's constraints. I have no doubt that, if judges must allow the Executive to act unlawfully in some circumstances, as the Court concludes today, executive lawlessness will flourish, and from there, it is not difficult to predict how this all ends. Eventually, executive power will become completely uncontainable, and our beloved constitutional Republic will be no more.[37]

Donald Trump proclaimed that the SCOTUS verdict was a big win. His words, incredible though they are, deserve notice too:

> The Supreme Court has delivered a monumental victory for the Constitution, the separation of powers, and the RULE OF LAW in striking down the excessive use of nationwide injunctions. . . . I was elected on a historic mandate, but in recent months, we've seen a handful of radical left judges effectively try to overrule the rightful powers of the president to stop the American people from getting the policies that they voted for in record numbers. It was a grave threat to democracy.[38]

The American Dream depends on dissent against the myriad distortions and lies in those few words from Trump. In no way is *Trump v. CASA, Inc.* a victory for the Constitution, the separation of powers, and the rule of law. The SCOTUS decision is the opposite of all that. Trump got no historic mandate. Some of the judges who rightly used nationwide injunctions to rule against him are Trump-appointed. Most Americans reject Trump's policies. He is a grave threat to democracy.

In her dissent in *Trump v. CASA, Inc.* Ketanji Brown Jackson was right when she asserted that the SCOTUS decision created "a zone of lawlessness within which the Executive has the prerogative to take or leave the law as it wishes, and where individuals who would otherwise be entitled to the law's protection become subject to the Executive's whims instead." Sonia Sotomayor understood that SCOTUS's creation of this zone of lawlessness did not originate with *Trump v. CASA, Inc.* Its precursor is *Trump v. United States*, the 2024 decision in which this same Roberts Court essentially handed Trump permission to do as he wishes without fear of criminal indictment, no matter how corrupt, immoral, and antithetical to American democracy his acts might be. That decision was top of mind when Sotomayor took a rare step. In addition to reading aloud from the bench, she strengthened her *Trump v. CASA, Inc.* dissent by adding an unscripted indictment: "The other

37. United States Supreme Court, *Trump v. CASA, Inc.* (2025).

38. Trump, "'A BIG WIN.'"

shoe has dropped on executive immunity."[39] Her statement underscored that *Trump v. United States* and *Trump v. CASA, Inc.* are two of the most disastrous decisions in SCOTUS history.

Erwin Chemerinsky, a leading legal scholar, concurred. On the SCOTUS decision against nationwide injunctions by district courts, he asserted that "nothing in any federal law or the Constitution justifies this restriction on the judicial power. . . . Never before has the Supreme Court imposed such restrictions on the ability of courts to provide relief against unconstitutional acts. . . . Let there be no doubt what this means; the Supreme Court has greatly reduced the power of the federal courts. And it has done so at a time when the federal judiciary may be our only guardrail to protect the Constitution and democracy."[40] Meanwhile, Chief Justice John G. Roberts Jr. decamped to a judicial conference in Charlotte, North Carolina. His audience full of lower court federal judges, the ones he and his conservative allies had castrated the day before, Roberts said nothing about *Trump v. CASA, Inc.* Instead, he condemned "violence, intimidation, and defiance directed at judges."[41]

Less than two weeks later, on July 10, Judge Joseph N. Laplante of the US District Court for the District of New Hampshire countered the Roberts Court's ruling against nationwide injunctions. In a case called *Barbara v. Donald Trump*, Laplante issued a preliminary injunction against Trump's executive order opposing birthright citizenship. Importantly, the judge certified the lawsuit as a class action, an option left open by the Roberts Court, which meant that the lawsuit represented all individuals who would be affected by Trump's order. This saga is far from over. On December 5, 2025, SCOTUS announced that it will hear the case to decide whether Trump's effort to ban birthright citizenship is constitutional. Meanwhile, Laplante snatched some recompense from the voracious jaws of *Trump v. CASA, Inc.*[42]

Overturned and Discredited

It should be hoped that federal courts will yet be a bulwark against Trump's reckless disregard for the rule of law, but the Roberts Court shows that such trust may be forlorn. The future of the American Dream hangs in the balance. So, it is good that there are reasons not to despair, a proposition that

39. Fritze et al., "Takeaways."

40. Chemerinsky, "Stunning and Tragic." See also Chemerinsky, *No Democracy Lasts Forever.*

41. VanSickle, "Chief Justice Urges."

42. VanSickle, "Supreme Court Agrees to Review Trump Order."

invites historical perspective about other landmark SCOTUS cases that have impeded or advanced the American Dream, sometimes before that term existed.

First, consider crucial SCOTUS decisions that had to be overturned or discredited for the American Dream to survive and thrive. Prior to *Trump v. CASA, Inc.*, the July 1, 2024, decision in *Trump v. United States* is the most recent member of that dismal group.[43] It belongs there not only because it disrespects the foundational principle that no American is above the law but also because it reflects and advances the pernicious *unitary executive theory* (UET), an interpretation of the Constitution, embraced and practiced by Trump, which holds that the President of the United States has sole authority over the executive branch of government.

Supporters of the UET include Russell Vought, director of Trump's powerful Office of Management and Budget and a mastermind behind the malevolent Project 2025 scheme about which Trump has denied knowledge while he steadily works to implement its antidemocratic policies.[44] Under Chief Justice Roberts, the conservative SCOTUS majority (Justices Alito, Barrett, Gorsuch, Kavanaugh, and Thomas) tilts toward the UET too. Advocates for the theory believe that it is grounded in key provisions of Article II of the US Constitution. That article not only vests executive power in the president and no one else but also mandates that the president is responsible to ensure that the nation's laws are faithfully executed.

UET backers interpret these fundamental Article II provisions to mean that Trump and subsequent presidents have immense power to remove and replace any federal employee and to impose their will on every decision in every agency in the executive branch. That interpretation is no small matter. The executive branch of the federal government includes agencies that employ millions of Americans: the Departments of State, Justice, Defense, and Treasury, for example, and entities such as the Central Intelligence Agency, the Environmental Protection Agency, and the National Aeronautics and Space Administration (NASA). UET proponents believe that the Constitution and the needs of the country presently call for an extremely strong president. Donald Trump tenaciously agrees with that proposition. Critics and opponents push back. The UET invites, they judiciously contend, an imperial presidency that threatens the separation of powers, the rule of law, and democracy itself in ways that the Founders would find abhorrent.[45] Defending UET, at least by

43. United States Supreme Court, *Trump v. United States* (2024). See also Sands, "Trump's Immunity."

44. Brown, "Why Trump Thinks."

45. Sunstein, "This Theory." See also Hutzler, "Trump and the 'Unitary Executive.'"

implication, escalates the danger to democracy and to the American Dream; the executive continues to assume more and more unchecked power thanks to the disastrous SCOTUS decision in *Trump v. United States*, making it one of the worst SCOTUS rulings in American history.

As noted earlier, in deliberations during *Trump v. United States*, Justice Sonia Sotomayor rightly asked, "If the president decides that his rival is a corrupt person and he orders the military or orders someone to assassinate him, is that within his official acts for which he can get immunity?"[46] She sensed that SCOTUS would grant—in this case, Donald Trump—immunity that would make the answer yes. That meant that no one is safe in the United States. Five other SCOTUS cases have taken similarly egregious positions. Fortunately, they were discredited if not overturned. *Trump v. United States* is already discredited. Saving the American Dream requires that it should be overturned as well. We can see why by noting cases that are its closest relatives.

1. *Dred Scott v. Sandford* (1856) held that people of African descent, whether enslaved or free, were not and could never be citizens of the United States.[47] This ruling withheld from them the rights and protections afforded to citizens under the Constitution. One can scarcely imagine what the United States would be today if the Thirteenth Amendment (1865) had not abolished slavery and the Fourteenth (1868) had not overturned *Dred Scott v. Sandford* by redefining citizenship to ensure that all individuals born or naturalized in the United States, including those formerly enslaved, are citizens. The overturning of that decision is bedrock for the American Dream and foundational for our democracy. For similar reasons, *Trump v. CASA, Inc.*, which moves in the direction of disallowing birthright citizenship, should be overturned as well.

2. *Plessy v. Ferguson* (1896) embedded racism in American life by upholding the legality of racial segregation in public facilities, including transportation, schools, restaurants, and other public accommodations as long as they were supposedly equal in quality.[48] The pernicious principle of "separate but equal" had the potential to endanger Americans time and again. Its overturning in *Brown v. Board of Education* (1954) was too long in coming, but it did arrive, saving the American Dream and the country, although not from every threat or kind of damage that SCOTUS could do.[49]

3. *Korematsu v. United States* (1944) threatened the American Dream by showing how SCOTUS can act in ways that cancel the rights of American

46. Bomboy, "Supreme Court Tackles."

47. United States Supreme Court, *Dred Scott v. Sandford* (1856).

48. United States Supreme Court, *Plessy v. Ferguson* (1896).

49. United States Supreme Court, *Brown v. Board of Education of Topeka* (1954).

citizens.[50] Decided on December 18, 1944, this case emerged in wartime. For months, Nazi Germany dominated Europe and committed genocide against the European Jews before the United States declared war against Germany as well as Japan after Japanese forces attacked Pearl Harbor on December 7, 1941. Under the Alien Enemies Act (AEA) of 1798, about 11,000 German Americans and German nationals were detained in camps across the country due to fears of espionage and disloyalty.[51] That law states that when the US is at war or facing an "invasion or predatory incursion" by another nation, the president can detain and deport citizens of the enemy nation. Unconstitutionally, Donald Trump invoked the old and little-used AEA to round up and deport alleged members of Tren de Aragua, a Venezuelan gang. According to Trump's propaganda, the president of Venezuela, Nicolás Maduro, unleashed the gang against the United States.[52]

During World War II, the AEA was used constitutionally, but it was considered insufficient to combat alleged threats from Japanese Americans because, while allowing for the detention of alien enemies, the AEA did not specifically apply to US citizens. The result was Executive Order 9066, which President Franklin Roosevelt issued on February 19, 1942.[53] It did not refer explicitly to Japanese Americans, but it authorized the military to exclude "any or all persons" from designated military areas, primarily the West Coast. Roosevelt's order was used to legitimate the detention of more than 120,000 ordinary citizens and immigrants of Japanese descent in ten relocation centers at places such as Tule Lake and Manzanar, California. These centers were American concentration camps.

A series of "exclusion orders" implemented Executive Order 9066 by specifying when and where Japanese Americans had to report in order to be in compliance with it. When a Japanese American citizen, Fred Korematsu, 23, disobeyed Civilian Exclusion Order No. 34 by failing to report for relocation, he was arrested on May 30, 1942, in San Leandro, California. Standing trial in a federal district court, he was convicted on September 8, 1942, and incarcerated. When Korematsu appealed all the way to SCOTUS, the result was one of the worst decisions by that body.

In a 6–3 decision, SCOTUS upheld both the constitutionality of internment camps for Japanese Americans during World War II and Korematsu's conviction, affirming that the need to protect against espionage outweighed

50. United States Supreme Court, *Korematsu v. United States* (1944).

51. United States National Archives, Alien and Sedition Acts (1798).

52. Montoya-Galvez, "Trump Invokes 1798 Alien Enemies Act."

53. Roosevelt, Exec. Order 9066 (1942); United States National Archives, "Executive Order 9066."

Korematsu's individual rights. Writing for the majority, Justice Hugo Black made a problematic argument:

> All legal restrictions which curtail the civil rights of a single racial group are immediately suspect. That is not to say that all such restrictions are unconstitutional. It is to say that courts must subject them to the most rigid scrutiny. Pressing public necessity may sometimes justify the existence of such restrictions; racial antagonism never can. . . . Korematsu was not excluded from the Military Area because of hostility to him or his race. He was excluded because we are at war with the Japanese Empire, because the properly constituted military authorities feared an invasion of our West Coast and felt constrained to take proper security measures, because they decided that the military urgency of the situation demanded that all citizens of Japanese ancestry be segregated from the West Coast temporarily.

Writing for the dissenters, Justice Robert H. Jackson, who later served as the US Chief Prosecutor at the International Military Tribunal, which prosecuted Nazi war criminals at Nuremberg, Germany, identified the long-term as well as immediate danger in the SCOTUS decision:

> A military order, however unconstitutional, is not apt to last longer than the military emergency. Even during that period a succeeding commander may revoke it all. But once a judicial opinion rationalizes such an order to show that it conforms to the Constitution, or rather rationalizes the Constitution to show that the Constitution sanctions such an order, the Court for all time has validated the principle of racial discrimination in criminal procedure and of transplanting American citizens. The principle then lies about like a loaded weapon ready for the hand of any authority that can bring forward a plausible claim of an urgent need. Every repetition imbeds that principle more deeply in our law and thinking and expands it to new purposes.

Jackson anticipated how a version of the Korematsu decision would echo in Trump's 2025 deportation initiatives against immigrants and dissenters.

4. *Citizens United v. Federal Election Commission* (2010) keeps endangering the American Dream by reversing long-standing election campaign financing restrictions and by enabling, and thereby encouraging, corporations, unions, and other groups to spend unlimited funds to influence elections.[54] The result has been the establishment of vast political action

54. United States Supreme Court, *Citizens United v. Federal Election Commission* (2010).

committees (PACs) that funnel immense sums into political campaigns, without needing to disclose the identity of donors. Private wealth and political power collude in ways that corrupt democracy and imperil fair and free elections.

In a 5–4 decision, SCOTUS found that limits on independent spending from corporations, unions, and other groups are equivalent to limits on free speech. The court's reasoning, taking corporations as an example, entailed that corporations are not literally people, but people form them and pursue goals through them. With that understanding at play, corporations speak, and they have a right to do so freely. Spending money—spending it on politics—is one way corporations speak. On those grounds, the justices reasoned, spending restrictions limit freedom of speech.

A counterargument held that restrictions on political spending are important to prevent abuse and corruption. Especially problematic is "dark money," which leaves the sources, and thus the interests, of its donors unidentified and hidden. The SCOTUS majority did not find such problems to be sufficient or compelling enough to modify its position. Nor was it persuaded that the immense wealth of corporations might in some instances overwhelm freedom of speech. On the contrary, said the Court's majority, the voices of the most significant sectors of the economy would be stifled by spending restrictions, and that limitation would be unjustified.

The decision in *Citizens United* stands, but it remains significant that an ongoing effort to rid the country of it also stands and may be growing. That development's success would be good for the American Dream and for the country overall. The overturning of *Citizens United* would restore confidence that elections are at least freer and fairer than they are now, swayed by "dark money" from unfettered PACs and corporations-as-persons, in a climate where tortured interpretations of the First Amendment equate the spending of money with freedom of speech. Such mystification helps to explain why Donald Trump, a convicted felon, occupies the White House.

5. On May 9, 2023, a Manhattan jury found Donald Trump liable for sexually abusing and defaming the journalist E. Jean Carroll. She was awarded $5 million in damages. When Trump persisted in defaming Carroll, a second trial resulted in a federal judge's order on February 8, 2024, that Trump owed Carroll $83.3 million more. The list of allegations of abuse that women have brought against Trump is as disgusting as it is long. In the 2024 presidential campaign, Trump claimed he would protect women, ominously adding "whether the women like it or not."[55] Few of Trump's claims

55. Nehamas and Green, "Trump Says."

are hollower. *Dobbs v. Jackson Women's Health Organization* (2022) testifies to that.[56]

Running for the presidency in 2016, Trump boasted that his appointment of SCOTUS judges would assure the overturning of *Roe v. Wade* (1973), which had given American women the autonomy that came with the right to abortion.[57] The die was cast when Trump successfully maneuvered the appointment of Justices Neil Gorsuch, Brett Kavanaugh, and Amy Coney Barrett, who joined Justices Clarence Thomas and Samuel Alito in a 5–4 *Dobbs* ruling that found no constitutional right to abortion, overturned *Roe v. Wade*, and left decisions about abortion and attendant women's health issues to the states, ensuring chaos and cruelty, endangered health and unnecessary death for many American women. For the first time in decades, a fundamental federal right was taken away. Daughters lost the right their mothers had possessed. Granddaughters lost what their grandmothers had held. Fathers and grandfathers, husbands and partners felt the loss as well. Far from making anyone safer, *Dobbs* showed that Trump's influence over SCOTUS is malign. He bears direct responsibility for one of the worst SCOTUS decisions in American history.

Better Landmarks

Fortunately, SCOTUS has had better days than the ones marred by its worst decisions, including *Trump v. United States* and *Trump v. CASA, Inc.* Checks and balances among the three branches of the federal government, the rule of law, the defense of democracy, and the expansion of the American Dream have all been enhanced by five SCOTUS cases that merit recognition.

1. Neither the Declaration of Independence nor the US Constitution contains the signature of John Marshall, but he remains one of the most important founders of the country because President John Adams named him chief justice of SCOTUS on February 4, 1801. He held that office until his death on July 6, 1835. No SCOTUS case is more important than *Marbury v. Madison* (1803), which was decided early in Marshall's term.[58] The details of the case are significant but even more so is the ruling that emerged from them.

In 1801, Adams appointed William Marbury to be a justice of the peace in the District of Columbia, but the president died before the appointment

56. United States Supreme Court, *Dobbs v. Jackson Women's Health Organization* (2022),

57. United States Supreme Court, *Roe v. Wade* (1973),

58. United States Supreme Court, *Marbury v. Madison* (1803).

papers were delivered. Thomas Jefferson succeeded Adams as president and did not want Adams's appointment of Marbury to be honored. So, Jefferson instructed James Madison, his secretary of state, to withhold it. Marbury sued Madison, appealing for a court order to give him his due. When the case reached SCOTUS, Marshall, writing for the unanimous majority, found that Marbury did have a right to his appointment. But the part of the Judiciary Act of 1789 under which Marbury was suing, said Marshall, was unconstitutional because it expanded the Supreme Court's jurisdiction beyond what the Constitution allowed, specifically in Article III, Section 2. Marbury lost his case, but SCOTUS triumphed because Marshall's decision established the decisive principle of judicial review, which empowers SCOTUS to strike down laws that violate the Constitution.

2. The Constitution itself does not grant SCOTUS this power, but Marshall's decision in *Marbury v. Madison* nonetheless established SCOTUS's power to interpret the Constitution and to declare laws unconstitutional. Judicial review checks the power of the legislative and executive branches of government. It brings balance to the three branches by underscoring the power of the judicial branch, and SCOTUS in particular, to interpret the Constitution and to find, as Marshall did in his key decision, "that a law repugnant to the Constitution is void, and that courts, as well as other departments, are bound by that instrument."[59] SCOTUS does not always get its decisions right, but, overall, the power of judicial review does more to save the American Dream than to harm it.

Evidence for that claim is found in *Brown v. Board of Education* (1954). The case began in 1951 when the public school system in Topeka, Kansas, refused to enroll the daughter of Oliver Brown, a local Black father, at the school closest to their home, instead requiring the child to ride a bus to a segregated Black school farther away. The Browns and twelve other local Black families in similar situations filed a class-action lawsuit in US federal court against the Topeka board of education, alleging its segregation policy was unconstitutional. When the case reached SCOTUS, the court overturned *Plessy v. Ferguson*, saying that "separate educational facilities are inherently unequal," and ruling that racially segregated schools are unconstitutional.[60]

This SCOTUS decision encountered widespread resistance, especially in southern states, which raised a thorny question, one very much present again with regard to Donald Trump's lawlessness: What happens when a SCOTUS ruling is defied and disobeyed? In 1955, a second SCOTUS

59. United States Supreme Court, *Marbury v. Madison* (1803).

60. United States Supreme Court, *Brown v. Board of Education* (1954). See also United States National Archives, "Brown v. Board of Education."

ruling directed states to implement desegregation plans "with all deliberate speed,"[61] but even then, obstruction persisted. Private schools for Whites only were established. Harassment and violence greeted some Black students who tried to integrate previously segregated schools. On September 23, 1957, President Dwight D. Eisenhower issued Executive Order 10730, which sent federal troops to maintain peace and order while the integration of Central High School in Little Rock, Arkansas, took place.[62]

As the Little Rock episode made clear, SCOTUS lacks enforcement power, which leaves the rule of law vulnerable if the American people and, in our own time, President Donald Trump thumb their noses at SCOTUS, echoing Andrew Jackson's alleged taunt in 1832 that "John Marshall has made his decision; now let him enforce it." In *Worcester v. Georgia* (1832) the Marshall Court ruled that the Cherokee Nation was a distinct political entity with its own sovereignty, and therefore Georgia's laws could not apply within Cherokee territory.[63] Jackson's refusal to enforce the ruling led to the "Trail of Tears," the forced and lethal removal of Cherokee people to Oklahoma, a shameful chapter in American history.

The struggle for racial justice and minority rights is far from over in 2025 and beyond. The division, cruelty, and disregard for judicial authority that mark Trump 2.0 bear witness to that, but nevertheless *Brown v. Board of Education* is a landmark that advances the American Dream's commitment to resist racism and to defend liberty and justice for all.

3. Donald Trump's lawlessness far exceeds Richard Nixon's, whose presidential term, January 20, 1969–August 9, 1974, ended in well-deserved disgrace when he resigned in his second term rather than facing criminal charges on which he surely would have been convicted. Now widely recognized as mistaken, Gerald Ford's subsequent pardon of Nixon has done little to redeem Nixon or, for that matter, his successor Ford, who was never elected either vice president or president but rose to those positions because corruption deposed then–Vice President Spiro Agnew and then Nixon himself.

United States v. Nixon (1974) stands as a crucial landmark because it defended the principle that no person, not even the president of the United States, is above the law.[64] The origins of the case go back to June 17, 1972, when police apprehended burglars at the Democratic National Committee facilities in the Watergate office complex in Washington, DC. The thieves'

61. United States Supreme Court, *Brown v. Board of Education* (1955).

62. Eisenhower, Exec. Order 10730 (1954–1958); Encyclopedia of Arkansas, "Desegregation."

63. United States Supreme Court, *Worcester v. Georgia* (1832).

64. United States Supreme Court, *United States v. Nixon* (1974).

aim was to steal information that would help Nixon's upcoming reelection campaign. A few days later, Nixon ordered the FBI to curtail its investigation of the Watergate break in. Unfortunately for Nixon, the paranoid president's office recording system preserved the directive. The tape recording became the "smoking gun" when it confirmed that Nixon was engaged in criminal cover-up.

Nixon balked when prosecutors sought to obtain the damning audio tapes. He argued that executive privilege gave him the power to withhold sensitive information, such as the tapes, from other government branches in order to maintain confidential communications within the executive branch and to secure the national interest. Nixon's defense did not persuade SCOTUS. When the court received the matter on July 8, 1974, it decided on July 24—in the words of Chief Justice Warren Burger—that "neither the doctrine of separation of powers nor the generalized need for confidentiality of high-level communications, without more, can sustain an absolute, unqualified Presidential privilege of immunity from judicial process under all circumstances." Burger added a telling comment, citing a decision by John Marshall in an 1807 treason case against Aaron Burr: "Marshall cannot be read to mean in any sense that a President is above the law."[65]

The tapes showed that Nixon had committed crimes. Knowing that impeachment and conviction awaited him, with the likelihood of criminal proceedings against him on the horizon as well, Nixon resigned about two weeks later. *United States v. Nixon* set matters right. *Trump v. United States* did not. The former is justly celebrated. The latter deserves overturning. The Harvard legal scholar Neil Eggleston supports these points when he says:

> The Nixon case made clear that the notion that the president's communications are absolutely privileged and cannot be reviewed by a court was wrong. It determined that President Nixon was a witness, just like any other witness in connection with a criminal trial. But in the Trump immunity case, the Court took the opposite view, essentially determining that the criminal laws don't apply to the president at all, as long as official conduct is involved. So, although they're not directly at odds, the way the Court looked at the role of the presidency and our constitutional system could hardly be more different.[66]

4. Meanwhile, American calendars designate June 14 as Flag Day. Unlike Thanksgiving, Memorial Day, or the Fourth of July, Flag Day means business as usual for banks, post offices, and other establishments. Still, even

65. Reed, "Are Presidents Above the Law?"
66. Reed, "Are Presidents Above the Law?"

if "a flag is only a bit of cloth," sociologist Émile Durkheim was right when he added, "a soldier will die to save it."[67] The American flag is one of the nation's most potent symbols. Quite literally, people will kill and die for it.

The exact origins of the Stars and Stripes are obscured by legend and tradition. Historians, for example, have never documented that Betsy Ross first made "the American flag" at the request of George Washington. Yet the story persists. Every year thousands of visitors to Philadelphia track down the Ross house to pay respect. Better proved than the Betsy Ross legend, a resolution was adopted by the Continental Congress on June 14, 1777. It specified that the flag of the United States should be "thirteen stripes, alternate red and white; that the Union be thirteen stars, white on a blue field, representing a new constellation."[68] A century later, Congress called for public displays on June 14, 1877, to commemorate the flag's one-hundredth anniversary. World War I was under way on May 30, 1916—Decoration Day (later Memorial Day)—when President Woodrow Wilson proclaimed Flag Day an annual national observance.

The flag is designed to be a symbol of national unity, although its power in that regard is often questioned. As an act of political protest, public desecration of the flag has a long and widespread history. Flag burnings, for example, were frequent during the Vietnam War protests of the late 1960s. Later, in 1984, a man named Gregory Lee Johnson burned a flag in front of the city hall in Dallas, Texas, to protest policies of President Ronald Reagan. A Texas law banned such flag desecration. Arrested, tried, and convicted, Johnson was sentenced to a year in jail and fined $2,000.

After the Texas Court of Criminal Appeals reversed the conviction, the case went to SCOTUS. The 5–4 decision in *Texas v. Johnson* (1989) held that flag burning was protected under the First Amendment's guarantee of free speech.[69] This landmark decision established that the government cannot prohibit the expression of ideas, even if those ideas are offensive or unpopular.

Texas v. Johnson was decided on June 21, 1989. Opposition was strong and swift. On October 28, Congress enacted the Flag Protection Act of 1989, which stipulated: "Whoever knowingly mutilates, defaces, physically defiles, burns, maintains on the floor or ground, or tramples upon any flag of the United States shall be fined under this title or imprisoned for not more than one year, or both."[70] SCOTUS, however, was not having it. In

67. Durkheim, "Value Judgments," 87.

68. Library of Congress, "Today in History—June 14."

69. United States Supreme Court, *Texas v. Johnson* (1989).

70. United States Congress, Flag Protection Act of 1989, Pub L. No. 101-131, 103 Stat. 777 (1989).

United States v. Eichman (1990), the same five-justice majority from *Texas v. Johnson* again upheld the right to flag burning, striking down the Flag Protection Act as a violation of free speech.[71] Together, the two flag-burning cases are immensely important to American democracy and the American Dream because they so strongly defend the right to criticize and protest against an administration, such as Trump 2.0, that will muzzle free expression on a march toward dictatorship.

5. The final top-five honor goes to *Roe v. Wade* (1973), which was unjustly overturned in *Dobbs v. Jackson Women's Health Organization*. The origins of *Roe v. Wade* are found in 1969, when Norma McCorvey was blocked by Texas law from obtaining the abortion she wanted. Using the pseudonym Jane Roe, McCorvey sued Henry Wade, the district attorney of Dallas County, and the case was tried in federal district court. Appeals took the case to SCOTUS, which reached a decision on January 22, 1973.

The US Constitution does not contain the word *abortion*, but in a 7–2 decision, SCOTUS found that women in the United States had a fundamental right to choose to have an abortion without excessive government restriction; the ruling struck down the Texas abortion ban as unconstitutional. A key factor in the SCOTUS decision was the affirmation that the Constitution contains, at least by implication, a right to privacy. Prior to fetal viability, the majority reasoned, this right to privacy was sufficient to protect a woman's freedom to choose, her right to decide whether to abort a pregnancy. A key provision in the decision put the fundamental point as follows: "This right of privacy, whether it be founded in the Fourteenth Amendment's concept of personal liberty and restrictions upon state action, as we feel it is, or, as the District Court determined, in the Ninth Amendment's reservation of rights to the people, is broad enough to encompass a woman's decision whether to terminate her pregnancy."[72]

For fifty years, an American woman had a fundamental right to choose, to make decisions about her own body and reproductive health. But in *Dobbs v. Jackson Women's Health Organization*, a 6–3 SCOTUS decision on June 24, 2022, overturned *Roe v. Wade*. SCOTUS took fundamental rights away. Its action not only denied the existence of a constitutional right to abortion but also effectively removed the federal guarantee of privacy in reproductive health care decisions, allowing individual states to regulate or ban abortions and thus to diminish a person's bodily autonomy and freedom in making personal decisions. The American Dream defends and expands basic rights. It seeks good health and amplifies the chances for it.

71. United States Supreme Court, *United States v. Eichman* (1990).

72. United States Supreme Court, *Roe v. Wade* (1973).

Roe v. Wade supported the American Dream. The *Dobbs* decision does not. A majority of Americans are right in their opposition to *Dobbs* and in their support for a renewal of the freedom to choose that *Roe v. Wade* advanced.

Good Judges

Writing collectively as Publius, Alexander Hamilton, James Madison, and John Jay made substantial contributions toward ratification of the US Constitution by coauthoring *The Federalist*, commonly called *The Federalist Papers*. Published between October 1787 and May 1788, that series of eighty-five essays urged support for the Constitution. In *Federalist* 78, Hamilton argued that the federal judiciary, including SCOTUS, a necessary final arbitrator of the law, has "neither force nor will, but merely judgment."[73] He told his readers that the federal judiciary is the "least dangerous" of the three branches of American government.

As the 2026 and 2028 elections approach and beyond them as well, Americans need to reconsider Hamilton's judgment. It is risky to think that any branch of American government is least dangerous. In the wrong hands, the three of them—each and all, and with no exception for SCOTUS—can be extremely dangerous to the American Dream. Polluted by hyperpoliticized appointments to the bench, dubious and sometimes leaked opinions, and conflicts of interest unchecked by a credible code of ethics, SCOTUS flexes more muscle than Hamilton imagined or than most Americans prefer. For good reason, trust in SCOTUS has been near a record low.[74]

As history shows, however, SCOTUS often makes decisions that are good and right. We need that to be the case. We need good judges, arbiters who are the opposite of the young and lawless hatchet man Emil Bove, Donald Trump's former personal lawyer, whom feckless MAGA Republicans confirmed by a party line Senate vote of 50–49 on July 29, 2025, to take a lifetime seat on the 3rd Circuit US Court of Appeals.[75] If Trump has his way, the aging SCOTUS justices Samuel Alito and Clarence Thomas, both well into their seventies, will retire during the president's second term. Then Trump will name two young, conservative, and compliant jurists—like Bove—to succeed them.[76] Resistance against that bleak scenario requires defenders of the American Dream more than ever to be the good judges that Trump's judicial loyalists are not.

73. Hamilton, *Federalist Papers*, no. 78.
74. Copeland, "Favorable Views of Supreme Court Remain Near Historic Low."
75. Jurecic, "Emil Bove."
76. Bennett, "Inside the Preparations."

Usually, SCOTUS judges are less dramatic or colorful than presidents or senators. The qualities they exhibit are integrity and seriousness; they typically do not engage in campaign charades or make inflated promises. To work well, our democracy requires that "We the People" are serious and conscientious judges: critical of our own causes as well as of those pursued by others. We must be committed to the Constitution, even as we realize that our readings of it may differ. We need to look long and hard at the cases before us, ferreting out the evidence, and then make a decision, but only after we have deliberated as carefully as time and energy allow. And then perhaps most difficult of all, we have to trust each other enough to abide by a majority decision even as we work to alter it if it is unwise and to resist and overturn it if it is unjust.

Few things are more difficult than being a good judge. The framers of our national life could have opted for an easier system, one that left decisions to only a few. But even though they expected no utopia, their dreams soared high in thinking that Americans could make wise and fair choices, that sovereignty belongs to the American people—not to any appointed or elected official, not even to the president. That confidence is their major challenge to us in the late 2020s. Accepting it self-consciously entails tremendous self-discipline and persistence.

It would be a utopian dream to imagine that all Americans will be good judges who always make sound decisions. Nevertheless, the quality of our life together will be directly proportional to the quantity of good judges in the land and the quality of their decisions. "We the People," we Americans, share freedom and responsibility, share in preserving our system's stability and in assuring justice. We separate the powers and tasks, we try to check them against excess and abuse, we work to balance interests equitably—at least those are some of our best ideals. They support the American Dream, and the Dream advances them. "We the People" are the start and finish. We can function as a nation only through representatives, but the people have to save themselves from bad government, from tyrants and tyranny. No one can give us good government except ourselves. Article III of the Constitution creates and guides the judicial branch of government, and it confers upon us all the responsibility to be good judges.

4

Full Faith and Credit

April 2025 included the 250th anniversary of major events in the American Revolution. In colonial Boston, for example, Paul Revere, an American silversmith, took action on April 18, 1775. Following a tip that British troops would raid American military supplies stored in nearby Concord, Massachusetts, he made his storied "midnight ride" to Lexington to warn the rebels that the Redcoats were coming.

Fought on April 19, 1775, the battles at Lexington and Concord were among the first of the American Revolutionary War. As news spread that the Americans had forced the British to withdraw, support for independence grew. Soon, on July 4, 1776, the Declaration of Independence was signed by the Continental Congress in Philadelphia. From Lexington and Concord in 1775 and Philadelphia in 1776, half a decade passed before the British surrendered at Yorktown, Virginia, in 1781. The United States and the American Dream were born from violence, suffering, and death. Long and brutal, successful only with support from France, the Revolutionary War pitted Americans not only against the British but also against one another in a battle between rebels and loyalists. A lethal smallpox epidemic compounded the carnage and suffering.[1]

About 6,800 Americans were killed in Revolutionary War combat. A heavier toll on the military, some 17,000 deaths, resulted from disease. If those dead could speak now, would they say that the cost was worth it? Their answer might depend on whether Americans in 2026 and 2028 rally to make day-to-day life affordable, to defend American democracy, to protect the rule of law, and to save the American Dream.

1. For important perspectives and timely analysis, see Ken Burns's distinguished 2025 PBS documentary, *The American Revolution*. See the series website and specifically the web page called "American Revolution Facts."

The 250th anniversary of the Declaration of Independence comes in a decisive election year that will do much to determine whether the United States will be, in the Declaration's words, a nation of "free People" or subjects of some version of "an absolute Tyranny over these States." In April 2025, Trump 2.0 was still in its early stages, and the darkest times were yet to come. With his popularity and approval ratings in decline during the dwindling of his first one hundred days in office, Donald Trump faced economic turmoil of his own making. Engulfing the country in chaos, his ill-conceived policies on trade and tariffs tanked the stock market, driving it to the worst April performance since the Great Depression of 1932. Trump alone bore responsibility for cratering the value of bonds essential for financing American government and for crippling the dollar's international value. The world's as well as Americans' confidence in the stability of the US economy plummeted.[2]

As spring turned to summer, the economy seemed to improve, but Trump 2.0 is still in its early stages. Expecting an upward economic trend to continue during Trump 2.0 is likely a fool's forecast. Meanwhile, a poll of more than five hundred American political scientists found a large majority saying that under Trump the United States is moving swiftly from liberal democracy toward authoritarianism.[3] His thirst for revenge against his opponents intensified distrust of him at home and abroad. Deepening the decay, Trump's noxious arrogance, incompetence, and cruelty were mated with escalating Epstein-file evidence of Trump's long-practiced sexual decadence and disrespect for women.

Especially concerning was Trump's fawning, red-carpet reception of the Ukraine-invading war criminal Vladimir Putin at Joint Base Elmendorf-Richardson in Alaska on August 15, 2025. That Trump-touted "summit" accomplished little beyond handing Putin a huge public-relations bonanza. Trump's submissiveness to Putin, an international pariah, was exemplified by the grand welcome the Russian dictator received at a key American military base and his ride alone with Trump in the US president's limousine.[4] Sometimes, as the saying goes, a picture is worth a thousand words. On August 18, as Trump kept bumbling and as Russia's brutal, unrelenting war against Ukraine continued, Russian media released video footage reputedly showing a US-made M113 armored personnel carrier bearing Russian and American flags during an attack on Ukrainian positions.[5] That image

2. Barajas, "Trump Gets an 'F' on His First 100 Days."
3. Langfitt, "Hundreds of Scholars."
4. Haberman and Pager, "6 Takeaways."
5. Zadorozhnyy, "Russian Media."

is emblematic of Trump's smarmy deference to Putin. By warmly shaking his hand, Trump signaled that the Russian's killing and torture of Ukrainians and the kidnapping of their children do not matter. Trump's embrace of Putin betrays our allies, endangers national security, and imperils the American Dream.

Widespread anti-Trump protests grow across the country. *USA Today*, once called "America's newspaper," provided one sign of the unrest on April 4, 2025, when it reprised a full-page open letter by Grant Grissom, published a month earlier in the *New York Times*. The author, an old-school Republican in his eighties, brought grievances against the flailing but dangerous president. Echoing rising numbers of Americans, Grissom wrote bitterly against Trump on topics that ranged from the president's praising and pardoning the "thugs" who attacked police officers at the Capitol during the insurrection on January 6, 2021, to his showing "contempt for poor and middle-class Americans, allowing Elon Musk to dismantle agencies they rely on." Directly addressing Trump, the letter added that "you have fed us a diet of your anger and hatred. It has divided us and made us sick." The boldfaced conclusion minced no words: "Many patriotic Americans voted for you. You have betrayed them. For the sake of God and country: Resign."[6]

Grissom got the grievances right. Unfortunately, resignation is not likely to be Donald Trump's final presidential act. He sought the office to stay out of jail. He will cling to it as long as he can, likely trying for an unconstitutional third term if his power and health permit. Dying unscathed in the Oval Office would be his ultimate cruel joke on the America he says he loves but shows he hates.

Trump could be impeached again and convicted on the third try. Although the chances for that scenario are slim, a rebellious populace supported by the federal judiciary and growing congressional opposition in 2026 might sustain the American Dream until the 2028 elections, which will either provide relief or cause irreparable harm.

Somber and sobering, those prospects should make us Americans recall that, along with the Constitution, the Declaration of Independence is as close to a sacred text as any American writing can be. Americans know that the Declaration was proclaimed on July 4, 1776, but most of us are deeply aware of only one of its thirty-two sentences. Consisting of less than forty of the Declaration's words, which total about 1,320, that memorable sentence says: "We hold these truths to be self-evident, that all men are created equal, that they are endowed by their Creator with certain unalienable Rights, that among these are Life, Liberty and the Pursuit of Happiness."

6. Grissom, "Plea for Donald Trump to Resign."

Repeated Injuries

Beyond those hallowed propositions, the Declaration alleges and details "a long train of abuses and usurpations" inflicted on the American colonies by George III, "the present King of Great Britain." The Declaration judges that these "repeated injuries" are sufficient to make it not only a right but also a duty "to throw off such Government," whose goal is "the establishment of an absolute Tyranny over these States."[7]

During Trump 2.0 it is amazing but not surprising to find that many of the injuries inflicted on Americans more than two centuries ago are meted out again by Donald Trump, a wannabe dictator if not king in the United States. "To prove this," as the Declaration puts its point, "let Facts be submitted to a candid world."

The charges have eighteenth-century tones, but with little commentary, at least nine of the offenses apply to Donald Trump.

1. "He has refused Assent to Laws, the most wholesome and necessary for the public good." As federal court decisions reveal, Trump breaks American law on an almost daily basis. Two examples, Trump's executive order purporting to end birthright citizenship and the firing of fraud-finding inspectors general across the government without providing notice or a rationale to Congress, only scratch the surface.

2. "He has endeavored to prevent the population of these States; for that purpose obstructing the Laws of Naturalization of Foreigners; refusing to pass others to encourage their migration hither." Trump's bans on entry to the country—based on religion or nationality—are combined with unconstitutional attacks on birthright citizenship, the revoking of visas for foreign university students, the arrest and deportation without due process of people who have entered the country legally or illegally, and hostility to the American Dream's affirmation that we are "a nation of immigrants." The eighteenth-century protest against King George III can be leveled no less against Trump, the man who would be king.

3. "He has obstructed the Administration of Justice." Repeatedly, Trump refuses to comply promptly with federal court orders, violating the constitutional system of checks and balances and the rule of law.

4. "For cutting off our Trade with all parts of the world." Trump's tariff policies have muddled international trade, eroding American prosperity and damaging every nation's trust in our country's economic

7. For material here and below, see United States National Archives, "Declaration of Independence (1776)."

reliability. Nor is confidence inspired by Trump's follow-up plan to offer tariff exceptions to industries and countries that bend the knee to him.[8] On the contrary, Trump's "exceptions" are invitations to grift and corruption. Trump puts the US government up for sale. Pay to play is the game: Quid pro quo.

5. "For imposing taxes on us without our Consent." Trump's tariffs are a tax on every American consumer, but the tax falls especially hard on the least able to bear it. The tariffs and Trump's tyranny are inseparable. No American voted for them. Trump's tariff impositions rest on shaky if not false legal ground.[9]

6. "For depriving us in many cases, of the benefits of Trial by Jury." Trump's deportation schemes have led to arrests and imprisonment, including incarceration in homegrown concentration camps such as the swampy Alligator Alcatraz in Florida.[10]

7. "For transporting us beyond Seas to be tried for pretended offenses." On this point, Trump rivals King George III. Trump has illegally used an ancient law, the Alien Enemies Act of 1798—it provides for detainment and removal of citizens or subjects of a hostile nation in times of war or invasion—as the excuse for deporting foreigners without due process of law, indicating further that he would "love" to send American "homegrown criminals" to foreign prisons.[11] Apparently, King George III seized people to stand trial. Trump's intentions are worse: Deportation and imprisonment abroad; no due process necessary.

8. "He has excited domestic insurrections amongst us." Trump did nothing less than that on January 6, 2021, when, spreading his Big Lie (still persistently embraced by him and his collaborators), he claimed that the 2020 presidential election was stolen from him. His pardon of the perpetrators, his revenge and retribution against political opponents—especially the press ("the enemy of the people," as he repeatedly smears them), and judges who rule against his lawlessness—all these actions and more encourage domestic upheaval that endangers American democracy.

9. "A Prince, whose character is thus marked by every act which may define a Tyrant, is unfit to be the ruler of a free People." Thomas Jefferson, John Adams, Benjamin Franklin, and arguably all the fifty-three

8. Trump, "Fact Sheet: President Donald J. Trump Modifies."
9. Jouvenal, "Supreme Court Appears Skeptical."
10. Olmsted, "Sickening Living Conditions."
11. Johansen, "Trump Says He Would 'Love' to Send."

other men who signed the Declaration of Independence would stand in judgment of Donald Trump in precisely those terms.

Judged and found unacceptably wanting by the sacred standards of the Declaration of Independence, Trump shows himself "unfit to be the ruler of a free People," notwithstanding his 2024 election by a slim margin, which garnered less than a majority of the popular vote. According to a new measure called the Determinative Popular Vote (DPV), which reveals the minimum number of votes (placed across the right states) that a candidate would have needed to change the Electoral College outcome, merely 0.15 percent of voters nationwide gave Trump his victory.[12] That result is far from the "mandate" that Trump falsely boasts he received.

Despite Trump's wins, he is a loser as far as the Constitution's hopes for the "general Welfare" and "the Blessings of Liberty" are concerned. Sooner rather than later, Americans must make that judgment to save the American Dream. Doing so will be a bitter pill for all of us—those who voted for Trump, those who voted against him, and those who chose not to cast a ballot in 2024. But unless we forsake the Declaration of Independence and the Constitution, Americans cannot responsibly side with Donald Trump and his MAGA enablers, who will ruin our country and its good name.

The *E Pluribus Unum* Article

Article IV of the US Constitution seems dry as dust. Its provisions scarcely arouse current interest let alone inspire passion. But more is at stake than contemporary eyes see at first glance. That claim is valid because Article IV—it can rightly be called the *e pluribus unum* article—focuses on one of the things that Trump wants to destroy: a pluralistic, inclusive, democratic sense of national unity. To explore that claim, return to Inauguration Day, January 20, 2025.

After taking the oath of presidential office—emblematic of his infidelity to the words he carelessly mouthed, Trump never put his hand on the Bible before him—the new president pronounced that "national unity is now returning to America, and confidence and pride is soaring like never before. . . . We are one people, one family, and one glorious nation under God. . . . The American Dream," he added, "will soon be back and thriving like never before."[13] No one should think that Trump really believes those words. They mean little to Trump but are meant to motivate his

12. Haidar and Calvelli, "Landslide?"

13. Trump, Inaugural Address.

now-shrinking MAGA base,[14] without which his mystique and power evaporate.

Since taking the 2025 oath of presidential office in a deeply divided country, Trump has unleashed chaos that mocks one of the nation's mottos—*e pluribus unum* ("out of many, one"). On July 4, 1776, immediately after adopting the Declaration of Independence, the Continental Congress established a committee—including Benjamin Franklin, John Adams, and Thomas Jefferson—to create an official seal to affix on documents and to certify the new nation's independence. Not until June 20, 1782, however, was a design approved. One of its features, which can be seen on the reverse side of the US one-dollar bill, is the still-aspirational motto—*e pluribus unum*—which underscores the importance of unity in spite of ongoing, contentious division.

Its thirteen letters reminiscent of the thirteen original states in the Union, *e pluribus unum* encircles the base of the Statue of Freedom atop the dome of the US Capitol in Washington, DC. The words served as the de facto national motto until July 30, 1956. On that date, two years after pushing to have the phrase "under God" inserted into the Pledge of Allegiance, President Dwight D. Eisenhower signed a law declaring "In God We Trust" to be the nation's official motto. This step took place during the height of the Cold War and was intended to signal opposition to the feared secularizing ideology of communism. The law also mandated that the phrase, which had been placed on US coins since the Civil War, should be printed on all American paper currency as well.

Trump respects neither motto, mocking them both instead. In his Easter Sunday, April 20, 2025, posting on Truth Social he vowed to make the United States "bigger, better, stronger, wealthier, healthier, and more religious than ever before."[15] But Trump trusts in only himself. Mouthing "In God we trust" is part of the grift to keep Christian nationalists by his side. Instead of "out of many, one," Trump destroys and divides, putting the integrity and authority of the US Constitution at risk.

Unlike the Declaration of Independence, the US Constitution contains no reference to God, save for mentioning "the year of our Lord" in dating its 1787 signing. The religious views of the founders were pluralistic. If they shared a conviction that fundamental human rights were God-given, they did not think alike about divinity. Whatever their beliefs concerning Christianity might have been, their political project was not to establish

14. Blake, "Cracks in Trump's Base."

15. See the third post in Trump, "Truth Social Posts of April 20, 2025," compiled as part of the American Presidency Project.

"a Christian nation." Instead, their aim—the Preamble to the Constitution summarizes it—was to establish government rooted in the sovereignty of "We, the people." The Founders may have hoped that "higher powers" would favor that cause, but their fundamental commitment was that government derives its legitimacy from the consent of the governed, not from a king or even from God, and least of all from some individual's or group's Christian nationalism.

So, to save the American Dream from dogma and division, to save it from Trump and his gang, it is worthwhile to keep Article IV, the *e pluribus unum* article, in view. Start by noting that its key stipulations include these: (1) Each state must respect and honor the state laws and court orders of the other states, even when its own laws are different. (2) States cannot discriminate against citizens of other states. A state must give people from other states the same fundamental rights it gives its own citizens. (3) Only Congress can admit new states into the Union, and a single state cannot create a new state within its boundaries. (4) The United States must ensure that each state has a "republican form of government."

A deep flaw is that Article IV legitimated chattel slavery by giving slave owners autonomy to recapture "fugitives from labor"—the original Constitution's deceptive euphemism for slaves—who had fled to other states, even to states that prohibited slavery. It took the 1865 passage of the Thirteenth Amendment, which abolished slavery and involuntary servitude ("except as a punishment for crime whereof the party shall have been duly convicted") to make that odious part of Article IV null and void.

A much better feature of Article IV is its stipulation that every state must have a "republican form of government." Obviously, the term *republican* does not refer to a political party. The Republican Party, founded by antislavery activists, did not exist until 1854. Article IV did not define the term *republican form of government*, but the Founders intended that every state should emulate the form of government that the Constitution itself was creating for the country. That outlook highlighted ingredients such as (1) a government of laws, not rulers, to secure liberty and justice; (2) the sovereignty of a people who are free; (3) representative democracy; and (4) a mixed political structure that checks and balances legislative, executive, and judicial authority.

Article IV's provisions attempt to make one out of many. Several states there would be. Recognizing that plurality was essential for forming the United States of America and agreeing on a constitution. But likewise, no constitution could be agreed to, and no country called the United States of America could exist unless the states honored and respected the existence of all the other states in the union.

Commonalities among the states, such as a shared form of government, would improve the chances for mutual support and strength, providing a bulwark against the intrusion of tyrannical domination from outside or within. A deeply shared "republican form of government" would be necessary though not sufficient to keep the Union from rupture during the Civil War, which left the rebel southern states in ruined condition. Constitutional provisions do not ensure that unity will prevail over division, but that fact means that strong allegiance to understanding and sharing the value of republican government becomes even more important. That insight is where Article IV's intriguing concept of "full faith and credit" becomes crucial.

First Words

Full faith and credit—that phrase, the first words of Article IV, explicitly requires states to respect the laws, records, and judicial decisions of other states. That respect, necessary for stability and predictability, resists chaos, lawlessness, and actions that take advantage of people who do not know what they can count on or what to expect. But if the concept of full faith and credit is explored beyond narrow confines, it becomes a helpful ethical guideline as well. The meaning of those words extends not only to what is but also to what ought to be. True, that suggestion goes beyond a strict, tightly focused view of the phrase's placement and meaning in Article IV, but an expanded grasp of its connotations and implications has its place because awareness of and respect for Article IV is a key part of saving the American Dream.

What deserves full faith and credit? What does not? The concept is not only about one state's accepting another's laws and transaction rules. If that were the sole meaning, then states' rights could be exploited harmfully. Slavery, for example, would have been, and might still be, acceptable. The Civil War and especially the Thirteenth, Fourteenth, and Fifteenth Amendments made clear that not everything that states may do is acceptable, legal in a particular state though the provisions and acts might be. As a citizen of Washington state, for example, I may have to give full faith and credit to elections in another state, but from an ethical perspective, the words "full faith and credit" may help me to see that the election practices in, say, highly gerrymandered states, where the best forms of republican government are neither honored nor practiced, do not deserve full faith and credit and must be resisted accordingly.[16]

16. On these points, see Bouie, "Madison Saw Something."

That last word, *accordingly*, is fraught. Trump knows that the narrow Republican majority in the House of Representatives could be lost, opening the door for a Democrat majority to impeach him. So, on July 15, 2025, Trump—growing as desperate as he is dishonest—urged Texas Republicans to violate existing norms and take unprecedented early steps to reconfigure congressional districts. That step would problematically flip five Democrat-held US House seats in the 2026 elections. Another state—California, for example—cannot prevent Texas from taking that undemocratic step, but California will resist by congressional-district reconfiguration of its own, creating more US House seats for Democrats.

Debates about redistricting strategies, including how they impact the health of already ailing American democracy, will swirl beyond the boundaries of Article IV.[17] Meanwhile, little if anything that Donald Trump says or does deserves full faith and credit. In early April 2025, Trump's press secretary, Karoline Leavitt, inflamed the relentless gaslighting by proclaiming, "trust in President Trump. This is a president who is doubling down on his proven economic formula."[18] To warrant receiving full faith and credit, a genuine basis for trust must exist. That basis includes honesty, consistency, fairness, and treating people with respect. The opposite of that basis includes lying, making contradictory assertions or taking contradictory actions, making exceptions that capriciously favor one person or group and disadvantage others, and using people instead of helping and serving them.

Where the basis exists for giving full faith and credit, then the responsibility is to honor the laws and relationships that embody that foundation, to support the conditions and traditions that advance that cause, to encourage actions and policies that strengthen honest, consistent, fair, and respectful practices. If individuals as well as states act and relate in those ways, then the chances for mutual prosperity and well-being are enhanced. Aspirations toward making one out of many are improved. Article IV tells us that states must give full faith and credit to one another in order to ensure the "more perfect Union" that the Constitution seeks to create. In mandating the states to grant full faith and credit one to another, Article IV also entails, at least implicitly, that "We the People" must strive to deserve, to be worthy of the profound and precious gift of full faith and credit, which should never be granted lightly, let alone taken for granted.

17. NPR Network, "Fight Is On."

18. See Hutzler et al., "Trump Says."

Privileges and Immunities

Article IV contains what is often called the privileges and immunities clause. It requires that citizens of one state are treated equally with citizens of other states with regard, for example, to trade and commerce. The clause promotes *e pluribus unum* by requiring states to treat out-of-state citizens with equal respect and, with reasonable exceptions, in the same way they would treat their own residents.

If I am a citizen of Washington state, and I go to California, Article IV ensures that I can give full faith and credit to the belief that I will be treated essentially the same as a citizen of California. If I am an out-of-state student, I might have to pay higher tuition at a university, and I would have to establish residence before I could vote in state elections or get a driver's license, but in most cases, I would enjoy the same privileges and immunities as the citizens of that state. These understandings are crucial for the American Dream, which has long included the idea that one's life might be improved by relocating to a new place, making a new beginning somewhere else, taking the chance that better times and opportunities may be found out west, down south, up north, or back east.

Article I of the Constitution gives Congress power to regulate commerce "among the several states." Article IV supports that provision by promoting a unified national market. States must recognize one another's "acts, records, and judicial proceedings." That provision helps to establish a framework for interstate cooperation and limits on state discrimination, facilitating the free flow of goods, services, and people across state lines. Restrictions against that free flow would diminish opportunity and constrain new beginnings.

Privileges and immunities: that concept central to the American Dream depends on understanding and honoring Article IV, but the meanings, implications, and responsibilities of the Dream extend and expand beyond those specific constitutional duties. In 1931, for example, when James Truslow Adams defined the American Dream during the Great Depression, he might not have been thinking explicitly about Article IV, but implicitly he was reflecting on "privileges and immunities" when he stressed that the Dream included the hope and promise of a "richer" life. He did not mean "richer than a king," as the American poet Edwin Arlington Robinson depicted Richard Cory, an invented figure whose name became the title of Robinson's perceptive 1897 poem.[19] But Adams did understand, as Americans have done persistently and insistently, that a basic standard of

19. Robinson, "Richard Cory."

living—adequate food, reliable health care, safe shelter, clean air and water, steady income from a worthwhile job, good education, realistic hopes for upward mobility, opportunity for children's lives to be better than their parents'—was necessary, indeed imperative for the Dream's integrity and future. If the concept of privileges and immunities and indeed the Dream itself do not take such equitable considerations into account, then they both are morally bankrupt.

When we are at our best, Americans understand that the Dream is not about Trumpism's art-of-the-deal transactions where power is leveraged to gain advantage over others in a winner-take-as-much-as-possible struggle. It is not about commerce—international, interstate, interpersonal—in which might makes right, in which what's mine is mine and what's yours is negotiable.

Yes, the Dream involves buying and selling—it has to do so because the Dream is inseparable from economics and from successful trade and business. Achieving a version of it requires hard work and determination. Once, those virtues were considered enough to give a person a fair shot at the Dream, but less so now. A Pew Research Center survey from the summer of 2024, for example, found that "half of Americans (53%) say that dream is still possible. Another 41% say the American dream was once possible for people to achieve—but is not anymore. And 6% say it was never possible."[20] Reasons for the skepticism are easy to find. Tariff-obsessed Donald Trump promised repeatedly to make America affordable again.[21] Instead, Trump has done just the opposite, piling uncertainty on hopes for the future and worsening estimates that the Dream's costs are out of reach. If the Dream consists of common milestones, including getting married, raising two children, buying a home, having a new car from time to time, saving for retirement, and going on a yearly vacation, then the lifetime household cost might be $4.4 million.[22] Trump's economic policies have made matters worse. In early April 2025, another Pew Research Center poll found that "just 23% of Americans rate national economic conditions as excellent or good, while 42% say they are only fair and 34% rate the economy as poor. . . . 45% of Americans say they expect economic conditions to be worse a year from now, up from 37% in February."[23]

Secretary of the Treasury Scott Bessent was right on March 6, 2025, when he said that "the American Dream is rooted in the concept that any

20. Borelli, "Americans Are Split."

21. Doggett, "Trump's Economic Promises Timeline."

22. De Visé and Procell, "American Dream Now Costs."

23. Pew Research Center, "Economic Ratings and Concerns."

citizen can achieve prosperity, upward mobility, and economic security." He was also correct when he said that "access to cheap goods is not the essence of the American Dream."[24] Not its essence, for sure, but the wealthy, advantaged Bessant was disingenuous when his comment downplayed the importance of low-priced, high-quality goods for American consumers. They are not sufficient for the American Dream, but they are necessary.

Donald Trump was even more calloused and cruel. "I couldn't care less," he said in response to questions about the foreign-car price spikes his tariff scheme inflicts. "I hope [foreign automakers] raise their prices, because if they do, people are going to buy American-made cars. We have plenty."[25] Much hinges on the price of cars, as far as the American Dream is concerned. The Dream will not get much mileage if the cost of a new car, or at least of a reliable late-model used one, is out of reach. Ahead of the Trump tariffs in the spring of 2025, car dealers saw an uptick in business as buyers took advantage of pre-tariff deals. Post-tariff car prices will be thousands of dollars higher. Trump's "I couldn't care less" is emblematic of his undermining of the Dream.[26]

Privileges and immunities: progress in dealing with the Dream's affordability crisis requires, at the very least, serious and sustained commitment to improve equitable economic conditions in the United States. The Dream cannot be credible in circumstances where income and wealth disparities are the way they are in 2025: According to the nonpartisan Congressional Budget Office, the share of wealth held by families in the top 10 percent has reached 69 percent, while the share held by families in the bottom 50 percent is only 3 percent.[27] The Dream has little chance to be anything but a snare and delusion for more than 36 million Americans living below the poverty line in April 2025, an annual income threshold of $15,650 for an individual or $32,150 for a family of four.

Living from paycheck to paycheck does not fulfill the American Dream. Nor is the path to it improved by a Trump administration hell-bent on massive tax cuts for American oligarchs and their corporations while the majority of "We the People" find that Elon Musk and his twentysomething DOGE aides have gutted government services, shredded basic safety nets such as Medicaid and the Supplemental Nutrition Assistance Program

24. Kochi, "Treasury Secretary."
25. Wootson, "Trump Says He 'Couldn't Care Less.'"
26. Wootson, "Trump Says He 'Couldn't Care Less.'"
27. Smith, "America Has Never Been Wealthier."

(SNAP), and coldheartedly slashed funds for health research and treatment that make life-or-death differences.[28]

The American Dream is not about making the rich richer. It is about amplifying opportunity, promoting what the Constitution calls "the general Welfare," and securing "the Blessings of Liberty to ourselves and our Posterity." Steps in those directions require dealing with climate change, which must be addressed lest it undermine everything we Americans hold dear when we are at our best. Saving the American Dream requires election results in 2026 and 2028 that deter Trump and his cronies. Preserving the Dream also requires creative thinking and constructive planning to guide the American economy in ways that resist the effects of despair and cynicism, which result from believing that the American Dream may be beyond saving. On the *Bulwark Podcast*, Senator Cory Booker, of New Jersey, put that point well on April 24, 2025:

> This is a time when I can't surrender to cynicism about America. . . . There are wretched, dark corners in our history, but people didn't give up believing in who we are. . . . As the great poet Langston Hughes said, "America never was America to me, / And yet I swear this oath—/ America will be!" This is the kind of conviction that is needed. I refuse to stop believing in us. Just because we have a demagogic leader who is such an affront to the values I think this country most adheres to, this is the time when we should be speaking and affirming with even greater conviction who we are and fighting against the forces that have been here from the beginning, that seem to want to undermine the highest values and ideals of our nation.[29]

Build and Invent

Article IV, the *e pluribus unum* article, envisioned national unity as essential for the building and invention that would make the United States and its citizens prosperous. As the specter of a Trump-inflicted economic decline grew during the first year of Trump 2.0, recovering that spirit is essential for saving the American Dream. It is required for the project that two influential American dreamers, Ezra Klein and Derek Thompson, urge the country to pursue. In addition to *build* and *invent*, the table of contents for *Abundance*, their influential, action-packed 2025 bestseller, includes three

28. Schliefer et al., "Young Aides."

29. Booker, "Cory Booker." Slightly edited for concision and clarity.

more verbs—*grow*, *govern*, *deploy*—that can revive and sustain the American Dream at a critical time in the nation's life.

The thesis of *Abundance*, the authors say, is "a simple idea: to have the future we want, we need to build and invent more of what we need."[30] The book reveals that its basic proposition is easier said than done; its governing idea is scarcely simple. Nevertheless, Klein and Thompson are correct: Things should not be as hard as we think or make them. Scarcity, unaffordability, impossibility: these obstacles to human flourishing are real, but they are also states of mind as much as they are hard, immoveable inevitabilities. That is where the verbs—*grow*, *build*, *govern*, *invent*, and *deploy*—come in. People and their projects do these things, usually against stiff odds.

"I dwell in Possibility," the great American poet Emily Dickinson emphasized.[31] The Dream encourages all Americans to believe and enact that conviction. Good chances to build and invent more of what we need are within our grasp, and if we reach for them, we may come closer to the future we want, which is not hard to envision. As Klein and Thompson see, that vision focuses on production more than consumption. If we think better about what can be built rather than about what can be bought, then we can discern that the possibility we inhabit includes abundance—"enough of what we need to create lives better than what we have had."[32] With that conviction top of mind, Klein and Thompson want Americans to focus now on housing, transportation, energy, and health, all essentials for fulfilling the Dream.

Homelessness defeats the American Dream. Saving the Dream requires growing the economy to reverse the cause of that effect: "the availability and cost of housing"[33] Few conditions will wreck the future of the American Dream more than ruinous climate change. The Dream's survival depends on giving full faith and credit to what we know how to do: "power economies without using fossil fuels."[34] No, can't, won't—those negations stop the Dream in its tracks. Yes; can do; we're on it—those affirmations are more the American way.

Lawsuits and vetoes have their place, but the American Dream can't advance on them alone. Meeting the nation's needs in housing, transportation, energy, and health will not be done by slowdowns and shutdowns. The Dream's future pivots on speeding up the steps we must take to "promote

30. Klein and Thompson, *Abundance*, 4.
31. Dickinson, "I dwell in Possibility."
32. Klein and Thompson, *Abundance*, 20.
33. Klein and Thompson, *Abundance*, 40.
34. Klein and Thompson, *Abundance*, 64.

the general Welfare" before it is too late. We do not have decades, let alone forever, to turn the tide of problems that may swamp us. Regulations, rules, restrictions: yes, they have their place, but it is not to make housing unaffordable or transportation inefficient; it is not to leave climate change unchecked or put the costs of health care out of reach.

We Americans are smart and good enough to figure things out better than that. At its best, the American Dream says so and then holds us accountable to achieve goals worth pursuing. Alone, neither government nor the private sector can do what is needed. Together, the chances are better. "Whether government is bigger or smaller is the wrong question," Klein and Thompson argue. "What it needs is to be better. It needs to justify itself not through the rules it follows but through the outcomes it delivers."[35] What they underscore about government pertains to every institution in American life.

On April 13, 2016, President Barack Obama hosted a White House science fair for American students, an initiative he started in 2010. As he marveled at the students' ingenuity, Obama underscored that "we belong on the cutting edge of innovation. That's an idea as old as America itself. We are a nation of tinkers, and dreamers, and believers in a better tomorrow."[36] Klein and Thompson echo Obama: "Invention—the act of solving problems by bringing new products, systems, and ideas into existence—is the basis of human progress."[37]

A crucial problem, however, looms large. Not only in science but also in a host of human endeavors, as Klein and Thompson suggest, "progress is a blessing that comes with a curse. The unsolved problems are typically harder than the solved ones."[38] Saving the American Dream is like that. As in scientific discovery, it will require invention, which entails risk-taking and ambition, focused on the question, What must we do to move toward the American society we want?

Identifying and emphasizing good responses to that question are not enough. As Klein and Thompson point out—they are far from naively utopian optimists—"the ten-thousand-year story of human civilization is mostly the story of things not getting better: diseases not being cured, freedoms not being extended, truths not being transmitted, technology not delivering on its promises."[39] So much depends on implementing what we invent, on

35. Klein and Thompson, *Abundance*, 128.
36. Obama, "We're a Nation."
37. Klein and Thompson, *Abundance*, 133.
38. Klein and Thompson, *Abundance*, 145.
39. Klein and Thompson, *Abundance*, 172.

deploying what we dream, and on whether we can do so competently at "warp speed."[40]

If we want more democracy, we must be more democratic—now. If we want the rule of law, we must practice it—today. If we do not want dictatorship and oligarchy, we not only have to reject them in the 2026 and 2028 elections. We have to defend and support—with no wasted time—a free press and schools and universities that teach students to inquire critically, follow where evidence leads, and respect truth. At every point, the authors of *Abundance* contend, we must encourage "bottleneck detectives," whose insistent curiosity and persistent impatience remove restrictions that should not exist, scrap plans that do not work, envision new paths that should be tried, and encourage experimentation that could lead the way. Careful attention should go to Artificial Intelligence (AI) in these considerations. Klein and Thompson are likely right when they opine that AI "might be the most important technology of the decade."[41]

Abundance and the American Dream are interrelated and inseparable. The Declaration of Independence emphasizes the pursuit of happiness. The Constitution, including Article IV, was written to "secure the Blessings of Liberty." The Dream enshrines the aim of a life that is better, richer, and fuller for all Americans. Thanksgiving Day is rightly our most loved national holiday. All these realities, and more, depend on abundance, which Klein and Thompson conclude, "is the promise of not just more, but more of what matters."[42] That proposition deserves our full faith and credit.

The Law Is King

The first one hundred days of chaos-laden Trump 2.0 came and went on April 29, 2025.[43] During that destructive time, the president's manic delusions of grandeur reached highs and lows new even for him. "I run the country," he fraudulently boasted, arrogantly adding "and the world."[44] Later, on January 7, 2026, he compounded the danger of such pompous nonsense. Asked if there are any limits on his global powers, Trump said: "Yeah, there is one thing. My own morality. My own mind. It's the only thing that can stop me."[45] Never minding the countless disconnections between

40. On this theme, see Klein and Thompson, *Abundance*, 184–89, 199–202.
41. Klein and Thompson, *Abundance*, 196.
42. Klein and Thompson, *Abundance*, 222.
43. Yourish et al., "All of the Trump Administration's Major Moves."
44. Parker and Scherer, "'I Run the Country.'"
45. Sanger et al., "Trump Lays Out a Vision of Power."

his campaign promises to lower prices and tame inflation when just the opposite took place, Trump contended that "what I'm doing is exactly what I've campaigned on." Presuming that his saying so made it so, the dogmatic Trump insisted, "I've been right. If you look at all of the years that I've been doing this, I've been right on things."[46]

Thomas Paine, the eighteenth-century antimonarchist revolutionary, would have none of Trump's conceited autocracy. In writings such as *Common Sense* (1776), Paine, one of the great political influencers of his day, argued persistently to convince Americans that their revolution against Great Britain and King George III was right and favored: "The sun," he urged, "never shined on a cause of greater worth."[47] The American cause—his American Dream—was economically expedient; it was in accord with divine will; it was logical from a geographical point of view. Above all, it was just and righteous because of the hope that would emerge if a people could break the shackles of tyrannical rule to form a new society based on a democratic compact that honored reason and conscience.

Americans, urged Paine, had a right to rebel. Indeed, it was their duty to do so as a symbol of promise. "The cause of America," he contended, "is in great measure the cause of all mankind."[48] Full faith and credit could be given to that proposition, however, only to the extent that Americans were virtuous. That meant rejecting the lying, grifting, self-serving corruption, and self-dealing greed, which are poisonous at any time but rarely more so than in Trump 2.0. Power governed and governing by those impulses destroys trust at home and abroad. Paine's good advice for a new, isolated nation in the eighteenth century—"a fair national reputation is of as much importance as independence"—is even more to the point in today's older, interlocking world.

I run the country. I run the world. Such hubris offended Thomas Paine. He associated it with absolutism—monarchial in his day, authoritarian in ours. His rejection of it in 1776 should be ours in 2026 and beyond. Paine's impassioned eighteenth-century plea bears remembering.

> But where says some is the King of America? I'll tell you Friend, he reigns above, and doth not make havoc of mankind like the Royal Brute of Britain. Yet that we may not appear to be defective even in earthly honors, let a day be solemnly set apart for proclaiming the charter; let it be brought forth placed on the divine law, the word of God; let a crown be placed thereon, by which the

46. Cortellessa and Jacobs, "Full Transcript of Trump's '100 Days' Interview."
47. Paine, *Common Sense*.
48. Paine, *Common Sense*.

> world may know, that so far as we approve of monarchy, that in America the law is king. For as in absolute governments the King is law, so in free countries the law ought to be King; and there ought to be no other. But lest any ill use should afterwards arise, let the crown at the conclusion of the ceremony be demolished, and scattered among the people whose right it is.[49]

In America, the law must be king. The Constitution, including Article IV, stands on that bedrock. Acting in ways that give, create, and sustain full faith and credit to those principles can save the American Dream and increase the abundance on which it depends.

Between 1776 and 1783, Thomas Paine bolstered American resolve during often dark times by publishing a series of pamphlets called *The American Crisis*. Widely read in the American colonies, such publications were key elements in the social media of the day. Paine's first *American Crisis* pamphlet appeared on December 19, 1776. A series of defeats had demoralized George Washington's army. The Revolutionary War was not going well as Americans tried to overcome tyranny. Tradition holds that Washington ordered officers to read Paine's essay to the embattled troops before they crossed the Delaware River on December 26, surprised the British at Trenton, and achieved a tide-turning victory.

In December 1776, Paine wrote: "These are the times that try men's souls. The summer soldier and the sunshine patriot will, in this crisis, shrink from the service of their country; but he that stands it now, deserves the love and thanks of man and woman. Tyranny, like hell, is not easily conquered; yet we have this consolation with us, that the harder the conflict, the more glorious the triumph."[50] Paine's words then inspire us now to rally against Trump's tyranny in defense of American democracy and the American Dream.

49. Paine, *Common Sense.*

50. Paine, *American Crisis*, No. 1.

5

Intents and Purposes

Article V of the US Constitution is brilliant and flawed. Its brilliance is in the article's openness to change. Its flaw is in refusal to change, at least for a time. First, consider the flaw, which has two dimensions—both compromises needed to secure approval and ratification of the Constitution. Without mentioning the word *slavery*, Article V stated that prior to the year 1808, no change to the document could overturn provisions in Article I that protected chattel slavery, including the importation of new slaves from abroad. For too long, the Constitution embedded slavery in the United States. It took a bloody Civil War and the Thirteenth Amendment (1865) to atone, but only in part, for the nation's "original sin."

The second flaw in Article V may be even harder to correct because it eludes amendment. To set the context, note that often the US Constitution problematically supports minority rather than majority rule. For instance, while the term *electoral college* does not appear in the Constitution, Article II established a mechanism for presidential election—a compromise between the election of the president by a vote in Congress and election of the president by a popular vote of qualified citizens. The resulting Electoral College, as it came to be called, entailed that presidential ballots are cast for electors in states, their number equal to a state's senators and representatives in the US Congress. The Electoral College system dishonors a fundamental principle of democracy—one person, one vote—by permitting the American president to be elected by a minority of American voters, which has happened five times in American history, most recently in 2016 when Hillary Clinton won approximately three million more votes than Donald Trump but lost in the Electoral College.[1]

1. Lerer, "Clinton Wins Popular Vote."

In only one respect does Article V deal explicitly with elections, but that instance also problematically supports minority rather than majority rule. Each American state elects two senators to Congress. In 1787, James Madison argued that Senate representation should be based on population. Not only did he lose that debate but also Article V stated that the rule—two senators for each state—was scarcely subject to amendment: "no State, without its Consent, shall be deprived of its equal Suffrage in the Senate." Those provisions favor land over people, because a senator from Vermont or Wyoming, for example, represents about 648 thousand or 587 thousand persons, respectively, compared to one who represents California with a population of more than thirty-nine million people or Texas with a population of more than thirty-one million. Small-population states punch unfairly above their weight when it comes to affecting policy.

The Living Document Provision

Despite its flaws regarding change, Article V is brilliantly open to change as well, so much so that it could be called the US Constitution's living document provision. As the historian Jill Lepore argues in her magisterial *We the People: A History of the US Constitution*, that document, which "ingeniously . . . accounted for the passage of time . . . was intended to be amended."[2] Article V ensures that when stated requirements are met, the US Constitution can be changed. That means it is not carved in stone but can be updated and corrected. Crucially, Article V specifies that such amendments "shall be valid to all Intents and Purposes, as Part of this Constitution." Underscoring legal finality, the phrase means that a proper amendment to the Constitution is fully part of the original document. The meaning of the First Amendment, for example, is different from the meaning of Article V, but both elements are equally parts of the Constitution. Article V proclaims the framers' intents and purposes to make that equation possible and then to see it honored when it occurs.

Intents and purposes are important. The terms connote related but not identical features of human thought and action. Usually *purpose* refers to an aim, goal, or project. The Constitution's purpose is to "form a more perfect Union." Usually, *intent* refers to a specific step that is part of a larger goal. Article V expresses the framers' intent to keep the Constitution up-to-date. Means and ends—intents and purposes relate and interact like that.

Some intents and purposes are good and just. Others are not. On May 4, 2025, for example, NBC's *Meet the Press* moderator, Kristen Welker, asked

2. Lepore, *We the People*, 1–2.

Donald Trump, "Don't you need to uphold the Constitution of the United States as president?" Trump replied, "I don't know."[3] Those three words speak volumes. The Constitution specifies that the president must swear to "preserve, protect and defend the Constitution of the United States." The constitutionally ordained purpose of every American president is to ensure that "the Laws be faithfully executed." The intent of the oath of office is to ensure that the president's responsibility includes preserving the Constitution, which entails obeying and honoring it.

For Trump to say "I don't know" in response to a question about his sworn duty to uphold the Constitution is unacceptable but also emblematic of his intents and purposes. Contrary to his sloganeering, Trump's purpose has never been to "make American great again." Instead, it has been to serve himself, to increase his power, to take revenge on his opponents, and to line his pockets. The means to those ends—his intents—are adroit uses of fraudulent promises, unrelenting grievances, torrential falsehoods, and unending lies. The United States is distressed and the American Dream is endangered because far too many Americans have trusted Trump.

At our best, we Americans defend the Constitution, especially when our corrupt president does not, and often we take an oath to do so, because the Constitution's intents and purposes are good and just. Its purpose is to advance "a more perfect Union." Its provisions are intents to serve that end. We seek to save the American Dream because, at its best, the Dream's intents and purposes are also good and just. The Dream's purpose is to envision what James Truslow Adams called "a land in which life should be better and richer and fuller."[4] Its encouragements are intents to do what needs to be done to advance that goal. We rightly assess character, evaluate policy, and judge action by gauging how well we Americans, including our presidents, are doing with regard to the intents and purposes enshrined in the Constitution and the American Dream.

The framers wisely understood that the strength, stability, and sustainability of the Constitution entailed allowing for its adaptation to changing circumstances. At least implicitly, their understanding assumed that the meaning and significance of the Constitution's propositions depended on interpretation, on keeping as clear as possible their sense and scope, especially in evolving circumstances.

Although the Constitution does not specify exactly how it is to be interpreted, its preamble provides overall guidance. All the Constitution's provisions should be understood in ways that are consistent and constructively

3. Terkel and Hurley, "Trump, Asked."
4. Adams, *Epic of America*, 415.

engaged with that vision. No interpretation of the Constitution's provisions, moreover, should undercut the fundamental principle that the Constitution is what Article VI calls "the supreme Law of the Land."

Beyond those broad internal guidelines, however, latitude for theories of interpretation as well as differences of opinion about specific interpretations stand out. Writing in *Federalist* 78, Alexander Hamilton implied as much when he argued that "the interpretation of the laws is the proper and peculiar province of the courts. A constitution is, in fact, and must be regarded by the judges, as a fundamental law. It therefore belongs to them to ascertain its meaning, as well as the meaning of any act proceeding from the legislative body."[5] The power of judicial review is not expressly granted in the Constitution, but such acts of interpretation, following Hamilton's counsel in *Federalist* 78, gained legitimacy through the Supreme Court's decision in *Marbury v. Madison* (1803). Ahead of the *Marbury v. Madison* decision, the framers of the Constitution took crucial steps to keep it relevant and responsive to the nation's needs. The amendment provisions stated in Article V have been crucial for the Constitution's evolution and authority to address new challenges.

The amendment requirements are not easily met, a conservative measure that discourages hasty changes and encourages thoughtful deliberations. An amendment can be proposed by Congress with a two-thirds vote in both the House and the Senate, or by a convention called for by two-thirds of the state legislatures. Once proposed, the amendment must be ratified by three-fourths of the states, either through their legislatures or by conventions held within each state. These high thresholds check tyranny by preventing amendments from being easily passed by a dominant political faction or a temporary majority. The Constitution has been amended a modest twenty-seven times—most recently in 1992—since its ratification in 1788. The amendments are additions to the original text. Sometimes they repeal constitutional provisions, but most often they modify constitutional requirements or add new ones.

It did not take long for the constitutional amendment process to be at play. Already during the constitutional convention and shortly after the Constitution's ratification, debate swirled about whether the document sufficiently protected individual rights against federal government overreach. Initially, James Madison, who eventually championed the Constitution's famous Bill of Rights, opposed such amendments but changed his mind because he became convinced that popular loyalty to the Constitution as well as justice itself would be enhanced by them. Following his eloquent

5. Hamilton, *Federalist Papers*, no. 78.

address in the House of Representatives on June 8, 1789, Madison worked tirelessly to obtain ratification of the first ten amendments to the Constitution, the Bill of Rights, which was achieved on December 15, 1791. On that day, Virginia became the eleventh state to endorse the amendments, meeting the required three-fourths of the states needed for ratification.

Madison supported the intents and purposes of the Bill of Rights because encouragement was at stake. Adoption of those amendments was a means toward the end of greater loyalty to the Constitution and the dreams, individual and communal, that it supported. Adoption of those amendments was also a means toward the end of sustaining a courageous citizenry, toward encouraging individual Americans to put their rights and respect for them into practice, to do so with confidence that the new federal government would support and defend them in those efforts. Advancing civil courage is one way to identify what the intents and purposes of the US Constitution and the American Dream always ought to be.

Civil Courage

On February 19, 2025, JB Pritzker, the governor of Illinois, embodied and exemplified civil courage when he gave a State of the State address that captured national attention because of the way it ended. Less than thirty days into Donald Trump's second presidential term, Pritzker drew upon history to underscore where Trump 2.0 might lead. The governor said:

> It took the Nazis one month, three weeks, two days, eight hours and 40 minutes to dismantle a constitutional republic. All I'm saying is when the five-alarm fire starts to burn, every good person better be ready to man a post with a bucket of water if you want to stop it from raging out of control. . . . Tyranny requires your fear and your silence and your compliance. Democracy requires your courage.[6]

Pritzker referred to the Enabling Act passed overwhelmingly by the German parliament on March 23, 1933. In little more than fifty days after Adolf Hitler became Germany's chancellor on January 30, the Enabling Act gave him authority to consolidate Nazi power, remove constitutional checks and balances, and establish a dictatorship. Trump could not match Hitler's amassing of power in one hundred days, let alone fifty, but his trampling of the rule of law and his disrespect for democracy—including his deportation

6. NBC 5 Chicago and Pritzker, "'State of the State' Address."

and "disappearance" of persons he identifies, without evidence, as criminals—are too close to Hitler's for comfort.

When Pritzker underscored that fear, silence, and compliance are tyranny's breeding ground, when he emphasized that courage is essential to defend and sustain democracy, he echoed the resisting German theologian Dietrich Bonhoeffer. Arrested in Nazi Germany on April 5, 1943, Bonhoeffer was judged complicit in the July 20, 1944, assassination plot against Hitler. He was executed by hanging on April 9, 1945, less than a month before Hitler killed himself on April 30 and a ruined Nazi Germany unconditionally surrendered on May 8.

In December 1942, a few months before his arrest, Bonhoeffer wrote a brief but powerful essay called "After Ten Years." It assessed what had happened after the Nazis took control of Germany in the winter of 1933. His thoughts crafted in seventeen short reflections, Bonhoeffer shared them only with a small circle of close friends. In the penultimate section, he wondered whether he and his friends were still of any use.

Then and now, the importance of Bonhoeffer and his friends has been huge. The example of their resistance to tyranny remains, and Bonhoeffer's writings continue to be studied because they are timely, perceptive, and prophetic. "After Ten Years" fits that description, especially in its reflections on *civil courage*. Bonhoeffer had seen not only that a political culture could collapse quickly and completely but also that there is no way to understand such failure or to move beyond it unless people find their "way back to simplicity and honesty," defining characteristics of what he meant by civil courage.[7]

"We have been silent witnesses of evil deeds," Bonhoeffer wrote.[8] Simplicity and honesty require saying that his assessment applies to many Americans as Trump 2.0 unfolds. "We are in the midst of a process of coarsening at every level of society," Bonhoeffer said.[9] Trump's callousness and cruelty are amplified because Bonhoeffer's simple, honest judgment applies to American life in the mid-2020s. "The air in which we live is so poisoned with mistrust that we almost die from it."[10] Again, Bonhoeffer's description of Germany in 1942 fits the United States today, and Bonhoeffer is right again when he adds that "to sow and to nourish mistrust is one of the most reprehensible things."[11] Trump's culture of lies testifies to that. So does

7. Bonhoeffer, *"After Ten Years,"* 20–21, 30.
8. Bonhoeffer, *"After Ten Years,"* 30.
9. Bonhoeffer, *"After Ten Years,"* 26.
10. Bonhoeffer, *"After Ten Years,"* 25.
11. Bonhoeffer, *"After Ten Years,"* 26.

what Jonathan Alter rightly called the "jaw-dropping corruption" invited by Trump's tariff "exemptions," an endless pay-to-play grift.[12] And then there is sheer stupidity.

In Bonhoeffer's understanding, stupidity is not primarily about gross ignorance, lack of intelligence, or mental deficiency. As Bonhoeffer simply and honestly evaluated it, stupidity is a moral defect. It is deaf to sound reasons. It ignores, disbelieves, or pushes aside facts that honesty and simplicity recognize to be irrefutable. Nazism, Bonhoeffer believed, was lethally stupid. Trump, Musk, and their fawning followers are too. Their cuts to foreign aid starve African children to death and sentence Ukrainian civilians to murderous attacks by Vladimir Putin. Their demolition of medical research and health care networks and their embrace of anti-vaccine quackery doom American citizens, young and old, to unnecessary sickness and death. Civil courage says so, but more is required than individual speaking out.

When Bonhoeffer lamented the lack of civil courage around him, he did not deny that individual Germans resisted tyranny bravely and at great sacrifice. Culturally, however, Germans were used to obeying authority. Absent a different culture, the chances to overthrow Hitler from within were scant. Resignation was not Bonhoeffer's position. True, he said, "what remains for us is only the very narrow path, sometimes barely discernible, of taking each day as if it were the last and yet living it faithfully and responsibly as if there were yet to be a great future." He found at least two sources for a communal, culture-changing insistence that "never abandons the future to the opponent but lays claims to it."[13]

The first was what Bonhoeffer called "the view from below."[14] I believe he would counsel us Americans to take "the perspective of the outcasts, the suspects, the maltreated, the powerless, the oppressed and reviled" and then to consider what those outlooks tell us about the quality of life that the United States should pursue, what the American Dream is *for* when those viewpoints come to the fore. With Trump 2.0, cruelty is an end in itself, deprivation is a means to power, taking from the poor to give to the rich affirms that might makes right. These depredations are disguised as preludes to a golden age of prosperity, but Bonhoeffer aptly called such deception a "huge masquerade of evil."[15]

As Trump 2.0 unfolds, cultural shifts that disobey such authoritarianism are on the rise. They should be because of the second source of

12. Alter, "Trump's Huge Tariff Exemption Grift."
13. Bonhoeffer, *"After Ten Years,"* 28–29.
14. Bonhoeffer, *"After Ten Years,"* 30–31.
15. Bonhoeffer, *"After Ten Years,"* 18.

emboldened cultural resistance that Bonhoeffer identified. "The younger generation," said Bonhoeffer—our children and grandchildren—have much to teach their parents and grandparents about "living responsibly, for it is their future that is at stake."[16] Bonhoeffer's point is not that they can articulate the policies and enact the plans required for a future worth having. Saving American democracy, however, requires seriously envisioning the society we want and do not want for our children and grandchildren and then acting together to move toward it.

Bonhoeffer's emphasis on simplicity and honesty guides us Americans in such directions. The American Dream resists devastating climate change and defends clean air and water for the young. It refuses gutted education and insists that excellent public schools and world-class universities and colleges are the lifeblood of a healthy society. The American Dream denies that a free press is the enemy of the people and supports open inquiry against all attempts to stifle it. As we Americans approach the crucial elections of 2026 and 2028, Bonhoeffer's emphasis on "the view from below" and on the young, whose future is at stake, can help us to pursue the right kinds of intents and purposes, to advance civil courage and cultural resistance, to save the American Dream, and to see how Article V of our Constitution is pivotal in those causes.

Dream Amendments

Three amendments to the Constitution are especially important for the American Dream. Before celebrating them, however, it must be said that one amendment remains especially problematic for the Dream. Perhaps appropriate for the eighteenth-century revolutionary times in which it emerged, the fraught Second Amendment—"A well-regulated Militia, being necessary to the security of a free State, the right of the people to keep and bear Arms, shall not be infringed"—has had unintended consequences that plague "the general Welfare." A malign coalition of economic, political, and judicial interests has successfully interpreted the Second Amendment in ways that make nearly uncontrolled gun ownership more important than the unalienable right to life itself.

The United States has far more guns than people. Scores of school shootings take place annually. Tens of thousands die from gun violence in the United States every year, Since 2020, firearm-related injuries are the leading cause of death for American children and adolescents (ages one

16. Bonhoeffer, *"After Ten Years,"* 22.

to nineteen).[17] Outcries mount for stricter gun control, but the Second Amendment stifles them.

The Second Amendment will not go away. Nor will the fact that it does much more harm than good for the American Dream. Stricter gun control, which most Americans want, is essential. But hopes for its success depend not only on courageous legislation but also on the willingness of federal courts to uphold commonsense gun laws that are necessary to "establish justice" and "insure domestic Tranquility."

On much better notes, the Nineteenth Amendment (1920), late though it was in arriving, granted women the right to vote. Unfortunately, American women are still denied basic rights of autonomy over their own bodies. The overturning of *Roe v. Wade* (1973) by SCOTUS on June 24, 2022, in the case of *Dobbs v. Jackson Women's Health Organization* bears witness to that in its cancelling a national right to abortion that had been in place for more than fifty years. The nation's failure to ratify the Equal Rights Amendment (ERA)—"Equality of rights under the law shall not be denied or abridged by the United States or by any state on account of sex"[18]—sadly compromises the American Dream too. Introduced in Congress in 1923, the ERA met all the Article V ratification requirements on January 27, 2020, when Virginia became the thirty-eighth state to approve it. Political and legal wrangling about the binding effect of an earlier deadline for ratification has snarled and thus far prevented the ERA from taking its deserved place as the Twenty-Eighth Amendment.

Prior to the Nineteenth Amendment, numerous states gave women the right to vote, at least if they were White, but the constitutional change guaranteed, at least in principle, that women's suffrage was the law of the land. The struggle to reach that point was long. One of its milestones is found at Seneca Falls, New York, where five American women—Elizabeth Cady Stanton, Lucretia Coffin Mott, Martha Coffin Wright, Mary Ann McClintock, and Jane Hunt organized the Seneca Falls Convention (July 19–20, 1848), the first women's rights convention in the United States. It produced a Declaration of Sentiments and Resolutions, including the affirmation that "all men and women are created equal" and the imperative that "it is the duty of women of this country to secure to themselves their sacred right to the elective franchise."[19] The Seneca Falls Declaration stands with the Declaration of Independence as bedrock of the American Dream.

17. Johns Hopkins Bloomberg School of Public Health. "2025 National Survey"; Washburn, "Guns Are the Leading Cause of Death"; Matthews et al., "School Shootings."

18. United States Congress, Joint Resolution of March 22, 1972.

19. Stanton et al., "Declaration."

The Fourth of July, a treasured national holiday, should not be celebrated without remembering the Twentieth of July as well.

Second, in addition to the Nineteenth Amendment, the Fourteenth, ratified five decades earlier on July 9, 1868—another midsummer date that deserves remembering—is also essential for the American Dream. The Fourteenth Amendment grants citizenship to all persons "born or naturalized in the United States, and subject to the jurisdiction thereof," including formerly enslaved people. It requires that no person in the United States or any state shall be deprived of "life, liberty, or property, without due process of law"—the phrase is identical with the Fifth Amendment. It guarantees that individuals within a state's jurisdiction shall receive "equal protection under the laws," a measure taken to extend to the states most provisions of the Bill of Rights, which explicitly safeguards citizens and states against the overreach of federal power. The due process and equal protection clauses are as crucial as they are interconnected. The equal protection clause ensures that everyone is treated equally under the law, while the due process clause ensures that government actions do not deprive individuals of their rights without fair procedures.

With reckless regularity, Trump 2.0 has not only violated the constitutionally mandated due process requirements but also evaded court orders that find Trump and his administration in violation of that principle. Obsessed with ridding the nation of people he does not like, especially but not necessarily only undocumented immigrants, Trump has lawlessly invoked a problematic eighteenth-century law, the aforementioned Alien Enemies Act (1798), enacted when the new nation believed that war with France was imminent. The act states that "whenever there shall be a declared war . . . or any invasion or predatory incursion shall be perpetrated, attempted, or threatened" against the United States, all "subjects of the hostile nation or government" could be "apprehended, restrained, secured and removed, as alien enemies." Previously, the act has been used just three times in American history, all in wartime and most notoriously when it was used to legitimate the internment of tens of thousands of Japanese Americans during World War II.

In spring 2025, Trump and his draconian ICE agency lawlessly invoked the Alien Enemies Act to deport—"disappear" is more accurate—238 Venezuelans and twenty-three Salvadorans to El Salvador, primarily to the dreaded Terrorism Confinement Center (CECOT). These deportees were accused of being members of Tren de Aragua (TdA), a Venezuelan gang, and MS-13, a Salvadoran gang. Most of these people had no established criminal records or evidence of gang affiliations. None of them were engaged in war, invasion, or predatory incursion against the United States. Nevertheless, they were arrested and deported without due process of law.

The best-known case is that of Kilmar Abrego García, a Maryland man unlawfully deported by the Trump administration to the notorious CECOT prison in El Salvador, where his captors abused and tortured him.[20] His wife and three children are American citizens. He is not but was legally living and working in the United States before he was arrested and deported without due process of law. SCOTUS ordered the Trump administration to "facilitate" his return to the United States, but Trump and his minions stonewalled. Well into the second hundred days of Trump 2.0, García's future remained in suspense while Trump flouted the law. Then, on June 6, 2025, the Trump administration abruptly flew García back to the United States but only to face charges of transporting undocumented migrants. A month earlier (on May 4, 2025), NBC's Kristen Welker had asked Trump whether citizens and noncitizens in the United States are entitled to due process. His disgraceful answer was, "I don't know. I'm not, I'm not a lawyer. I don't know."[21]

On December 12, 2025, federal judge Paula Xinis blocked US immigration authorities from further detaining Abrego García—she had released him from detention hours earlier—without due process of law.[22] Meanwhile, if Trump again pays no price for his criminality, the United States has moved closer to dictatorship, and no one in the United States can take personal safety for granted. On the contrary, American citizens could be arrested on trumped up charges, and without due process, they could be swept away never to be seen again. Augmented by the Fifth Amendment, the Fourteenth Amendment reminds Americans how important it is to muster civil courage and cultural resistance against Trump 2.0, to defend due process and equal protection, and thereby to save the American Dream.

Third, when James Madison and his allies advanced a Bill of Rights to supplement the Constitution in 1791, they chose wisely to write the First Amendment as they did:

> Congress shall make no law respecting an establishment of religion, or prohibiting the free exercise thereof; or abridging the freedom of speech, or of the press, or the right of the people to peaceably assemble, and to petition the Government for a redress of grievances.

The American Dream would not and cannot exist without those provisions. In the dark times of Trump 2.0, however, much of the First Amendment is under attack, because its provisions stand against despotism, corruption,

20. Feuer, "Abrego Garcia."
21. Swan, "Trump Says 'I Don't Know.'"
22. Kunzelman, "Immigration Officials Can't Re-detain."

oligarchy, lawlessness, economy-weakening tariffs, and nearly everything that Trump and his MAGA crowd is attempting to do in and to the United States.

On September 21, 2025, more than sixty thousand Americans, including Donald Trump and leading officials in the Trump 2.0 administration, flocked to State Farm Stadium in Glendale, Arizona, to pay tribute to Charlie Kirk. The thirty-one-year-old conservative activist, a Christian nationalist, and the cofounder of Turning Point USA, which regularly drew thousands of younger Americans to "Prove Me Wrong" debates on university and college campuses, was assassinated at Utah Valley University on September 13. His murder plunged the United States into growing fear about political violence and alarm about restrictions on freedom of speech. The latter concern was intensified when Vice President JD Vance urged Americans to inform on one another if anyone celebrated Kirk's murder.

Kirk was remembered and eulogized in a memorial that blended evangelical Christianity and MAGA politics in ways that illustrated the importance of the First Amendment's guarantee of freedom of speech, which Kirk valued. His wife, Erika, who spoke for twenty-eight minutes, tearfully said of her husband's killer, "I forgive him. I forgive him because it was what Christ did and what Charlie would do." Her words drew a standing ovation. So did Donald Trump's when he followed with a forty-minute homage that will be remembered only for the threat it contained. Charlie Kirk, said Trump, "was a missionary with a noble spirit and a great, great purpose. He did not hate his opponents. He wanted the best for them. That's where I disagreed with Charlie. I hate my opponent, and I don't want the best for them. . . . I can't stand my opponent."[23]

Past was prologue; the day before, Trump had pressured Pam Bondi, his compliant if not criminal attorney general, to move faster and go farther in prosecuting his opponents. "We can't delay any longer, it's killing our reputation and credibility," Trump said. "They impeached me twice, and indicted me (5 times!), OVER NOTHING. JUSTICE MUST BE SERVED, NOW!!! President DJT."[24]

Kirk's horrific killing damaged the American Dream, which depends on honoring the rights to life, liberty, and the pursuit of happiness. An assassin's bullet robbed Charlie Kirk of those rights and put them at risk for every American. The latter happened partly because Donald Trump and his minions weaponized Kirk's death in support of their campaign to silence criticism. A word against Kirk became a word against Trump 2.0.

23. King, "Erika Kirk and Donald Trump."

24. Rahman, "Trump Calls on Pam Bondi."

The Trump regime understood that in death as well as in life Kirk remained their staunch ally. Not only had Kirk's Turning Point USA rallied many young people to the MAGA cause but also Kirk stood on the Trump 2.0 side of major political issues, criticizing gay and transgender rights, opposing gun control, expanding Christian nationalism, downplaying climate change, deploring civil rights legislation, labeling and attacking liberal perspectives as "woke," and smearing academic opponents by naming them on a Professor Watchlist.[25] Trump could not have conjured a more useful ally than Charlie Kirk, whose influence grew because Kirk appeared to defend and practice freedom of speech while arguably if not hypocritically serving up content and holding commitments that undercut it.

Like Donald Trump, Charlie Kirk has attracted many followers. Most Americans, however, are not among them, and the number of Trump's supporters, if not Kirk's, declines.[26] That fact, plus robust defense of the First Amendment's guarantee of freedom of speech, shows that revival of the American Dream and the democratic pluralism it supports could be at hand if enough Americans campaign strongly and vote wisely in 2026 and 2028. American young people, especially those in Gen Z, will be better served by that revival than by Charlie Kirk's Trump-tainted legacy.

In addition to enshrining freedom of speech, the First Amendment grounds the long-standing principle that in the United States there is and always ought to be a separation of church and state. That principle amplifies freedom all around. But in the darkness of Trump times, Christian nationalism seeks domination, and religious schools aim to expand and tighten their grip on funds that should go to public schools. Trump's attacks on language are emblematic of his anti–free speech authoritarianism. Words that speak about diversity and inclusion, racism and gender, are damned as "woke." The pronouns that the LGBTQIA+ community can use to identify themselves are censored. The incompetent Secretary of Defense Pete Hegseth uses his ill-gained power to trash academic excellence at the service academies and to ban books from their libraries.[27] Trump has long smeared the press—journalists and reporters—as enemies of the people. He aims to defund National Public Radio and the Public Broadcasting Service, whose voices do not bend to his.[28] In June 2025, Trump ordered about four thousand National Guard troops and seven hundred US Marines to Los Angeles on the

25. Ahn and Joselow," "Where Charlie Kirk Stood."

26. Brenan, "Trump's Approval Rating Drops"; Perry and Trussler. "Poll: Trump's MAGA Base Is Still Behind Him."

27. Cohen, "Hegseth's Headlong Pursuit."

28. Mullin. "NPR and PBS Vow to Fight."

bogus pretext that protection for federal buildings and ICE personnel was needed in response to the peaceful anti-Trump protests in that California city. Nothing would please Trump more than to find or provoke an excuse to invoke the Insurrection Act and unleash military force against Americans who assemble peacefully to protest against the corruption, incompetence, stupidity, and fawning "Dear Leader" accolades of Trump 2.0.[29] Far from surprising, it should be expected that, sooner or later, Trump will viciously and violently seek to quell public protest against him.

The First Amendment is anathema to Trump, because the rights it enshrines and defends oppose him, even though he and his acolytes try to use them to suggest if not claim—blasphemously—that his power is divinely given and God-blessed. For Trump and his followers, freedom of speech is primarily about the freedom to lie, deceive, gaslight, grift, inflame division, evade prosecution, exact revenge, and promote economic fantasies. Trump equates freedom of the press with Fox News and Truth Social. Anything different deserves harsh treatment, if silence or compliance cannot be bought. Peaceable assembly? For Trump, MAGA rallies are what that is about, if not cabinet meetings of loyalists. In one such gathering, Attorney General Pam Bondi claimed that Trump in his second term saved "258 million lives" due to the amount of fentanyl that his justice department has taken off the streets, adding "your first 100 days has far exceeded that of any other presidency in this country ever, ever. Never seen anything like it. Thank you." Not to be outdone, Interior Secretary Doug Burgum declared absurdly that Trump was "not just courageous, you're actually fearless" in taking on issues that other presidents dare not touch. "All of us can sprint, because you're running ahead," Burgum said.[30]

Petitioning for redress of grievances? None of that against Trump 2.0, but plenty of "I am your retribution" policies, as Trump pardons insurrectionists who fomented a coup against the country on January 6, 2021. Trump continues to protest without a scintilla of evidence that the 2020 election was stolen from him; continues to gaslight Americans to accept that the country's economic woes are former President Joe Biden's fault, not his; continues to crow that his misbegotten tariff policies will bring us a Golden Age of prosperity after only a bit of pain. Trump likes the First Amendment when he can use it to undermine the rights it proclaims, but he really hates it, because he knows that those same rights can be his undoing. His attacks on education bear witness to that.

29. Brookings Institution, "Reference Sheet."
30. Kim, "Lovefest or Cabinet Meeting?"

A Speech

The Constitution does not contain the word *education*. But the Constitution's existence, meaning, authority, and living character all depend on education. Thomas Jefferson knew that when the epitaph he wrote for himself emphasized not only that he had authored the Declaration of American Independence and the Virginia statute for religious freedom but also that he was "Father of the University of Virginia." Had he witnessed what happened on that campus on June 27, 2025, Jefferson surely would have shed angry tears when Trump 2.0 engineered the resignation of James E. Ryan, president of the University of Virginia, because of the university's DEI efforts—a shameful removal in which the university's caving board was complicit.[31]

Some of the most famous and distinguished universities in the world were established in the American colonies decades before the United States existed: Harvard (1636), Yale (1701), Princeton (1746), and Columbia (1754). Presently, there are more than 4,700 colleges and universities in the United States, including about 2,700 public institutions and 2,000 private ones. Overall, no nation in the world has better higher education than American universities and colleges provide. The First Amendment undergirds that fact. Absent the right of people to peaceably assemble, no university or college could exist. Absent freedom for and from religion, the American university and college network could not be imagined. Above all, absent freedom of speech, which facilitates freedom of inquiry and thought, academic freedom would perish, and no university or college would enjoy much of a future on American ground. Fortunately, the First Amendment's necessary conditions for higher education, indeed for sound education of any kind, have prevailed, and the nation's universities and colleges have flourished, supporting and advancing the American Dream in the process. Those intents and purposes, however, must not be taken for granted, because Donald Trump's campaign of American carnage targets American higher education.

On his dubious way to becoming Trump's vindictive vice president, JD Vance gave a keynote speech on November 2, 2021, at the National Conservative Conference in Orlando, Florida. Titled "The Universities Are the Enemy," his talk, far from conserving anything of value, was a vengeful assault on American higher education. Ignoring the hypocrisy in decrying institutions—The Ohio State University and Yale Law School—that had

31. Schmidt and Bender, "University of Virginia President Resigns."

paved his way, Vance declaimed that "we have to honestly and aggressively attack the universities in this country . . . the professors are the enemy."[32]

According to Vance, the venom and vengeance were warranted because universities and professors "control"—his word—knowledge, truth, and falsity in the United States. Vance resorted to a thinly veiled conspiracy theory to advance the proposition that universities and professors were manipulating and lying to the American people because they did not bend the knee to support the National Conservative Conference's agenda, which, minus tariff madness, was very much the same then as Trump's agenda is now. Vance's plan included discouraging young people from aspiring to university or college education. Who needs that, he pontificated, when the result will be brainwashing and debt? One does not have to be Thomas Jefferson to see through the disingenuity, which includes awareness that a poorly educated citizenry can be manipulated and lied to with impunity.

The seeds that Vance sowed in Orlando grew into noxious weeds soon after Trump and Vance took office in 2025. They seized on student unrest that roiled American campuses after Hamas—provoked by Israel's long-standing siege of Gaza and its expansion of settlements in the West Bank—launched a gruesome surprise attack against Israel from Gaza. In the deadliest single-day attack on Jews since the Holocaust, Hamas killed more than 1,200 Israelis and foreign nationals, including at least thirty-five US citizens living in Israel. Hamas also took more than 250 hostages—including children, women, and elderly people, as well as men and soldiers. Israel responded with massive force, killing tens of thousands of Palestinian civilians in Gaza while attempting to destroy Hamas. Gaza became a wasteland, its population, refugees with nowhere safe to go, engulfed in an ongoing humanitarian crisis that has been widely condemned as genocidal.[33]

As the Israel-Hamas war escalated in the spring of 2024, eventually leading to Trump's Israeli-encouraged June 21, 2025, orders to bomb Iran's nuclear facilities, protest and disruption, antisemitism and anti-Palestinianism, encampments and arrests beset American colleges and universities from coast to coast. On more than one hundred campuses, demonstrators demanded an end to Israel's war in Gaza, insisted that their colleges and universities scrap financial ties with Israel, and upset commencement ceremonies. Jewish students and faculty members felt besieged as antisemitism skyrocketed. Palestinian protesters and their allies complained that

32. Vance, "Universities Are the Enemy."

33. For further discussion of these matters, see Rittner and Roth, *Stress Test*. See also Tharoor, "Leading Genocide Scholars."

administration reactions, including interventions by police, were heavy-handed and in violation of free-speech rights.

Trump, Vance, and their anti-higher education allies saw and took advantage of their opening. They weaponized antisemitism to undermine American universities and colleges. On March 10, 2025, for example, the US Department of Education's Office for Civil Rights (OCR) sent letters to sixty institutions indicating that "enforcement actions" would be coming to any that were found wanting in their protection of Jewish students on campus.[34] Professional wrestling promoter Linda McMahon, the unqualified secretary of education whose portfolio includes destruction of the agency she is sworn to serve, amplified the extortionist threat: "The Department is deeply disappointed that Jewish students studying on elite US campuses continue to fear for their safety amid the relentless antisemitic eruptions that have severely disrupted campus life for more than a year. University leaders must do better. US colleges and universities benefit from enormous public investments funded by US taxpayers. That support is a privilege and it is contingent on scrupulous adherence to federal antidiscrimination laws."[35] The threat's recipients included Harvard, Yale, Princeton, and Columbia as well as Thomas Jefferson's University of Virginia. As Harvard soon learned, it was the prize target in a barely disguised extortion scheme aimed at requiring Harvard and other influential universities and colleges to comply with Trump-Vance ideology or be crippled if not destroyed.

On April 3, 2025, Harvard received notice from the Trump administration specifying "immediate next steps that we regard as necessary for Harvard University's continued financial relationship with the United States government." In addition to mandating that Harvard prevent antisemitism and punish those who discriminate against Jewish people, the letter demanded that the university "cease all preferences based on race, color, or national origin" in admissions and hiring and "shutter" DEI programs. A few days later, on April 11, another Trump administration letter alleged that "Harvard has in recent years failed to live up to both the intellectual and civil rights conditions that justify federal investment." To atone for these sins, said the second directive, Harvard had to, among other things, hire a "critical mass of new faculty" to ensure "viewpoint diversity."[36] Pending compliance, the Trump administration would hold hostage billions of dollars of federal funding, much of it used for cutting-edge scientific and health-related research.

34. United States Department of Education, "Office of Civil Rights Sends Letters."
35. United States Department of Education, "Office of Civil Rights Sends Letters."
36. Rose, "Attacks on Harvard."

Harvard pushed back. On April 14, President Alan M. Garber declined to meet the Trump administration's demands. Writing to the Harvard community, he said:

> The University will not surrender its independence or relinquish its constitutional rights. The administration's prescription goes beyond the power of the federal government. It violates Harvard's First Amendment rights and . . . it threatens our values as a private institution devoted to the pursuit, production, and dissemination of knowledge. No government—regardless of which party is in power—should dictate what private universities can teach, whom they can admit and hire, and which areas of study and inquiry they can pursue.[37]

The next day, Donald Trump threatened to revoke Harvard's tax-exemption. Harvard responded on April 21 by suing the Trump administration, underscoring that its threats to Harvard's federal funding were not only "arbitrary and capricious"[38] but also in violation of the First Amendment. The following day, hundreds of American university and college presidents and other higher-education leaders issued "A Call for Constructive Engagement," in which they spoke "with one voice against the unprecedented government overreach and political interference now endangering American higher education."[39] By May 9, more than six hundred influential educators had signed the protest. Their outlooks found widespread support among the American public. In early May 2025, more than half of Americans, 56 percent, rejected Trump's attacks on higher education.[40]

Harvard's example of civil courage, its commitment to build a culture of resistance against Trump's tyranny, is essential. Of course, antisemitism must be combatted, especially on American university and college campuses, and those institutions must lead in that important work. But no one should be confused that Trump's intents and purposes make him care much about antisemitism. With it, as with everything, he is transactional. He will dine with Holocaust deniers, back neo-Nazis for significant posts in government, and slur Chuck Schumer, the leading Jewish elected official in the United States, by calling him a "Palestinian," when such actions serve his interests.[41] He will use antisemitism to bludgeon American higher educa-

37. Garber, " Promise of American Higher Education."

38. Crimson News Staff, "Read Harvard's Complaint."

39. American Association of Colleges and Universities, "Call for Constructive Engagement."

40. Gecker and Sanders, "Most Americans Disapprove."

41. Gross, "Rights Groups Condemn Trump."

tion—agreeing with his sidekick JD Vance that universities and professors are the enemy. Saving the American Dream depends on saying no to Trump as Harvard has courageously done. Doing that, of course, is risky. Litigation is lengthy, its results uncertain.

Meanwhile, the Trump 2.0 onslaught against Harvard—the academic "trophy" that Trump's attack most wants to claim—continued its relentless course. Trump 2.0 tried to rescind Harvard's right to host some seven thousand international students, but a federal judge blocked that attempt on June 20, 2025. Other matters had been under negotiation between Trump 2.0 and Harvard for some time when, on June 30, 2025, the Trump administration reignited acrimonious threats in a lengthy letter sent to the university by Paula M. Stannard, who directs the Office for Civil Rights within the US Department of Health and Human Services.[42] The document accused Harvard of violating Title VI of the Civil Rights Act of 1964 by acting with "deliberate indifference" toward harassment of Jewish and Israeli students by other students and faculty from October 7, 2023, through the present. Harvard strongly disputed the accusations, but with billions of dollars of federal research funding at play, the stakes in this conflict are high. Trump wants to take Harvard down. Harvard wants to sustain its integrity, autonomy, and international reputation as a world leader in research and education.

Trump's vendetta against leading American universities continued when he signed the so-called One Big Beautiful Bill Act (OBBBA) on July 4, 2025. While it exempted colleges with fewer than three thousand students, the bill included a hefty tax of 4–8 percent on the endowment earnings from flagship universities such as Harvard, Yale, Princeton, and Stanford.[43] Nothing in the bill does much to improve access to or support for higher education. Instead, it reduces university support for students and increases their financial burdens. The Trump administration's specific harassment of Harvard continued into early July, with further attempts to interfere with the university's international students and its accreditation.[44] By mid-August, it appeared that Harvard and Trump 2.0 were nearing a settlement. In exchange for Harvard's agreement to spend $500 million on vocational and educational programs and research, the university's billions of dollars of federal research funding would be restored.[45] More than 14,000 Harvard-related protesters urged the university to reject the "deal" because

42. United States Department of Health and Human Services, "Notice of Violation."
43. Patel, "What the Republicans' New Policy Bill Means."
44. Blinder and Bender, "Trump Administration Renews Attacks."
45. Blinder et al., "Harvard and White House Move."

it would compromise "the university's autonomy in unconstitutional or unlawful ways."[46]

Transcendence

On April 23, 2025, two days after Harvard sued the Trump administration, litigation that moved toward a September 3 court ruling that favored Harvard but left final settlement details uncertain, the Yale Symphony Orchestra (YSO) played the final concert of its 2024–25 season. The concert's theme was *transcendence*, a concept that evokes rising above and surpassing current conditions to recognize, seek, and pursue what is better, more beautiful, and more inspiring. Harvard's lawsuit aims to transcend Trump's venality and stupidity.[47] YSO and its music uplift spirits and enlarge horizons to help listeners and performers to feel and aspire to what people can do together when we are at our best.

Streaming technology permitted me to transcend the physical distance between my home in Winthrop, Washington, and Yale University's Woolsey Hall. The April concert was as poignant as it was beautiful for me because it was the last time that my graduating granddaughter, violinist Keeley Brooks, would play with her beloved YSO. She is one of that "younger generation," as Bonhoeffer acknowledged in his time, whose future "is at stake." In addition, it was the final conducting performance for William Boughton, a superior musician, who led YSO with distinction for many years.

A noted cellist whose orchestra experience inspired him to pursue conducting, this Englishman is an insightful educator. His final YSO concert honored that heritage by featuring Edward Elgar's elegant *Cello Concerto in E minor*, played brilliantly by Yale alumnus Henry Shapard, one of Boughton's protégés, and Gustav Holst's *The Planets*, whose musical explorations of the heavens expand awareness of Planet Earth as well. But Boughton also made sure that his final YSO concert included "Holy Dance" from *Four Black American Dances* by the contemporary American composer Carlos Simon. Consistently, Boughton insisted that the YSO repertoire should emphasize the music of American composers such as Florence Price and Aaron Copland, Joan Tower and Duke Ellington, because he wanted his Yale musicians to grasp the country's musical roots and legacy.

For the YSO repertoire to work, the musicians had to master it with individual brilliance and play it just as vividly together. The notes had to ring true, the phrasing had to be melodic, crisp, precise. This work is hard. It

46. Patel, "Thousands Ask Harvard."

47. Schmidt et al. "Why Trump and Harvard."

takes musical forms of civil courage to do it well. In a YSO concert—and in the disciplined practicing and rehearing that lead to it—no place exists for grifting, lying, waste, fraud, extortion, or abuse. On the contrary, William Boughton, stellar conductor-educator, taught his musicians that an excellent orchestra models what a flourishing society needs to be.

Individuals who love their instruments and passionately want to play them to the best of their ability are essential. So are individuals who strive together for good that transcends what they can ever do alone, who love community, who care especially about their community, and passionately want it to transcend itself, to be even and ever better than before. I expect William Boughton never spoke to his YSO musicians about the American Dream, but when I heard him talk about what he wanted them to learn, he taught me about important metaphorical ways to think about saving the American Dream: think, act, play like YSO at its best.

A few weeks after the April 23, 2025, YSO finale, a *New York Times* essay with a musical and transcendent theme riveted my attention. Coauthored by Jonathan Biss, a concert pianist, and Christopher Serkin, a professor at Vanderbilt Law School, the essay carried a title that invited me in: "A Pianist and a Law Professor Meet at the Bar . . ." The two compared the strictly textualist and "originalist" methods of constitutional interpretation with the challenges a pianist faces in interpreting a Mozart concerto, a Schubert piano trio, or a Beethoven sonata.

In both cases, a text—the constitutional document or a musical score—governs the interpretation. Signs of the authors' or composers' original intent can be seen, their aims inferred as well. In both the constitutional and the musical cases, information about historical context and previous interpretations is needed. Done well, for the good of all, Biss and Serkin aptly say,

> Interpretation—of Mozart or the Constitution—is neither mechanical reproduction nor unfettered creativity. It is about using your eyes and ears and lived experience and education and critical lens and passion and skepticism and, above all, humility, to tease out the text's infinite implications, and in doing so, to come closer to its essence.[48]

Resounding a note of transcendence that is applicable to saving the American Dream in dark Trump times, Biss and Serkin conclude their essay by observing that a performance of Mozart or a reading of the Constitution can never be beautiful enough, let alone perfect. More always remains to be

48. Biss and Serkin, "Pianist and a Law Professor." See also Dennie, *Originalism Trap*.

done. At least in part, the purpose of the Constitution or a Mozart score is to help us to respond well to that insight.

More always remains to be done. Embracing that truth, acting on that conviction—those commitments to transcendence, those intents and purposes, can build the civil courage and inspire the culture of resistance that reject Trump's tone-deaf chaos and repudiate his off-key arrogance. In their ugly place can be a symphonic American Dream that affirms again the old hymn's beautifully great refrain: "Let music swell the breeze, / And ring from all the trees / Sweet freedom's song."[49]

49. See Gilder Lehrman Institute, "My Country" for the third stanza (and all stanzas) of Samuel Francis Smith's "America" (1831), also called "My Country, 'Tis of Thee."

6

Binding Oaths

Binding oaths are promises and pledges. They hold Americans accountable and make us responsible for each other. In addition to underscoring that "this Constitution . . . shall be the supreme Law of the Land," Article VI affirms that "Senators and Representatives . . . and the Members of the several State Legislatures, and all executive and judicial Officers, both of the United States and of the several States, shall be bound by Oath or Affirmation, to support this Constitution." That provision echoes Article II, which states that before the president holds office, "he shall take the following Oath or Affirmation:—'I do solemnly swear (or affirm) that I will faithfully execute the Office of President of the United States, and will to the best of my Ability, preserve, protect and defend the Constitution of the United States.'"

While the Constitution provided wording for the presidential oath, it did not do so for any other government officers, leaving that determination to Congress. So, the first legislative act passed by the United States Congress after the ratification of the Constitution was "An Act to Regulate the Time and Manner of Administering Certain Oaths."[1] Signed into law by President George Washington on June 1, 1789, the act established the oath required by the Constitution for federal and state officials, promising they would support the Constitution. Simple and straightforward, the prescribed oath stated: "I, A.B. do solemnly swear or affirm (as the case may be) that I will support the Constitution of the United States."[2]

During the 1860s, this oath was altered several times before Congress settled on the text used today, which appears in the United States Code, the

1. Blackerby, "Oath of Office."
2. Blackerby, "Oath of Office."

compendium of the general and permanent laws of the United States, at 5 USC 3331:

> An individual, except the President, elected or appointed to an office of honor or profit in the civil service or uniformed services, shall take the following oath: "I, AB, do solemnly swear (or affirm) that I will support and defend the Constitution of the United States against all enemies, foreign and domestic; that I will bear true faith and allegiance to the same; that I take this obligation freely, without any mental reservation or purpose of evasion; and that I will well and faithfully discharge the duties of the office on which I am about to enter. So help me God.[3]

Since the first naturalization law in 1790, applicants for naturalized citizenship have also taken an oath to support the Constitution of the United States. The current Naturalization Oath of Allegiance to the United States of America was finalized in 1952. No immigrant can become a US citizen until she or he takes this oath at a naturalization ceremony. The oath deserves full quotation because it contains rigorous requirements.

> I hereby declare, on oath, that I absolutely and entirely renounce and abjure all allegiance and fidelity to any foreign prince, potentate, state, or sovereignty, of whom or which I have heretofore been a subject or citizen; that I will support and defend the Constitution and laws of the United States of America against all enemies, foreign and domestic; that I will bear true faith and allegiance to the same; that I will bear arms on behalf of the United States when required by the law; that I will perform noncombatant service in the Armed Forces of the United States when required by the law; that I will perform work of national importance under civilian direction when required by the law; and that I take this obligation freely, without any mental reservation or purpose of evasion; so help me God.[4]

Promises and Pledges

Significantly, while oaths to uphold and defend the Constitution are a central part of government and military service, neither Article VI nor any other constitutional provision mandates that every American citizen must swear to uphold and defend the Constitution. The founders understood

3. United States Code, USC 3331.
4. United States Citizenship and Immigration Services, "Naturalization Oath."

that government properly derives its power and authority from the consent of the governed, a condition that could scarcely require every citizen to formally swear allegiance to the Constitution, but they also emphasized that the liberties protected and rights undergirded by the Constitution presumed that citizens have a moral obligation to participate in and defend their government, though not necessarily through formal oaths.

Those qualifications, however, do not diminish the fact that we Americans are a nation of oath-takers and promise-makers. Our judicial system and the rule of law, for example, depend on witnesses taking and heeding an oath to tell the truth. Before witnesses testify in legal proceedings, a question confers an essential duty upon them: "Do you solemnly swear that the testimony you will give will be the truth, the whole truth, and nothing but the truth, so help you God?" If the response is the expected "I do," then deliberately failing to tell the truth about pertinent matters may be a felony called *perjury*. Lying under oath is a serious matter because the entire system of justice in the United States, and hence the American Dream as well, depends on truth-telling. What's more, democracy, indeed human civilization itself, depends on seeking and respecting truth. Failure to pursue and honor truth undercuts and betrays what is good and right.

How different American democracy and prospects for the American Dream would be if Donald Trump and his followers sought and respected truth, but they do not and will not. How much better the country would be if every American citizen told the truth and followed where tested evidence leads. The nation not only would have been spared the Big Lie that the 2020 election was stolen by voter fraud—it was not—but also Trump and his acolytes would never have regained the power in 2024 that undermines the American Dream. From Adolf Hitler to Vladimir Putin, from Viktor Orbán to Donald Trump—and with a long, sordid history preceding them—tyranny depends on lying, on disrespecting truth, on willful failure to seek and respect it. If we Americans are to save the American Dream, nothing is more important than seeking and respecting truth.

That commitment requires believing in truth, affirming that it exists. And that work requires taking facts seriously. Doing so may be hard and contrary to our wishes, but we do it all the time. Unless we are blind and stupid, we have no other choice, because facts are stubborn. They can be suppressed, ignored, and denied, but they do not go away, and democracy's survival depends on fidelity to them.

Although American citizens are not required to swear that they will uphold and defend the Constitution, most of us know and affirm the following oath: "I pledge allegiance to the flag of the United States of America and to the Republic for which it stands, one Nation under God, indivisible, with liberty and justice for all." The Pledge of Allegiance was noted in chapter 1, but it merits further consideration here. Probably like you, I cannot remember exactly when I committed the pledge's words to memory, but I expect that one of my early Midwestern schoolteachers taught them to me. We were expected to know the Pledge of Allegiance by heart. Daily repetition made that certain. For a long time, nearly every American child has had that experience.

Even if the pledge is taught and learned with care, most recitations of it are thoughtless. Nonetheless, the pledge's simple statement has much to say, and it highlights much that is needed to save the American Dream. The pledge can provide a compass that helps us to read a map of our country. Before those words can do so, however, attention to their meaning needs to be paid.

Consider, first, that the Pledge of Allegiance begins differently than other classical texts—the Declaration of Independence, for example, or the Constitution, or even the National Anthem—that are foundational for the American Dream. "We hold these truths to be self-evident," says the Declaration, as it identifies individual rights that people share equally. "We the People," affirms the Preamble that ordains and establishes a Constitution for the United States of America. As for the National Anthem, it begins by asking whether *you* can see the star-spangled banner. In contrast, the pledge's first word is *I*.

The current form of the pledge developed from a version that appeared originally on September 8, 1892, in a Boston weekly called the *Youth's Companion*.[5] Published initially as part of a national commemoration of the four-hundredth anniversary of Christopher Columbus's "discovery" of the "New World," Francis Bellamy's text was soon used widely in patriotic school exercises. Directed toward young Americans, its language was intended to be personal. Indeed, the original version simply spoke of "my flag," not "the flag of the United States of America," a substitution made in 1924.

A pledge is a promise. In the case of the Pledge of Allegiance, the promise is an oath of loyalty. Thus, it is no accident that it was wartime—1942—when the federal government officially recognized the pledge. Nor can it have been accidental that, for all its first-person significance, the pledge is rarely said silently or in private. The pledge is recited publicly. Others, but also oneself, are supposed to hear and be informed by the shared words. They confer responsibility on those who say them to profess loyalty to a country we inhabit together and to a Dream we should value.

The Pledge of Allegiance contains words that have helped to make the United States home to the American Dream. Originally, the pledge promised allegiance to a flag that stood for a republic that would be "one

5. Ravitch, *American Reader*, 182.

Nation, indivisible, with liberty and justice for all." Those few words express a dream of immense proportions, aspirations, and implications, especially when history and ideals collide, revealing contradictions between what is preached and what is practiced. The part about "liberty and justice for all" is the pledge's best remembered, most often quoted, and most problematic and unsettling phrase, especially during the dark times of Trump 2.0.

Individual liberty has long been a national watchword. But the pledge conjoins liberty with justice. The inseparability of the two accents the words *for all*, because individual freedom entails communal responsibility, while "justice" that disrespects individual rights is not justice at all. Liberty comes ahead of justice in the pledge's ordering of values, but no "pledge word" is more important than *justice*. Justice is crucial, because without it the Declaration's sense that people are created equal becomes a mocking abstraction. Only as Americans treat each other with respect and fairness does equality have practical significance. Only as equality has practical significance can the United States make good its dream of providing "for all" its citizens a sense of belonging to and of being at home in a country that can rightly be called "one Nation, indivisible."

Could putting the nation "under God" help to make it one and indivisible, with liberty and justice for all? Many Americans apparently thought so in 1954, the year that President Dwight D. Eisenhower convinced Congress to add those words to the pledge, requiring schoolboys like me to undo memory and to learn a different cadence in the words, one that at times still seems strange because it was not the way the words informed my memory first. For good measure, Congress also specified a code of conduct to govern the pledge's recitation: Allegiance to the flag was to be pledged standing tall, hats off, right hand over the heart.

The idea that the nation is "under God" is, of course, nothing new, although the Cold War conditions that prompted the pledge's 1954 revision may have been so at the time. Belief that the United States is "under God" has been a part of our nation's life from the beginning. The Declaration's signers, for example, put their names on a document that professed "a firm reliance on the Protection of Divine Providence." The meaning of that idea for those late eighteenth-century sons of the Enlightenment, the fervor and sincerity with which they endorsed it, no doubt varied considerably. But the fact that the Declaration enshrined such language illustrates how religion has permeated the American Dream—sometimes by legitimating, other times by subverting, and still other times by correcting, what Americans wanted the Dream to be.

Donald Trump's relations with religion are vexed and fraught. They subvert the American Dream. His grifting, for example, includes hawking

Lee Greenwood's "God Bless the USA" Bible (King James Version), which includes copies of the Constitution, Declaration of Independence, Bill of Rights, and Pledge of Allegiance. "All Americans need a Bible in their home, and I have many. It's my favorite book," conned Trump, adding, "I'm proud to endorse and encourage you to get this Bible. We must make America pray again." It sold for $59.99 and brought Trump $1.3 million in 2024. Thousands of those Bibles were printed in China.[6] Trump has said that people "can't be happy without religion, without that belief. Let's bring religion back. Let's bring God back into our lives."[7] If that happened, corruption and oligarchy would not infest Trump 2.0 as they do. If the choice is between God and another pocket-lining deal, Trump will be as disloyal to God as he is to anyone he tosses aside as no longer useful.

Announcing a new "golden age" for America during his inauguration speech on January 20, 2025, Trump also recalled the July 13 assassination attempt on his life during the 2024 campaign. "I felt then, and I believe even more so now," he claimed, "that my life was saved by God to make America great again."[8] Those words and Trump's deeds, however, do little to support the Pledge of Allegiance's ideal that the United States is "one Nation under God, indivisible." On the contrary, Trump divides the country, and his appeals to God and religion worsen the division.

Meanwhile, no president has done more to weaponize the American flag for anti-American purposes. From encouraging and pardoning the mob he unleashed on January 6, 2021, which included insurrectionists who used American flagpoles to beat police officers, to his boastful erection of two 88-foot flagpoles on the White House lawn—"a GIFT from me," he bragged—and his periodic smarmy hugging of the flag in the overwrought display of the Stars and Stripes that always swathes his rallies, Trump appears to love the flag but not the republic for which it stands.[9]

Trump may mouth the Pledge of Allegiance, but his violations of the Constitution are massive and growing. He has done little, if anything, to "preserve, protect and defend the Constitution of the United States." In fact, he has done the opposite. Resistance against that destructive folly and persistence in saving the American Dream require all truly loyal Americans to swear to tell the truth and to pledge allegiance to the aim of liberty and justice for all. "We the People" also need to do what the Constitution does not officially require: namely, to take our own oaths—individually

6. Colvin, "Trump Is Selling"; Lardner and Kang, "Printed in China '; and Lalljee, "Crypto, Wallets, Bibles."

7. Jackson and Whisnant, "Donald Trump Tells National Prayer Breakfast."

8. Jenkins, "At Inauguration."

9. Bedigan, "' These Are the Most Magnificent.'"

and communally—to preserve, protect, and defend the Constitution from the carnage that Trump and his lawless accomplices have wreaked and will worsen in his second presidential term.

Trump's Chaos and Carnage

As Trump's antics about the flag and religion show, he loves a spectacle. His self-aggrandizing "You have never seen anything like it" repeats incessantly, a sign of his ceaseless craving for attention. That craving accounts for his lack of attention to governing. As his erratic tariff policies reveal, he starts in one direction, then veers in another. The notion that he is in clever control is a mystifying mirage that blurs a pattern of gut-instinct initiative followed by declining interest and lost focus and then by moving on to the next eventful chaos that will keep the spotlight on him but not on his corruption and sexual decadence. Trump lives for those moments in the spotlight. So do his followers, who are addicted to Trump. As the insightful observer Kyla Scanlon suggests, "Trump is the first human-algorithm hybrid president—governing via Truth Social truths, bond market reactions, and direct market signals. A feedback loop in a suit."[10]

Enchanted followers get what they want, and Trump-the-algorithm-in-a-suit gives them new commotion to applaud. On and on, the feedback loops, but with traps and pitfalls along the way. If their accolades for the "dear leader" fall short, Trump's closest acolytes may be discarded. His lackeys are often picking up the slack and driving Trump-suggested policies that are very much their own (think Stephen Miller on deporting undocumented migrants), but their influence, power, and prestige, dependent on bootlicking, can nevertheless be stripped away.

Nothing in that profile minimizes let alone denies Trump's power. He is expert at getting attention. Truth Social, which he owns and controls, is an extension of his presidency. Trump's playbook of attention-through-chaos helps to explain why no one in the world today has more power. But enlarging that explanation requires understanding that Trump's carnage-producing chaos also embodies a "philosophy"—such as it is. Call it Trumpism. The antithesis of the American Dream at its best, the "principles" of Trumpism are derived and identified less from what Trump says than from what he does. They can be bulleted as follows:

- Recite mandatory words, such as the presidential oath or the Pledge of Allegiance, but never take them as binding.

10. Scanlon, "How the Attention Economy."

- Proclaim liberty and justice for all, but enact the principle that might makes right and show that the strong do whatever they choose while the weak suffer what they must.
- Broadcast "America First," but put "Me First"—always and forever. Duty that beckons differently is for suckers and losers.
- Wealth and power are the greatest goods. Nothing is better or more valuable. Monetize for personal gain as much as possible. Seek and demand public glorification. Put your name on buildings, ballrooms, currency—wherever doing so will make you the center of constant attention.
- Reward those who do my bidding, share my aims, and bend the knee to me. Impugn, discredit, attack, reject, and ruin those who do not.
- Require loyalty from others, but be loyal to others only if that serves me and my aims.
- Far from being prosecuted, corruption—especially and only if it benefits me—must not only be pardoned but also encouraged and normalized so that the concept of corruption becomes meaningless.
- Everything—economics and politics, war and peace, national security and the health of the American people—pivots on "deals" and quid pro quo transactions.
- Nothing in the political playbook is more useful than lies or more potent than lying. Relentless grievances, claims of persecution, and wedges of division bear witness to that. Allege political persecution. Play the victim card skillfully, aggressively, and ruthlessly. Inflame conspiracy theories when advantageous; snuff them when not.
- Have no religious belief, except that God chose me, but cultivate religious support to legitimate authority.
- Insist and boast that "I know best," that "I will make America great again," and that "I alone can fix it." Never apologize or admit wrongdoing. Deny every allegation and indictment. Do not obey the law, but use it to delay every judgment against me.

Encased in political power, backed by people who are deceived or profiting from the grift, or both, Trump's "philosophy," such as it is, and his perverse and perverted "ethics" are a recipe for disaster as far as American democracy and the American Dream are concerned. But Trump 2.0 has clout because the administration has learned how to use American institutions and traditions against themselves.

In late May 2025, the perceptive journalist M. Gessen warned Americans that Trump's corrupt authoritarianism was entering a new phase. The previous four months, said Gessen, had given the United States "an unremitting series of shocks: executive orders gutting civil rights and constitutional protections; a man with a chain saw [Elon Musk] trying to gut the federal government; deliberately brutal deportations; people snatched off the streets and disappeared in unmarked cars; legal attacks on universities and law firms."[11]

What worries Gessen is not just that "it's been everything everywhere all at once." As the onslaughts and outrages keep coming, Gessen fears that "fewer and fewer things can surprise us." Mounting reports of corruption, tragedy, and cruelty become routine. We may get "accustomed to what used to seem unthinkable." Authoritarian, oligarchic, kleptocratic regimes count on that numbing and the indifference that accompanies it, facilitating the destruction of democracy, the rule of law, and the American Dream of liberty and justice for all. What's more and arguably worse is that "when the unthinkable recedes at least a bit, . . . it's easy to mistake it for proof that the dark times are ending." The problem, however, is that "these comparatively small victories don't alter the direction of our transformation—they don't even slow it down measurably."

Gessen is no fatalist. The triumph of Trump and his "philosophy" is not inevitable, but Gessen does not want resistance against Trump to be lulled into complacency by "the sense that there is more air to breathe and more room to act than there was yesterday." On the contrary, these are the times when concerted opposition is most needed because there is more room to act than there was yesterday.

Small Victories

During the end-of-May week when Gessen's insightful essay appeared, several small victories buoyed the spirits of those who defend the American Dream against Trump's carnage. Here are three examples.

First, on May 28, Elon Musk announced that he was leaving the White House and the Department of Government Efficiency (DOGE). He had spearheaded that lawless office with devastating consequences for the American people as he and his "young tech" accomplices reduced many government agencies and indispensable services to rubble. Musk thanked Trump "for the opportunity to reduce wasteful spending." The *Washington Post* summarized part of Musk's reign of terror as follows:

11. Gessen, "Beware."

> Musk's team launched a chaotic blitz on Washington, dismantling some US agencies and terminating the employment of hundreds of thousands of civil servants. Through this work, Musk's agents were able to gain access to highly restricted government records on millions of federal employees, much to the chagrin of security officials. And Musk himself appeared to relish his role, brandishing a chain saw given to him by Argentine President Javier Milei at the Conservative Political Action Conference on Feb. 20."[12]

Arguably the most unpopular person in America, Musk departed Washington, DC, at odds with Trump, faced with cratering sales of his Tesla cars and another failure of the uncrewed SpaceX Starship. His company's double-speaking press release called its explosion an "unscheduled disassembly."[13] Unleashing his cruel retrenchment plans, Musk quashed the myth that wealth and intelligence, let alone moral integrity, go hand in hand.

Musk showed that no credible version of the American Dream can be equated solely with ambitions for wealth and power. He is neither an example nor a defender of the American Dream at its best. It is not enough, however, to say good riddance, because Musk did immense damage to the country. The power his wealth wields is still at play and may do much more harm. Gessen is right. Musk's departure is a small victory that should not lull true defenders of the American Dream into complacency.

Second, during the first one hundred days of Trump 2.0, more than two lawsuits per day—a total of more than 220 in courts across the country—were brought against the president, challenging executive orders, immigration policies, and the firing of government officials.[14] Trump lost most of this litigation. According to political analyst Adam Bonica, "in May 2025, federal district courts ruled against the Trump administration in 26 of 27 cases—a stunning 96% loss rate. . . . This isn't just another data point; it suggests a potential inflection point in the judiciary's engagement with an executive that has consistently tested constitutional boundaries."[15]

A stunning judicial rebuke of Trump took place on May 28, 2025, when a three-judge panel of the US Court of International Trade unanimously ruled that Trump had exceeded his constitutional authority in imposing sweeping tariffs on goods imported from China and many other countries.[16] Trump im-

12. Ho et al., "Chain Saw."
13. Robledo, "SpaceX Starship."
14. Charalambous, "220 Lawsuits in 100 Days."
15. Bonica, "The 96% Rebellion."
16. Khardori, "Supreme Court May Not Step In."

mediately appealed the decision. The Supreme Court's decision in 2026 may put Trump on the losing side again. The Court of International Trade's action was a win for the American Dream, which depends on free international trade, not the crippling, inflationary, and regressive taxes that are inflicted on the American people by Trump's unchecked and chaotic tariff delusions. But again, Gessen's caution remains valid. With the crucial national elections of 2026 and 2028 upcoming, now is the time to keep legal pressure on Trump in every way possible.

Third, when mocking humor skewers Trump, the derision gets under his thin skin. The *Financial Times* columnist Robert Armstrong contributed mightily to that resistance on May 2 when he coined the acronym TACO (Trump Always Chickens Out) to lampoon the chaotic debacle of Trump's yo-yoing, on-again, off-again tariff policy. Trump was furious on May 28 when Megan Cassella, a CNBC correspondent known for her no-nonsense economic coverage, asked him about Armstrong's barb: "Mr. President, Wall Street analysts have coined a new term called the 'Taco trade.' They're saying 'Trump Always Chickens Out' on your tariff threats. . . . What's your response to that?" Trump bristled: "I chicken out? I've never heard that," he said, adding in a dismal attempt to bully Cassella, "Don't ever say what you said. That's a nasty question. To me, that's the nastiest question."[17]

Flattery is Trump's lifeblood. Mocking his incompetence, ridiculing his buffoonery, laughing at his garbled and nonsensical speeches—those are important acts of resistance against his authoritarian aspirations. But Gessen's warning remains. Trump's reign of corruption, defiance of law, and shredding of the Constitution are not laughing matters because when Armstrong's TACO taunted Trump, the president's second term was scarcely four months old. It has a long way to go.

Satire and parody, caricature and derision—essential though humor's political tools are for undermining Trump and his MAGA agenda, they will not be nearly enough to neutralize, let alone banish, his threats to the American Dream. No substitute exists for voting Trumpism out of power in 2026, 2028, and beyond. Immediate steps in that direction require defending four American Dream principles and resisting four of the most destructive initiatives that Trump and his accomplices are pursuing.

Principles and Threats

Saving the American Dream depends on at least four principles: (1) Invigorate and sustain the economy. That means reducing poverty, expanding

17. Bigg, "Asked About 'TACO.'"

opportunity for persistent initiative and honest work to be fairly rewarded, and bolstering experimentation and invention that benefit all Americans. (2) Revitalize education. That means advancing critical inquiry; building respect for evidence, science, and truth; confronting honestly both the darkness and the glory in American history; encouraging respectful dialogue about the pressing issues of our times; and supporting academic freedom in our universities, colleges, and schools. (3) Unmask, prosecute, and despise corruption, which includes but is not limited to bribery, self-dealing, conflicts of interest, scams, and grifting. No enemy against liberty and justice for all is more toxic than corruption. To the extent that the American Dream succumbs to it, the Dream fails. (4) Encourage new beginnings, including chances to take risks, to learn from failure, to start over and try again. But never confuse those goals with corrupted "pardons," those debased presidential acts that reward criminality, condone disrespect for the law, excuse insurrection against the Constitution, and betray the mutual obligations and responsibilities that we owe to one another to make our country the strongest and best it can be.

Gessen keeps reminding us, however, that principles are not enough. That is true, she suggests, because fewer and fewer things may surprise us.

> Once you've absorbed the shock of deportations to El Salvador, plans to deport people to South Sudan aren't that remarkable. Once you've wrapped your mind around the Trump administration's revoking the legal status of individual students, a blanket ban on international enrollment at Harvard isn't entirely unexpected. Once you've realized that the administration is intent on driving thousands of trans people out of the US military, a ban on Medicaid coverage for gender-affirming care, which could have devastating effects for hundreds of thousands, just becomes more of the same. As in a country at war, reports of human tragedy and extreme cruelty have become routine—not news.[18]

Gessen does not oppose principles, but action must back them. Those who care about the American Dream must be firmly opposed to the cynical opportunism and scornful nihilism that infest Trump 2.0 and put our country in dire straits. We need to do all we can to come out victorious in four battles that Trump and Trumpism are waging against the Dream.

18. Gessen, "Beware."

1. Trump and Trumpism are robbing most Americans, but especially the poor, to enrich the wealthy few.

Speaking at a Butler County, Iowa, town hall on May 30, Joni Ernst—shrewdly, she is not running for relection to the Senate in 2026—disrespected voters' concerns about the fatal implications of impending massive cuts to Medicaid and other provisions of the social safety net. "Well, we are all going to die," she chided her audience. "So, for heaven's sakes. For heaven's sakes, folks." Her callous comment went viral. Ernst's response to the outraged national pushback was more condescension and cruelty. In a video filmed in a cemetery, Ernst mockingly declaimed that "I made an incorrect assumption that everyone in the auditorium understood that, yes, we are all going to perish from this earth. So I apologize, and I'm really, really glad that I did not have to bring up the subject of the tooth fairy as well." She added that "for those that would like to see eternal and everlasting life, I encourage you to embrace my Lord and savior Jesus Christ."[19]

The provocation for Ernst's claptrap was the so-called One Big Beautiful Bill Act (HR 1, OBBBA), the MAGA federal budget bill that eked its way through the House of Representatives by one vote, 215–214, on May 22, then through the Senate on July 1 by one vote, 51–50, with Vice President JD Vance casting the tiebreaker, and finally through the House again, by a vote of 218–214 on July 3. Trump signed it into law with fanfare on the Fourth of July. It betrays the American Dream by robbing most Americans, but especially the poor, to enrich the wealthy few. Cutting to the chase, journalist Jonathan Chait rightly excoriated the ugly legislation as "the largest upward transfer of wealth in American history. That is not a side effect of the legislation," Chait underscored, "but its central purpose," which is to give lavish tax cuts to the rich while slashing benefits for those who need them most.[20]

Trump may have said, "We're not cutting Medicaid, we're not cutting Medicare, and we're not cutting Social Security." Time will tell, but his budget director, Russell Vought, mastermind of the notorious Project 2025, was ecstatic about the megabill. "It is a home run," he raved. "There's like, no downside to this bill. This is not one where you have to say pros and cons. It's all good."[21] But watch what Trump and his MAGA cronies have done, not what they say.

19. Alfaro, "Ernst Posts Snarky Reply."

20. Chait, "Largest Upward Transfer."

21. Waldvogel, "Russell Vought."

For the wealthiest 10 percent of Americans, the megabill will make them even better off, but the poorest 40 percent of American households will lose income. Vulnerable Americans will have added pain inflicted on them. Trump's bill, for example, cuts $930 billion from Medicaid. Enrolling more than seventy million people, many of them in rural communities, Medicaid is the largest public health insurance program in the country. Many recipients will lose coverage if they do not meet cumbersome work and bureaucratic requirements. Hospitals that depend on Medicaid funding may be forced to close. Cynically hoping to soften the backlash they know is coming, Republicans backloaded the Medicaid cuts, which will go into effect after the 2026 midterm elections.[22]

Overall, the megabill is likely to swell the number of Americans lacking health insurance by 11.8 million. The bill includes the biggest rollback ever for federal health support. Support for food security provided by the Supplemental Nutrition Assistance Program (SNAP) will be cut by $186 billion, ravaging needy families and young children. The deep cuts, however, do not come close to mitigating the national debt incurred by tax cuts for the wealthy and well-connected. The national debt will increase by at least $3.3 trillion. That number reflects $158 billion in new defense spending, including $25 billion to start a "Golden Dome" missile-defense system (a system that has not been proven effective); that system will eventually cost billions more. In addition, the megabill includes more than $170 billion for immigration enforcement and mass deportations, which will make ICE the biggest American law enforcement agency and larger than most of the world's militaries.[23]

The journalist Ezra Klein's early assessment of the bill remains on target. The OBBBA, he stressed, is "grimly exact. The bill has $1.1 trillion in tax cuts for people who make more than $500,000 a year. And it has $1.1 trillion in cuts to Medicaid and food stamps. It is a straight transfer from people who cannot afford food and medical care to people who can afford to fly first class."[24] Klein's interviewee, the economic analyst Catherine Rampell, added: "Basically 94 percent of Americans will get some tax cut relative to what would have happened if Congress does nothing. But the very biggest benefits definitely go to higher income classes. . . . Two-thirds of the plan's tax cuts by dollar value go to those in the top quintile. People in the top 1 percent would get about a quarter of the tax cuts. So that's people making over $1 million basically—they get about a quarter of the benefits."

22. Legum, "7 Things Everyone Should Know."
23. Legum, "7 Things Everyone Should Know."
24. Rampell, "Trump's Big Budget Bomb."

Klein concluded: "I've been a policy journalist for more than twenty years. I've covered more bills than I can count. I cannot remember a more cruel or irresponsible piece of domestic legislation that has been seriously proposed. And its sins are compounded by its size. If the Republicans' Big Budget Bomb goes off, we are all in the blast radius." Rob the poor to serve the rich. Take from the young to gift the old. Vandalize the future to bankroll outworn practices and favored profiteers. Nothing could be further from the American Dream.

Signing his megabill on the Fourth of July, Trump gushed, "It's the most popular bill ever signed in the history of our country," adding "this is the single most popular bill ever signed. . . . Promises made, promises kept . . . after this kicks in, our country is going to be a rocket ship economically."[25] Public opinion was less exuberant. June polls taken by Fox News, Quinnipiac University, and the Pew Research Center showed that most Americans opposed the bill. On average as the bill became law, 54 percent of Americans were in that camp, while only 31 percent favored it. Data indicated that the bill was more unpopular than any major legislation since 1990.[26]

The public's reaction to the megabill mirrored the approval ratings for Trump at the seven-month mark of his second term.[27] Mid-August 2025 Pew Research Center polling showed a 38-percent approval rating overall for the underwater president. Only 36 percent found Trump honest. Even fewer Americans (29 percent) considered him a good role model. Still fewer (27 percent) thought he was making American government better. A majority of 61 percent disapproved Trump's tariff policies. Even before Trump's disastrous, bootlicking meeting with Vladimir Putin on August 15, 2025, Americans (59 percent) lacked confidence that Trump will make wise decisions about the Russia-Ukraine war. Trump remains powerful, but he is neither popular nor invincible. A caveat is nonetheless worth stating. Dictators do not depend on approval ratings, even if they find fraudulent ways to ramp them up. Trump's unpopularity must be a catalyst for resistance. Otherwise, the American Dream could succumb to totalitarian control, disapproval to the contrary being insufficient to prevent its demise.

In July 2025, evidence of Trump's vulnerability grew as his MAGA base fractured over Trump's handling of the so-called Epstein files, documents about the notorious sexual predator and trafficker Jeffrey Epstein, a long-time, "terrific guy" friend of Trump's.[28] For years, Trump fueled con-

25. Trump, "Promises Made"; Dale, "Fact Check."

26. Anderson, "Trump Signs Megabill."

27. Kiley et al., "Trump's Job Approval." See also *New York Times*, "Approval Rating."

28. Barrett and Cameron, "What to Know"; Chait, "Trump's Epstein Answers"; French, "MAGA Is Tearing Itself Apart"; and Wallace-Wells, "Epstein Story."

spiracy theories about Epstein's clients, wealthy and well-connected elites who (according to the theories) would be exposed for sexual crimes they had committed as corrupt avatars of the Deep State that Trump so vociferously claims to oppose.[29] But when poised to release the "evidence" to the public, Trump held back, did an about-face, and claimed there was nothing to see. Many of the MAGA faithful were not having it. Feeling betrayed, uneasy that Trump himself could be heading a devious Deep State, and even sensing a cover-up to prevent further revelations about Trump's sordid sexual history, Trump's followers cried out against his prevarications and revealed that they will not allow him to rob them to protect himself, at least not completely. Trump's popularity with his MAGA base, let alone with the larger American electorate, is unlikely to improve. Increasingly exposed, his vulnerability provides hope that resistance against him will mount and save the American Dream.

2. Trump and Trumpism are attacking education to quell criticism.

On May 28, 2025, as the Trump administration continued its relentless hostility toward Harvard University, Linda McMahon, the devious secretary of education, said the quiet part out loud during an interview on CNBC: "Universities should continue to be able to do research as long as they're abiding by the laws and in sync with the administration and what the administration is trying to accomplish."[30] Her blatant autocracy would require, as American Association of University Professors (AAUP) President Todd Wolfson said, that American higher education no longer serves the public good but instead "radical right-wing politicians that are attempting to control what can be said, taught, or researched on our campuses."[31]

Adam Serwer, the astute *Atlantic* analyst, rightly argued that statements like McMahon's are part of the attack that the Trump administration is launching on knowledge itself. His probing essay, "The New Dark Age," identifies the aims and dangers of the onslaught. Serwer shows that "a deliberate destruction of education, science, and history" is tragically underway.[32] The National Science Foundation and the National Institutes of Health have been decimated. Historical repositories such as the Smithsonian Institution and cultural foundations such as the Kennedy Center will be hijacked to serve "MAGA ideology rather than historical fact and free

29. Sisak, "What to Know."
30. Gooding and Whisnant, "Linda McMahon Says."
31. Gooding and Whisnant, "Linda McMahon Says."
32. Serwer, "New Dark Age."

expression." Libraries are threatened, and books are banned. Educators are censored. Aggressive antagonism aims to eliminate so-called wokeness (a term favored by right-wing critics). This fight against "wokeness," Serwer aptly says, "is destroying huge swaths of scholarship and research, for fear the results might make the case for racial or gender equality, the redistribution of wealth, or the regulation of industry."

Defund National Public Radio and the Public Broadcasting Service. Bury the evidence and deny climate change. Fire people who do research and manage archives. Decimate the National Oceanic Atmospheric Administration (NOAA) so that weather prediction and preparation against natural disasters are compromised. Gut the Federal Emergency Management Agency (FEMA) and shift disaster responses to states that are neither equipped nor financially able to cope with such emergencies. Tell young people that university and college education is not worth the money. Get rid of experts who could unmask fraud and junk science, who could bring empirical evidence to bear and hold criminal grifters accountable. Smear DEI initiatives as illegal abominations while fraudulently insisting that allegedly underrepresented conservative White men merit more influence and power. Make the American people less literate, less prosperous, less healthy, less equal, and less democratic. "All that matters to Trumpists," Serwer cogently concludes, "is that they can reign unchallenged over the ruins."

The American Dream affirms that the American people can and should be more literate, more prosperous, more healthy, more equal, more inclusive, and more democratic. Clarity about that entails determination to defang and derail Trump 2.0. Trump's dead-ender followers will not do so, but every American who cares about our country and its Dream must refuse to accept Trumpist tyranny. Decisive defeats for Trumpism at the polls in 2026 and 2028 are crucial. Public protests need to be their resounding prelude.

3. Trump and Trumpism are embracing and encouraging corruption not only for self-enrichment but also to eliminate resistance and accountability.

In 2021, Donald Trump thought that the cryptocurrency Bitcoin was a scam. That judgment was right, but corrupt scammer that he is, Trump and his family have gone all in on crypto because digital currency deals enrich them immensely, not least by selling access to the president. As Molly Roberts underscores, this vast grift depends on Trump's immense "experience in selling something when there's nothing really there—in turning air into a kind of religion."[33]

A cynical, perverse mentality reduces the American Dream to getting rich as fast and as much as possible. One way to do that is to create and sell something that is worthless but that can become valuable if enough people think it is. Ponzi schemes pyramid that way. Hyped sufficiently, the electronic elements that make up cryptocurrency entice investors with promises that its "value" will rise and keep rising. The real beneficiaries are the originators. Late arrivals profit only if more investors appear. The pyramid grows—until it doesn't. By that time, Trump and his family will be billions richer. It is a new version of an old scam, but many Americans are ready, as they have often been, to succumb to the "get rich quick" temptation.

Roberts is on target when she stresses that "as with pretty much every cryptocurrency, blind faith is what gives bitcoin value—because it has no intrinsic worth, no tether to the real world." But that fact has not stopped MAGA followers and favor-seeking investors at home and abroad from funneling tens of millions of dollars into Trump-family crypto schemes such as World Liberty Financial and their meme coin $TRUMP, often with the prospect that profitable influence with Trump 2.0 awaits. Crypto investment losses are less crucial than the quid pro quo gains from lining Trump's pockets.

Trump crypto schemes are a major part of the corruption he embraces and encourages, but they are only part of an even larger depravity. On the one-hundredth day of Trump 2.0, Senator Elizabeth Warren delivered a speech titled "One Hundred Days, One Hundred Acts of Corruption."[34] She began by stating that "today I'm reading into the congressional record 100 reports of corruption from Donald Trump's first 100 days in office. When he ran for office, Trump promised repeatedly that he would lower costs 'on day 1.' But instead of following through on his promise, Trump and his administration have paved the way for the president, his top officials, and his billionaire buddies to personally feed at the trough of government corruption." What followed was a litany of conflicts of interest; insider trading opportunities; instances of selling White House access; appointments of unqualified cronies and disqualified sycophants to key governmental agencies; and retributive firings of competent, honest governmental officials who would question and resist his wishes.

In an interview with David Frum on May 7, 2025, the prescient political analyst Anne Appelbaum underscored that the scale of Donald Trump's corruption is by far the worst in American history. It has put his administration,

33. Roberts, "Trump's New Crypto Business."

34. Warren, "One Hundred Days."

she said, "in a completely different league."[35] It is not only the scope of Trump's self-enriching corruption that validates Appelbaum's judgment but also the fact that Trump uses corruption to eliminate resistance and accountability. He uses corruption to normalize, legitimate, and encourage more corruption. The more extensive the corruption, the less likely Trump and his associates will be held accountable. Resistance to bribery, extortion, and violations of the constitutional ban on foreign emoluments becomes less effective.

Unchecked, Trump's corruption will destroy the American Dream. But anyone who affirms the Dream at its best will be outraged and defiant against the degeneracy and dishonor that Trump 2.0 brings to our country. Ahead of the 2026 and 2028 elections, every corruption enacted by Trump and his acolytes must be identified, called out, defied, and opposed. Increasingly American patriots should emulate Elizabeth Warren's example of standing up and speaking out.

4. Trump and Trumpism are pardoning criminals to kill the rule of law.

Donald Trump's felonious apostle, Steve Bannon, has long advised "flooding the zone" and using "muzzle velocity" to launch so many antidemocratic, corrupt, and illegal initiatives so fast that no one can investigate them all.[36] That policy is at play in Trump's wanton use of the president's constitutional "power to grant reprieves and pardons for offenses against the United States, except in cases of impeachment" (Article II). From a strictly legal perspective, the president's pardon power is unfettered, but until Trump took office, norms and traditions provided guardrails against abuse.

The Office of the Pardon Attorney exists within the Department of Justice. The Pardon Attorney's mandate includes advising the president on pardon cases. Norms and traditions indicate that a pardon is justifiable if in some reasonable pattern a person's postconviction behavior, conduct, and character are good; the person's offense was neither recent nor major; the person acknowledges and takes responsibility for the crime; the person's conviction carried undue penalties; and people of good character and influence offer recommendations for a pardon. Such guidelines are imprecise and subject to broad interpretation, but their existence shows that pardons ought not to be solely the president's prerogative. Pardons can be deserved; they can also be undeserved and corrupt, so much so that grounds for presidential impeachment include abuse of the pardon power.

35. Appelbaum, "Most Corrupt Presidency."
36. Cranston, "Will 'Muzzle Velocity' Backfire on Trump?"

With muzzle velocity, Trump 2.0 has bypassed the Pardon Attorney, disrespected the norms and traditions that govern presidential clemency, and flooded the country in undeserved pardons. On May 28, 2025, with Trump's corrupt pardon attorney, Ed Martin, trumpeting "no MAGA left behind," Trump pardoned or commuted sentences for more than two dozen felons—cronies and campaign contributors prominent among them—including the reality television stars, Julie and Todd Chrisley, who were convicted of evading taxes and defrauding banks of more than $30 million; Michael Grimm, a former Republican congressman found guilty of massive tax fraud; and Marian I. Morgan, who defrauded investors of more than $28 million.[37] More recently, Trump notoriously pardoned former Honduran President Juan Orlando Hernández, who had been convicted of massive drug-trafficking that brought tons of cocaine into the United States.[38]

Trump postures as a law-and-order president. He is nothing of the kind. His wholesale pardon of the January 6, 2021, insurrectionists who stormed the Capitol to steal the 2020 election for Trump testifies to that. So do the pardons and commutations during the spring of 2025, which aimed to normalize, if not erase entirely, white-collar crimes of the kind that Trump himself has routinely committed. Already Trump has shown leniency to Ghislaine Maxwell, the predator partner of child-abuser Jeffrey Epstein, by relocating the convicted felon to a minimum-security facility. If Trump commutes her sentence or pardons her, which he may do in exchange for her silence about or denial of Trump's compromising relationship with Epstein, that action would add insult to the pardon abuse injury that Trump's venality worsens.[39]

Trump's corrupt pardons undermine the rule of law. That erosion is their purpose. Mercy, second chances, new beginnings—all of those have their place in the American Dream, but Trump's so-called acts of clemency take revenge against acts and agents of justice, handing out—often for a bribing price—get-out-of-jail-free cards, and ensuring that no prosecution awaits the specially favored, including multiple and repeat offenders. Far from "draining the swamp," another Steve Bannon mantra, Trump's abuse of the pardon power floods the country in the stench of purposely corroded norms and traditions. Ongoing outcries and persistent protests against Trump's corrupt pardons must rally opposition to leave MAGA far behind in the 2026 and 2028 elections.

37. Thrush, "Trump's Flurry of Pardons." See also Kanno-Youngs and Broadwater, "Trump Gives Clemency."

38. Ordoñez, "Trump Pardons Honduran Ex-president."

39. Daniels, "Trump Reiterates"; Orden, "Ghislaine Maxwell Transferred."

Like Lions

At the end of May 2025, an ecologist named Carl Safina published a *New York Times* essay that went viral. Taking on Trump, he argued, requires thinking like lions. Safina recalled watching a pride of lions preparing to hunt. Before they pursued the strategy that would feed them even if it was not successful every time and had to be tried again, the lions, he observed, "licked one another, pressed bodies and indulged in much face rubbing. They reaffirmed: 'Yes, we are together. We remain as one.' Only then did they set off."[40]

The lions affirmed no oaths of loyalty. They recited no pledges of allegiance. But their deep-down instincts, confirmed as they rubbed noses, governed their well-founded hunting tactic, which depended on the pride's coordination and cooperation. "As the lions showed me," affirmed Safina, "community comes before strategy."

Saving the American Dream is like that. "As individuals," Safina discerns, "we cannot always formulate the full fix. But we can be a part of a movement to forge one." His insights from the lions go deeper and further:

> Acquiescence is futile. Keeping one's head down is stupid. . . . As the administration dismantles agencies and policies that protect people, we must all say, very publicly, what is on our minds. We must support the courts and people skilled at defending the Constitution. We can reverse fear and acquiescence, energize public engagement and demonstrate how unpopular these moves are. If the rule of law holds, if voters wake Congress, the country will come back on keel. We need a laser focus on election integrity for 2026 and 2028.

Safina's lions know nothing about the American Dream. But they have much to teach Americans, much that we need to learn to save the Dream. As Safina's essay suggests, the lions can remind us of the importance of reaffirming "our sense of pride, our shared purpose, our dedication to our common good."

Safina is right: Akin to the lions that he observed in "the tall golden grass along the ridge of a low hill . . . so many people are waiting in the tall grass of decency, ready to rush out to restore the nation that we have all loved, the great America that promises liberty and justice for all." Thinking and acting like lions can save the American Dream.

40. Safina, "To Take On Trump."

7

Subscribing Our Names

Article VII, the last of the US Constitution's original provisions, specified that ratification by nine states would put the Constitution into effect. It further indicated that the constitutional convention took this action on September 17, 1787, a date now commemorated annually as Constitution Day. Article VII would be the Constitution's shortest but for the important fact that it subscribes the names of the thirty-nine American men, most of them military veterans from the Revolutionary War, who unanimously approved the document. Some of them—George Washington, James Madison, Benjamin Franklin—are well known. Others—Nathaniel Gorham, Pierce Butler, William Few—are not. They all knew, however, that signing the US Constitution was a momentous, consequential decision. If those people had not taken that step, the American Dream would not exist. What if we twenty-first-century Americans do not subscribe our names to the Constitution, consciously and with purpose as those before us did? What if we do? Reflection on the Holocaust and the American Dream clarifies what is at stake.

Turning Points

In 1956, a New York City taxicab struck a Holocaust survivor. After enduring Auschwitz and Buchenwald, Elie Wiesel, a young journalist, was reporting on the United Nations for *Yediot Ahronot*, an Israeli newspaper, when the accident happened. His long convalescence prevented him from returning to France to renew expired papers. So, Wiesel, a "stateless person" at the time, applied for US citizenship. He affirmed that "the day I received

American citizenship was a turning point in my life."[1] That step required Wiesel to vow that he would "support and defend the Constitution and laws of the United States of America against all enemies, foreign and domestic." He fulfilled that promise.

Surviving Nazi Germany's genocide against the European Jews, Wiesel became an acclaimed author of novels, plays, and significant essays. A passionate humanitarian who received the Nobel Peace Prize in 1986, he also championed the building of the US Holocaust Memorial Museum in Washington, DC. Wiesel did not write about the American Dream, but he believed in and lived his version of it. His son, Elisha, provides evidence to support that claim.

Elisha Wiesel said that he could "count on one hand" the times he saw his father angry.[2] The younger Wiesel experienced one of them firsthand, "the only time I can remember him being angry at me." At dinner during a holiday weekend, the eighteen-year-old Elisha, a first-year Yale College student at the time, defended the right to burn the American flag. "We should be inspired when we see the flag being burned," Elisha Wiesel said with youthful confidence, "because it means we are free." His father had none of that outlook. "'If you had been there,' he said in a voice I had never heard him use before. 'If you had been there when Buchenwald was liberated, if you had seen that flag being carried that day. . . . If you knew what that flag meant to me then, and means to me now, you would never utter such foolishness at my table.'"

Elie Wiesel could not have been among the original signers of the US Constitution, but in word and deed he subscribed his name to it. Dying on July 2, 2016, he did not experience Donald Trump's presidencies, including the president's 2025 attempt to find loopholes to permit prosecution and punishment for burning the American flag, despite court rulings that permit flag-burning protests under the First Amendment's protection of free speech.[3] I am confident that Wiesel always protected and defended the US Constitution and never sided with those who disrespect and subvert it. That conviction is rooted in decades of studying his writing and in long friendship with him.

Those experiences remain turning points in my life.[4] They led me to become a Holocaust scholar and educator. They also influence my understanding of the American Dream and the Constitution that the Dream

1. Jacoby, "Wiesel's Love of America."
2. Wiesel, "My Father."
3. Quinn, "Trump Wants to Punish."
4. See, for example, Roth, *Consuming Fire*; and Roth, *Sources of Holocaust Insight*.

defends and advances. Consider, for instance, one of Wiesel's most penetrating imperatives: "The Holocaust demands interrogation and calls everything into question. Traditional ideas and acquired values, philosophical systems and social theories—all must be revised in the shadow of Birkenau."[5] The killing center at Auschwitz, Birkenau was the site of gas chambers and crematoria that destroyed 900,000 Jews, Wiesel's mother, Sarah, and his little sister, Tzipora, among them. If the Holocaust calls everything into question, as I believe it does, then the American Dream and the US Constitution should be interrogated from that perspective.

Fatal Interdependence

The commandant of Nazi death camps on Polish soil at Sobibor and Treblinka, a former Austrian police officer named Franz Stangl was sentenced to life imprisonment by a West German court on December 22, 1970. Early in April of the next year, Gitta Sereny, an insightful scholar-journalist, met Stangl for the first time. The result was a memorable series of interviews with Stangl, his family, and many of his associates. These interrogations drove home to Sereny what she called "the fatal interdependence of all human actions."[6] That memorable theme governed her study of Stangl, which remains one of the most instructive books about the Holocaust.

Sereny's inquiry emerged from the hope that it might reveal, as she put it, "some new truth which would contribute to the understanding of things that had never yet been understood."[7] Specifically, she wondered, could Franz Stangl have left the path that took him to Treblinka? And if he could have left that path, would it have made any difference?

As Sereny probed her findings, she drew the following conclusions: Individuals remain responsible for their own action and its consequences, but persons are and must be responsible for each other too. What we do as individuals, contended Sereny, "is deeply vulnerable and profoundly dependent on a climate of life" that reflects "the fatal interdependence of all human actions."[8] If Gitta Sereny is correct—and she is—then how might the American Dream and the Holocaust be related? That question keeps moving me. It compels me to wrestle with differences between right and wrong, good and evil, with fundamental values that include my identity as an American, a Christian, a son, brother, husband, father, and grandfather.

5. Wiesel, foreword to Cargas, *Shadows*, ix.
6. Sereny, *Into That Darkness*, 15.
7. Sereny, *Into That Darkness*, 23.
8. Sereny, *Into That Darkness*, 367, 15.

One question leads to others. To what extent can we Americans do what our Dream requires? What do we too easily take for granted? How well do we practice what we preach? Such questions are especially important in the dark times that the journalist Michael Tomasky aptly described on July 11, 2025.

> We're a week short now of the six-month mark of Donald Trump's return to the Oval Office, and while a lot remains to be seen (gulp), we should have a pretty clear idea of how a democracy becomes an authoritarian police state. The five key ingredients: lies, corruption, idiocy, loyalty, and most important, a blanket of sedating propaganda swaddling the first four and protecting the administration from any remote hint of democratic consequences or accountability. . . . This will get much worse . . . there's so much more to come. . . . We are all well aware that we're losing our democracy day by day. . . . There is still time to stop this.[9]

If Tomasky is right, and there still time to stop Trump 2.0 from doing its worst, then it is worth remembering that Adolf Hitler came to power when he was appointed chancellor of Germany on January 30, 1933. About five years later, on April 10, 1938, Germans—including citizens in recently seized Austria—went to the polls. Scarcely fair and free, that election for members of the Reichstag was the last for the German parliament during Nazi rule. The ballot contained one issue: Did voters approve a list of Nazi candidates for the Reichstag as well as the annexation of Austria—Yes or No? Nazi officials determined that the voter turnout was 99.6 percent of those eligible to vote, with 99.1 percent of them voting Yes.

Adolf Hitler despised democracy, taking it to be a deceitful, subversive outlook spread by Jews. Five years earlier, on July 14, 1933, he celebrated the Law against the Founding of New Parties, which established the Nazi Party as the only political party in Germany. By then, the civil liberties of German Jews, including the right to vote, were on their way to extinction, destroyed by the Nazis' racial antisemitism. When democracy dies, the costs are too much to bear.

Warnings

Tuesday, November 7, 2028, may surpass it, but November 5, 2024, was the most important Election Day thus far in my mideighties lifetime. Its

9. Tomasky, "Trump's Toxic Toolkit."

results remind me to take nothing good for granted. Teaching and learning about the Holocaust are crucial, especially after November 5, 2024, because American democracy is endangered as never before.[10] Too many ambitious, determined, and corrupt people, backed by compliant followers, are prepared to abandon if not destroy it.

History does not repeat, but it does reveal and instruct. It shows and teaches that the Holocaust is a warning. That has been said before, but during Trump 2.0 the Holocaust's warning for us Americans resounds with greater urgency. It does so because that catastrophe did not erupt out of the blue, nor was it fated to happen. Human decisions and policies in the 1930s led to disaster. Destructive versions of them are widespread in the mid-2020s.

I draw uncomfortable comparisons between Hitler's Germany in the 1930s and my United States in the 2020s. That is wrongly crossing a line, critics may complain. Americans are better, far more exceptional than that. Such comparisons are unwarranted. Rejecting that taboo, I agree with the historian Timothy Snyder's insight that "the reason why we keep alive the memory of Nazi crimes is not because it could never happen here, but because something similar can always happen anywhere."[11]

A related resistance to comparison has existed in Holocaust studies. For years, it was argued that the Holocaust was unique, unprecedented, and those claims buttressed privileging the Holocaust in the history of genocide and in commemorations of mass atrocities. Nothing was quite comparable to the Holocaust or to its perpetrators. So, for example, the suggestion that any American leader could be Hitlerian was wrong on two counts. Not only would it be unseemly to think any American could be like that but also the comparison would diminish the evil of Hitler and the genocide he unleashed. Time's passage, however, including endangered democracy in the 2020s is leading Holocaust scholars to see that where comparisons are apt, they should be made.

Hitler's rise to power in 1933 doomed the fragile post–World War I parliamentary democracy of Germany's Weimar Republic. The Holocaust historian Christopher Browning thinks that "Weimar's fate provides us with some instructive parallels and important warning signals."[12] Let us hope that Browning is right when he adds that "Trump is not Hitler, Republicans are not Nazis." Let us determine, too, that November 5, 2024, in the United

10. Rittner and Roth, *This Time*.

11. Snyder, "Trump's Hitlerian Month."

12. Browning, "How Hitler's Enablers." See also Hett, *Death of Democracy*; and Browning, "Hitler's Enablers," which helpfully discusses Hett's book.

States must never be akin to January 30, 1933, in Germany. That means it bears remembering that retired general Mark A. Milley, former chairman of the Joint Chiefs of Staff, found Trump "fascist to the core" and "the most dangerous person to this country."[13]

The warning signals that Christopher Browning discerns in the Weimar Republic's fate are Holocaust-related. Hitler's rise to power and the Nazis' devastation of democracy culminated in the destruction of the European Jews and Germany too. The Holocaust warns against autocracy and obedience to it. It cries out: Beware of big, repeated lies, conspiracy theories, disrespect for evidence and truth, disdain for democracy, and disregard for language—antisemitic and racist—that defames and thus inflames division and violence. If such alarms are ignored, the world is worse for it.

Absent lies and liars, especially big lies and liars with autocratic power, the Holocaust would not have happened. Nor could autocratic Nazi power, which undermined and destroyed German democracy in the 1930s, have advanced without the compliance and complicity it needed and received from enabling leaders in every sector of German life—education, the media, law, politics, science, medicine, business, sports, the arts, and religion. The Nazis' lethally racist antisemitism rested on falsehoods. Nazi power arose because Hitler and his followers bogusly and repeatedly insisted that Germany's defeat in World War I resulted from a "stab in the back" conspiracy that never existed. Nazi propaganda overrode contrary evidence, and Hitler's vows to destroy the Jews, who were slandered as a disease-spreading, blood-poisoning, toxic pestilence in the body politic, show how malignant language becomes deadly. The key point for us Americans is not that failure to heed the Holocaust's warnings destines a version of that genocidal history to be ours but that failure to heed them endangers everything we hold dear when we are at our best.

The Holocaust warns us that democracy, indeed human civilization itself, depends on seeking and respecting truth. Failure to pursue and honor truth undercuts and betrays what is good and right. Tyranny, dictatorship, hate-steeped divisiveness, hostility to democracy—all depend on lying, on disrespecting truth, on willful failure to seek and respect it. If we Americans want to do good for our democracy, nothing is more important than seeking, respecting, speaking, and defending truth. Failing to do so sounds the death knell for democracy and the American Dream.

Hitler's slogan was "Deutschland uber Alles." Trump's is "Make America Great Again." In the 1930s, Germans were easy prey for Nazism because they felt displaced, downtrodden, disrespected, wronged, left out, and

13. Cramer, "'Trump Is Fascist to the Core.'"

ill-treated in a rapidly changing world. The lie that Jews caused the misery, that removing them from the German body politic would set things right, was an easy sell. In the United States in the mid-2020s, many Americans—White men prominent among them—also feel left out and disrespected, wronged and ill-treated in a rapidly changing world. It grows increasingly doubtful that Trump and his allies have truthful answers to those problems. Meanwhile, Trump's relentless grievance politics has played on fear and deepened division, insisting that "we got a lot of bad genes in our country right now" and that mass deportations of undocumented immigrants will go far toward setting things right now and beyond.[14]

Nazism's "truths" denied basic human equality and human rights. Nazi antisemitism and racism identified "life unworthy of life" and then targeted it for annihilation. Those policies were the antithesis of life, liberty, and the pursuit of happiness. Education did not stop Nazism and its Final Solution. Education will not be sufficient to save American democracy either. But absent the questioning, inquiring, and learning, the encouragement and resistance that only sound education can provide, major threats to democracy—ignorance, overconfidence, arrogance, tribalism, and stupidity among them—will not be curbed until it is too late.

A Voyage of Discovery

The education of a young American dreamer named Stingo remains instructive. He experienced a "voyage of discovery" in William Styron's 1979 novel, *Sophie's Choice,* which explores how the Holocaust tests the American Dream.[15] Taught by Sophie Zawistowska, a fictional Polish Catholic who, like thousands of her actual Polish sisters and brothers, was deported to Auschwitz, Stingo learns in 1947 about a world very different from his own. As Sophie's story unfolds, Stingo undergoes shocks of recognition, including, as he relates one coincidence, "the absurd fact that on that afternoon, as Sophie first set foot on the railroad platform in Auschwitz, it was a lovely spring morning in Raleigh, North Carolina, where I was gorging myself on bananas."[16] On that day—Styron says it was April Fool's Day, 1943—Stingo was seventeen. He was desperately trying to make the weight requirement for enlistment into the US Marines. He squeaked by. He had not heard of Auschwitz.

The American Dream and the Holocaust—they seem as different as the experiences of Sophie and Stingo in April 1943. And yet those realities

14. Svitek, "Trump Suggests 'Bad Genes' to Blame."

15. Styron, *Sophie's Choice*, 25.

16. Styron, *Sophie's Choice*, 217.

intersect and challenge each other—sometimes producing shocks of recognition and warning—in ways that make one wonder about the interdependence of all human actions, about what is and is not sacred and deserving of loyalty. Exploring those relationships, including the absurdities they sometimes involve, invites and even compels us to take seriously what it should and should not mean to subscribe our names to the Constitution of the United States. Additional lines in Styron's narrative about Stingo and Sophie show how and why.

In Styron's novel, Stingo meets Sophie Zawistowska in "a place as strange as Brooklyn," but their shared experience climaxes in Washington, DC. "We walked through the evening in total silence," Stingo recalls. "It was plain that Sophie and I could appreciate neither the symmetry of the city nor its air of wholesome and benevolent peace. Washington suddenly appeared paradigmatically American, sterile, geometrical, unreal." The reason, Stingo adds, was that Auschwitz "stalked my soul."[17]

Stingo's experience in Washington, DC, would have taken place about eighty years ago. Although the city is still paradigmatically American and its symmetry remains, much about our nation's capital is misaligned and out of kilter. That's true because in the summer of 2025, Washington, DC, was militarized by Donald Trump. Using crime prevention as a pretext, Trump sicced federalized police on American citizens and especially on immigration suspects who were targeted for detention and deportation without due process. The campaign advanced ICE goals, backed by a massive funding infusion of $170 billion from Trump's megabill, to implement its bellicose director's boast: "Tom Homan is going to run the biggest deportation operation this country has ever seen. Take it to the bank."[18] The goal is to target and deport as many as possible of the more than ten million unauthorized migrants living in the United States. The thuggery in Washington, DC, by unnamed, masked agents is not a one-off campaign but, like the earlier military intimidation in Los Angeles, a step on Trump's path to martial law against threats to his autocracy.

Trump was not yet deterred, but in the summer of 2025, his draconian strategies were not popular with the American people. The historian Heather Cox Richardson accurately put the situation in perspective.

> Trump appointees insist they have a "mandate" to drive undocumented immigrants out of the US and prevent new immigrants from coming in, and are launching a massive increase in Immigration and Customs Enforcement officers and detention

17. Styron, *Sophie's Choice*, 493.
18. Ross, "Playbook."

> facilities to do so. But a poll released [July 11, 2025] shows that only 35% of American adults approve of Trump's handling of immigration, while 62% disapprove. The poll shows a record 79% of adults saying immigration is good for the country, with only 17% seeing it as bad. Only 30% of American adults say immigration should be reduced. The poll shows that 85% of American adults want laws to allow "immigrants, who were brought to the US illegally as children, the chance to become US citizens if they meet certain requirements over a period of time."[19]

As Trump and Homan looked for countries that would take their deportees, ominous developments in Florida suggested that another option was also at play, one called "Alligator Alcatraz."[20] This detention center, situated at a repurposed airstrip in the swampy Everglades, may be the first in an archipelago of American concentration camps, much worse versions of the camps that imprisoned Japanese Americans during World War II. As Michael Tomasky shows, "Alligator Alcatraz'" is part of an immense project funded by the recent megabill's $45 billion for detention camps. "Forty-five billion," he notes, "will build a lot of stuff." But his point of comparison is more staggering: "In 2023, the United States budgeted $12.8 billion to build new affordable housing. We're about to spend nearly four times on detention centers what we spend on housing."[21] As of mid-August 2025, more than 60,000 persons were in American immigration detention, a key step toward deportation.[22]

While these unjust, antidemocratic policies proceed from Trump's Washington, DC, Americans not so different from Stingo visit the US Holocaust Memorial Museum at the same time. Millions of Americans have done so since the museum was formally dedicated on April 22, 1993. The museum shows its visitors how Nazi Germany became a genocidal state, using forced emigration, deportation, concentration camps, and eventually shooting squadrons and killing centers to rid itself of unwanted Jews, people who were depicted as "the worst of the worst," a deadly threat to the purity of German blood and the sovereignty of the Third Reich. What should Americans think of their own country as they visit the now more than two dozen Holocaust museums across the United States? If Americans emerge from their Holocaust museum visits determined not to let our country

19. Richardson, "July 14, 2025." For the source of Richardson's data, see Saad, "Concern About Immigration Has Abated."

20. Aleaziz, "Florida Builds 'Alligator Alcatraz.'" See also Olmsted, "Sickening Living Conditions."

21. Tomasky, "Are We About to Have."

22. Cameron and Aleaziz, "Over 60,000."

become like *that*, such commitment could support Tomansky's hope that there is still time to stop Trump 2.0 before it is too late.

Denounce and Defend

On July 5, 2025, the Claremont Institute, a right-wing think tank that advances Trumpism, gave JD Vance its annual Statesmanship Award, putting the vice president in the company of SCOTUS judges Samuel Alito and Clarence Thomas. Such folks are not statesmen, unless that accolade is debased to legitimate those who disrespect American democracy and the Constitution that grounds it. Vance's acceptance speech provided little reason to retract that judgment. On the contrary, two of Vance's points illustrate how much he might learn if, like Stingo's, Auschwitz stalked his soul.

First, Vance decreed that "this country is not a contradiction . . . not some unfinished or contradictory project." Serving the corrupt and despotic Donald Trump, Vance himself is what the legendary American songwriter Kris Kristofferson called "a walking contradiction,"[23] a person claiming to defend American democracy and posturing respect for the Constitution while undermining human rights and the rule of law. Trump 2.0 contradicts the American Dream at its best. Vance embodies the fact that the American project must be reclaimed as unfinished but worth aspiring to improve.

Second, Vance emphasized his "profound sense of gratitude for this country . . . for its natural beauty, for the settlers who carved a civilization out of the wilderness."[24] He rightly wants his fellow Americans to share that thankfulness. But surely even Vance knows that questions lurk in gratitude. Should Americans be thankful that Donald Trump is president and JD Vance is his sidekick? Some will say yes; many will say no. Do Trump and Vance defend and advance the American Dream at its best? Those who say yes are deceived. Those who say no must resist. The Holocaust is a source of insight about such quandaries and challenges.

As Stingo could testify, and visitors to the US Holocaust Memorial Museum are reminded, American armed forces proved essential in bringing the Third Reich to its knees. Museum visitors also learn about what the scholar David S. Wyman called "the abandonment of the Jews" by the United States during the Hitler era.[25] In the late 1930s, restrictive immigration policies

23. For the phrase "a walking contradiction," see Kristofferson, "The Pilgrim, Chapter 33" on the 1971 album *The Silver Tongued Devil and I*.

24. Vance, "Transcript: JD Vance's Speech."

25. For elaboration on these points, see two of Wyman's books: *Paper Walls* and *Abandonment of the Jews*. See also Nadell, *Antisemitism*.

meant that the American Dream of Emma Lazarus—the Jewish poet whose words "Give me your tired, your poor, / Your huddled masses yearning to breathe free" are inscribed at the Statue of Liberty—would be a dream tragically deferred and denied for many of her own people who might have escaped the Holocaust. "Negative attitudes toward Jews," Wyman showed, "penetrated all sectors of wartime America."[26] Even after public governmental acknowledgment in December 1942 that European Jews were being slaughtered en masse, the American government was not moved to take action specifically directed at alleviating the Jewish plight. Not the least of the reasons for that inaction was American antisemitism, some of it deeply embedded in American Christianity. According to Wyman, polls taken from August 1940 until the war's end showed that 15 to 24 percent of the respondents "looked upon Jews as 'a menace to America.'"[27] Such ingredients conspired to yield a record that showed this country to be a contradiction and far from finished.

Nor does the Holocaust's shadow on American ground stop there. Formerly the director of the Office of Special Investigations, a division of the US Department of Justice established in 1979 to identify and prosecute Nazi criminals in America, Allan S. Ryan Jr. hoped the nation's "record on dealing with Nazi war criminals was not entirely beyond salvage," but he also estimated that hundreds, if not thousands, of German and Eastern European war criminals found a haven here after World War II. "The record is clear," asserted Ryan. "Preventing the entry of Nazi criminals to the United States was not a high priority, and was not taken seriously."[28] Should "We the People" have Vance's "profound sense of gratitude" for that? The American Dream encourages gratitude for the United States but not without qualification and determination to make the country better and stronger than it has been and is now.

Ryan's report would have saddened but not surprised the great American novelist Ralph Ellison. In 1945, he was working on a different narrative when what he identified as the "blues-toned laughter" of *Invisible Man*, his 1952 masterpiece, began to dominate his imagination. Eventually the laughter compelled him to give full expression to this voice, which belonged to the invisible man "who had been forged," the author noted, "in the underground of American experience and yet managed to emerge less angry than ironic."[29]

26. Wyman, *Abandonment of the Jews*, 12.

27. Wyman, *Abandonment of the Jews*, 15; Nadell, *Antisemitism*.

28. A. A. Ryan, Jr., *Quiet Neighbors*, 344.

29. Ellison, *Invisible Man*, xv.

Ellison's postponed story was to be about an American pilot. Downed by the Luftwaffe and interned in a Nazi prisoner-of-war camp, he was the highest-ranking officer there and thus, owing to war's conventions, the spokesman for his fellow prisoners. Like Ellison himself, the American pilot was Black. A prisoner of racists and the "leader" of prisoners who in normal American circumstances would not see him as their equal, let alone as their superior, Ellison's pilot would have to navigate his way between the democratic ideals he affirmed and "the prevailing mystique of race and color." This dilemma, Ellison adds, was to be "given a further twist of the screw by [the Black pilot's] awareness that once the peace was signed, the German camp commander could immigrate to the United States and immediately take advantage of freedoms that were denied the most heroic of Negro servicemen."[30]

Although Ralph Ellison never finished that story, still his pilot's voice seems to echo that of *Invisible Man*. In that novel's epilogue, one of the most insightful American writings about the fatal interdependence of all human actions, Ellison's nameless protagonist does not refer explicitly to the American Dream, but his reflections and dispositions apply to it nonetheless. He cannot forget certain ideas. "Nor will certain ideas forget me; they keep filing away at my lethargy, my complacency. . . . So it is that I denounce and defend, . . . I condemn and affirm, say no and say yes, say yes and say no."[31]

The Holocaust shadows the American Dream. As it does so, we Americans confront questions about our loyalties and policies, about what deserves gratitude and what does not. In William Styron's story about Sophie Zawistowska, an SS doctor gave her a cruel, choiceless choice: She could pick which of her two children, Jan or Eva, should go to the gas. "Ich kann nicht wählen! (I cannot choose!)," she screamed.[32] Sophie could not choose. And yet, so as not to lose them both, she let Eva go.

Limited though it was, Sophie's choice was real. So was her sense of guilt. Set free in 1945, she found her way to the United States, but liberation left Sophie in the shadow of Birkenau. She found inescapable the conclusion that her own life, even in America where she had hoped to find a new beginning, was not worth living. In 1947, Sophie let it go—also by choice.

Dreams die hard in America, and not least because the cruelty of the SS doctor on the ramp at Auschwitz might make us think of the cruelty we Americans see embodied in the deportation and separation policies of Stephen Miller and Tom Homan. Have we thought of ourselves as better

30. Ellison, *Invisible Man*, x.

31. Ellison, *Invisible Man*, 566–67.

32. Styron, *Sophie's Choice*, 483.

than that? Should we? In *Sophie's Choice*, Stingo, the White Presbyterian Southerner, cannot prevent Sophie's suicide. But Stingo endures, having learned much about himself, about American racial guilt, about his own American Dream.

Three fragments from a journal Stingo kept in 1947 form the novel's conclusion. "*Someday I will understand Auschwitz*"; like many versions of the American Dream, that vow, Stingo reflects years later, is "innocently absurd." "*Let your love flow out on all living things*"; that one is worth saving "as a reminder of some fragile perdurable hope." Finally, some poetry: "*Neath cold sand I dreamed of death / but woke at dawn to see / in glory, the bright, the morning star.*"[33] Facing despair, Stingo finds ways to revive determination to choose life and hope again. If freedom to choose destroyed Sophie, apparently Stingo tries to resist that fate by using choice against itself in a struggle to make life more worth living and not less so. Styron does not say whether Stingo succeeded, but the question remains: What will we Americans denounce and defend, condemn and affirm? In the darkness of Trump 2.0, to what and to whom will we say yes and say no?

Outraged Memories

Some twenty years ago, I was privileged to have a research year at the Mandel Center for Advanced Holocaust Studies in the US Holocaust Memorial Museum. The route to my office took me past the Washington Monument and then through an entry and corridors whose walls are inscribed with the words of American Dream idealism. They stand in sharp contrast to the aims of Nazi Germany and the Final Solution to the so-called Jewish question, which marked so indelibly the aspirations of that genocidal regime. Those inscriptions include Thomas Jefferson's July 4, 1776, affirmations in the Declaration of Independence: All men are created equal. There are inalienable human rights, including "Life, Liberty, and the Pursuit of Happiness."

The inscriptions also include a September 27, 1979, statement by Jimmy Carter, the American president who appointed the Commission on the Holocaust, chaired by Elie Wiesel, which led to the building of the US Holocaust Memorial Museum. "Out of our memory . . . of the Holocaust," said Carter, "we must forge an unshakable oath with all civilized people that never again will the world . . . fail to act in time to prevent this terrible crime of genocide. . . . We must harness the outrage of our own memories to stamp

33. Styron, *Sophie's Choice*, 513–15.

out oppression wherever it exists. We must understand that human rights and human dignity are indivisible."[34]

Carter's statement raises many questions. For example, to what extent does his phrase "never again" ring true, and what should be done with the word *must*, which is repeated three times? In addition, two other points are especially worth highlighting. First, Carter's statement emphasizes memory. That emphasis is important because memories (and I use the plural form intentionally to include our remembering of particular things) are so crucial to our humanity. Memories are not entirely in our control, but without them we would not be human or American. More particularly, absent memories we could not be moral creatures, for history would dissolve, there would be no United States, no American Dream, and we would be able neither to identify one another as persons nor to make the connections on which ethical decisions depend. Ethics, in short, cannot exist without memory, but given that we human beings have memories, responsibility is thrust upon us. Challenges to sustain and advance the American Dream at its best are among the most important responsibilities that the darkness of Trump time confers on American citizens who care about democracy and the US Constitution that supports it. Many of us Americans are old enough to remember how much better our country was before Donald Trump took power and how much work there will be to restore the nation's integrity once Trump 2.0 ends.

Second, Carter's statement about memory is memorable because it has an edge. He noted, for instance, that memories can be *outraged*. Indeed, he suggested that we would not be fully human or ethical if some events, the Holocaust in particular, failed to outrage us. If American memory is not outraged by Trump 2.0—its cover-up of the Epstein files and favored treatment for Ghislaine Maxwell prime among matters we must not forget—then the future dims toward desolation. Memories, of course, are a key ingredient in happiness. Without memories, celebration of good things would not make much sense; it could scarcely contain and express much joy. It is also true, however, that memories can be outrageous and outraging because history is so corrupt, lethal, and murderous. The German philosopher G. W. F. Hegel described history aptly when he called it a slaughter-bench. History charges memories with feelings. Outrage is high on the list of common human feelings. Absent such ingredients, ethics would lack passion, intensity, and urgency, although it might be less prone to melancholy and despair. The same must be said about the American Dream in dark times that will cancel it unless we Americans rise to the occasion in its defense.

34. Carter, President's Commission on the Holocaust.

When President Carter spoke about memories being outraged, he used two powerful verbs in that context. Outraged memories must be *harnessed*, he emphasized. *Harnessed* does not mean hamstrung or paralyzed. As Carter used the verb, I think he meant that outraged memory has to be focused, directed, and governed so that attention is paid and work is done in the service of what is good and right. The purpose of harnessing outraged memories, Carter went on to assert, is to *stamp out* oppression wherever it exists. What such a phrase means, how it might be put into practice, what policies it would energize—these are crucial issues to consider as Trump 2.0 threatens the American Dream.

Carter's statement and the questions it raises are part of what can be called the ethics of memory. Such ethics involves deciding what we ought to do with what we have experienced and with what we know. Those deliberations ought to include the manifest and ruinous conflicts of interest, corruption, and criminality that infest Trump 2.0. The ethics of memory requires holding one another accountable, challenging acquiescence, breaking silence, calling out indifference, protesting against corruption, and resisting the harm that Trump 2.0 multiplies. A sound ethics of memory, especially when rooted in Holocaust questions and American dreams, should orient American citizens to care for the common good, the "general Welfare" that the US Constitution aims to promote.

The Common Good

Where the common good is concerned, the Holocaust provides a dual warning: First, neither are the concept's meanings simple, nor should they be taken for granted. Visions of the common good are varied and contested. It takes power, force of will, assertion, and commitment to give the American Dream's best vision of the common good a chance to prevail. Second, memory of the Holocaust is crucial for clarifying and defending what that vision of the common good ought to mean.

The Holocaust and the American Dream at its best, Trump 2.0 and the common good—these juxtapositions are antithetical or none could be. But as we evaluate those relationships and do our best to advance the "general Welfare," we also need to drive our reflection deep by observing that Nazi Germany did not lack a vision of the common good. It emphasized a racially unified and hierarchically organized society where the rights of individuals were subordinate to the interests of the nation, where German identity was grounded in a blood-and-soil narrative that took nationality to be exclusive, rooted in tribal and racial superiority. That view of the common good undermined democracy, fueled antisemitism, promoted militaristic German supremacy, unleashed the Holocaust, and left Germany devastated after World War II. With a vengeance, Nazi ideology held that the common good, at least for Nazi Germany, entailed a world in which Jews and other allegedly inferior people would not exist. The world paid a huge price to defeat Nazism, but that outlook was not allowed to prevail.

Perverse and impoverished though it is, Trump 2.0 also has its vision of the common good:

- Authoritarianism is better than democracy.
- Oligarchy is better than equitable distribution of wealth.
- A Whiter, more evangelical Christian, and male-dominated country is better than one that welcomes ethnic diversity, religious pluralism, and gender equality.
- In the common good of Trump 2.0, the right to vote should be hard, not easy, to obtain.
- Based on the premise that one nation's economic gains come at the expense of its rivals, economic policy should be protectionist, tariff-based, and intent on maximizing dominant trade advantages over other nations.
- Trumpist ideology, not free inquiry and reliable research, should control education and health care. Government data that contradicts what Trump thinks should be rejected as "rigged" and the messengers fired.
- Exclusion of difference is better than inclusion. Birthright citizenship dilutes the purity of an American version of blood-and-soil citizenship, which assumes that the longer a person's generational presence and heritage, the more truly American a person is.

Insular and isolationist, xenophobic and hostile to science and the pursuit of truth, transactional rather than cooperative, this America First vision of the common good is regressive and reactionary, as well as a magnet for corruption. It may embrace technology, even Artificial Intelligence and cryptocurrency, but nothing about it is farsighted and forward-looking. A high price may need to be paid to sideline the Trump 2.0 version of the common good, but unless that step is taken, a polluted, nondemocratic, sickened, poorer, and less secure United States will be what is left of our country.

Much more than is the case today, American discourse often employed the term *commonwealth*, which the states of Kentucky, Massachusetts, Pennsylvania, and Virginia still use in referring to themselves. As that old word implies, people have shared interests and concerns, responsibilities and obligations, hopes and aspirations, or they can scarcely be a community at all. Some of those public interests involve respect for the fulfilment of private needs, but many of those interests show that our selves are public. They are constituted by communal ties.

No society exists without individual men and women, but as people live together, a social reality that is more than them, individually or collectively, manifests itself and exerts its influence. Individualistic outlooks—selfishness infests Trump 2.0—tend to lose sight of the fact that living together binds people together by social ties and mutual responsibilities that elude reduction to individual choices and decisions, liking and disliking. Nevertheless, even individualistic outlooks can recognize the importance of traditions that emphasize how the good of the whole is crucial. That emphasis contends that there is a public interest or, better still, a *common good.* This good refers to the basic features of life that every person needs to thrive, including a home that is safe and secure, sound education, worthwhile and good-paying work to do, respect for one's life and liberty, mutual trust, lawful justice, and insistence on the importance of evidence-based inquiry and dedication to seeking truth and following faithfully where it leads. Trump 2.0 disrespects and does not serve the common good, because its top dogs and their policies are oligarchical and kleptocratic, not democratic and benevolent.

The goodness of the common good is social. More than the sum of individual efforts and parts, this goodness cannot be entrusted to "invisible hands" that will secure it, let alone to the likes of Donald Trump, as individuals pursue materialistic self-interest. The tuning of human loyalties toward what deserves fundamental respect is essential for the common good to thrive. Such loyalties emphasize realities not only that all Americans or all Germans need but also that all people need—individually and collectively. This qualification is basic, for to the extent that one group's "common good" jeopardizes, intentionally or even inadvertently, the well-being of other groups, then critical scrutiny and correction must loom large.

Among the elements that all people need are justice, truth, and compassion. At its best, the American Dream defends and advances these traits, at home and abroad. American citizens should subscribe their names in support of those qualities. They are not abstractions. We feel their presence or absence in the particularities of our lives, even as those qualities transcend such particularities by giving us the perspectives we need to understand, judge, and improve the specific times and places in which we live. I meditate on those facts when I recall that my present American home is about as far from Birkenau as one can get.

Winthrop sits small in the Methow Valley, a place of spectacular beauty on the eastern slope of the majestic Cascade Range, far north in the State of Washington. Indigenous people knew this valley and its glistening rivers long before it became one of the last places in the American West to be settled by White men and women.

Shortly after moving to Winthrop almost twenty years ago, I discovered the poetry of William Stafford, one of America's national treasures. Stafford's poems focus on the natural world, often on our abuse of it. Also drenched in history, his verse laments the carnage we human beings inflict and encourages resistance against it. In works such as *Traveling Through the Dark* and *The Darkness Around Us Is Deep*, his poems wonder, as Elie Wiesel did in *Night*, his famous Holocaust memoir, whether dark times prevail. But neither Stafford nor Wiesel accepted resignation and despair. They voiced protest and the possibility of creative change instead.

In Washington, DC, the US Holocaust Memorial Museum stands close by the headquarters of the US Forest Service. So, it is worth observing that two federal forest rangers contacted William Stafford one day. They had an unusual request: Would he help them create "poetry road signs" for the North Cascades Highway, which wends its way to and from Winthrop? Winter snow buries that breathtaking road, and the threat of avalanches closes it for several months each year. But several of William Stafford's specially written poems are there to reappear and offer guidance when the road reopens, and travelers are on their way through the mountains again.

"Being a Person" is one of Stafford's poems.[35] It invites a reader/viewer to contemplate the Methow River as its clear, cold water rushes to the Columbia and then to the Pacific. Stafford urges his readers to listen and to discern what is happening. He urges us to breathe with awareness, to affirm that how and where we stand is important. Stafford's reflections and the meditations they encourage make a good ending/beginning for this chapter's call for American citizens to subscribe their names—in dark times—in support of the American Dream's best vision of the common good.

35. Stafford, "Being a Person." This poem is one in a small collection called *The Methow River Poems*.

Amendments

We're Asking

No part of the Constitution of the United States is more important than its Amendments. The document's final section, the Amendments comprise twenty-seven additions, which have the same status as every preceding part of the Constitution. The Bill of Rights, the first ten amendments, went into effect on December 15, 1791. Other amendments have joined them to advance the rights of individuals, expand social justice, and strengthen democracy. They remind "We the People" to defend the American Dream. They reinforce the importance of advancing democracy in 2026, 2028, and beyond those pivotal election years.

Amendment—including particular amendments—changes the Constitution. It is instructive to consider that term's multidimensional meaning. It denotes more than acts that modify a constitution or a statute. Amendment also entails awareness and conviction that change is needed to respect what is right, just, and true. In addition, amendment involves intention to correct what is wrong, unjust, and false. That intention's credibility, moreover, depends on resolution to make amends—to improve circumstances and to make situations better. Especially in those moral senses, amendment is needed to save the American Dream.

We Don't Know

In 1937, six years after the historian James Truslow Adams's bestseller, *The Epic of America*, popularized the concept of the American Dream and made it ubiquitous in our culture, another American writer, Archibald MacLeish, worked on a poem at Conway, Massachusetts. The Great Depression still wreaked havoc on the United States. Dispossessed, impoverished, anxious, and uncertain, most Americans wondered what the future might hold. They were not confidently hopeful. The Depression was a national defeat. Literally and metaphorically, it turned the land, including the dream of land ownership, into a desolate Dust Bowl. American writers such as Adams and MacLeish advanced self-examination and soul-searching about what had gone wrong and how amends could be made. That process focused on the American Dream.

Compiling eighty-eight Depression-era photographs by American camera greats such as Dorothea Lange, Walker Evans, Ben Shahn, and Margaret Bourke-White, MacLeish created *Land of the Free*. "The original purpose," he explained, "had been to write some sort of text to which these photographs might serve as commentary." Finding in them vividly what he called a "stubborn inward livingness," MacLeish reversed that plan and produced not "a book of poems illustrated by photographs," but "a book of photographs illustrated by a poem."[1]

The final page of *Land of the Free* pictures the face of a wizened old man. Hat torn, his soiled suit worn, he does not have it made. And yet he's looking squarely at the camera, jaw set, unsmiling, eyes glinting. It seems like he might be asking questions. If so, they are not without discouragement, but no one would confuse his expression with despair. It's got too much insistence, too much resistance, too much wonder and determination for that.

"The Sound Track" is what MacLeish called his poetic accompaniment to the Depression photos in *Land of the Free*. Like features of the old man's face, its closing lines wonder if liberty is done, dreaming finished. The mood is one of "can't say" and "don't know." It's one of asking. MacLeish's verse conveys scant optimism, and yet the yearning and wondering of his lines express neither despair nor a lack of courage and morale to continue. MacLeish apparently felt the urge for renewal, for a new beginning if one can be made, and he understood that such feelings may run deepest not when times are placid and all seems well but when events have disoriented one's sense of direction.

Forty years later, in 1977, the photography scholar A. D. Coleman wrote the introduction for the first paperback edition of *Land of the Free*. Underscoring how timely MacLeish's book remained, his words from almost fifty years ago ring true in the dark times of Trump 2.0.

> As a nation, we seem to have come cyclically to a stretch of our own history which is similar in many ways to the time in which *Land of the Free* was created, making it seem much less of a period

1. MacLeish, *Land of the Free*, 89.

> piece. We, too, are living in a depression. Economic and ecological crises abound. The relationship between the government and the governed is frighteningly far from ideal. Much power is in the wrong hands, and at the disposal of the unrightfully privileged. The finitude of our resources is dramatically evident. The fragmentation of the body politic is severe. The imperative of some restored sense of deep community is knocking.[2]

That same imperative is knocking again. If we hear, feel, and heed it, we more than have it in our power to save the American Dream.

How Will We Know?

On May 8, 2025, the political scientists Steven Levitsky, Lucan Way, and Daniel Ziblatt raised a crucial question in their *New York Times* essay: "How will Americans know when we have lost our democracy?"[3] These scholars study what they call "competitive authoritarianism." Such regimes suppress opposition, but instead of relying primarily on violence, they sustain the illusion that free and fair elections give them power, and they advance the deception that their autocratic agenda enacts the people's will. Disguised as competitive, the tyranny of this authoritarianism is difficult to discern until it is too late. Hence, the question "How will we know?" looms large when democracy and the American Dream are at stake.

Levitsky, Way, and Ziblatt cut to the chase. As "the cost of opposing the government rises," the closer authoritarianism comes. The United States, they contend, "has crossed the line into competitive authoritarianism." The evidence flows from Donald Trump's making good on his repeated promise to the MAGA faithful: "I am your voice, . . . I am your warrior, . . . I am your justice, and for those who have been wronged and betrayed, I am your retribution. . . . I will totally obliterate the deep state."[4]

Trump 2.0 intensifies harassment and reprisals, revenge and punishments against critics and challengers, real and imagined, who dare to stand in the way. The escalating attacks have targeted law firms, universities, the media, businesses, and individuals such as Christopher Krebs and Miles Taylor, former Trump appointees whose criticism included evidence that utterly contradicted and falsified Trump's Big Lie about election fraud in 2020.[5] Trump threatens contract cancellations, security-clearance suspen-

2. Coleman, introduction, ix.
3. Levitsky et al., "How Will We Know."
4. See, for example, Trump, Speech at the Conservative Political Action Conference.
5. Cho, "Trump Directs Justice Dept."

sions, research-funding freezes, tax-exemption revocations, and relentless investigations, lawsuits, and firings to force knee-bending and ring-kissing obedience to his wishes. Resistance to Trump's threats imposes costly legal defenses, fears about death threats and personal safety, and chilling effects on counterattacks. Changing how Americans behave—acquiescence, lying low, self-censorship—the high costs of opposition to Trump are rising "with stunning speed."[6]

"Americans are living under a new regime," say Levitsky, Way, and Ziblatt. "The question now is whether we will allow it to take root." They rightly think that most Americans want to live in a democracy, not under authoritarianism, competitive or otherwise. But saving the American Dream, they see, will not result from "acts of individual self-preservation" let alone from appeasement. "Societal opposition" and "collective defense of democracy," they argue, could reverse "America's slide into authoritarianism . . . but no one has ever defeated autocracy from the sidelines."

What if the question is not only "How will we know when we have lost our democracy?" but also "When would we know that the American Dream is saved and safe?" Levitsky, Way, and Ziblatt help to show that the credible, responsible answer to the latter query must be, "Never." That awareness, however, does not and must not lead to acquiescence, let alone to despair. On the contrary, it can and should rally us Americans to defend what is worth defending, to protect what is worth protecting, and to advance what is worth advancing. Saving the American Dream is emblematic of those good desires. James Truslow Adams recognized that there is "a long and arduous road to travel if we are to realize our American dream in the life of the nation, but if we fail, there is nothing left but the old eternal round. The alternative is the failure of self-government, the failure of the common [person] to rise to full stature, the failure of all that the American dream has held of hope and promise for humankind."[7]

Levitsky, Way, and Ziblatt call for an American awakening, one that makes amends for the shortcomings and failures that have driven the United States toward an American nightmare personified by Donald Trump and Elon Musk. The June 2025 breakup of their "bromance" put into bold relief that such men and people who allow themselves to be subservient to them disrespect and deny the American Dream at its best.[8] The Dream is not about wealth and power, at least not primarily—and especially not when they are acquired by lying, corruption, crime, and greed that savage

6. Levitsky et al., "How Will We Know."

7. Adams, *Epic of America*, 428.

8. Pager et al., "Trump's Relationship with Musk."

the poor to enrich the already advantaged and well-connected. Trump and Musk embody everything that the American Dream should not be.

Not Finished, Unfinished

A voice in Archibald MacLeish's *Land of the Free* wonders if liberty is done and dreaming is finished. The faces in its photos convey plenty of experiences and reasons to say yes, but their expressions say no, at least in the sense that liberty and dreaming had better not, must not be done and finished. Too much good, justice, and truth is at risk for that.

Most of the faces in MacLeish's photo compilation are White. Another volume also called *Land of the Free*, a more ironic one, could feature Black faces and voices. They would have even more experiences and reasons to answer yes to the question of whether liberty and dreaming are done and finished. Yet they say no, at least in the sense that liberty and dreaming had better not be done and finished, must not be that way, because there's too much goodness, justice, and truth at stake for that.

- In his 1938 poem "Let America Be America Again," Langston Hughes underscored that America never was America to him.[9] But the poem swears, takes an oath, that America will be. The dream of America, Hughes affirms, lies deep in his heart.

  When Hughes said that America's dream lies deep in his heart, it lived in him with persistence and resistance, because the dream also kept lying to him there—not telling the truth, often intending not to do so, or at least not succeeding soon enough, faithfully enough, to make good on its promises. So, Hughes rightly implied, Americans must make amends. We need to remake America by redeeming, defending, and expanding democracy and the Dream.

- Twenty-five years later, on August 28, 1963, more than 250,000 Americans went to the Lincoln Memorial in Washington, DC, to advance civil and economic rights for Black Americans and other marginalized groups. No statement about the American Dream is more resolute, determined, aspirational, and iconic than the masterful "I Have a Dream" speech delivered on that occasion by Martin Luther King Jr. "In spite of the difficulties and frustrations of the moment," King began, "I still have a dream. It is a dream deeply rooted in the American dream."[10]

9. Hughes, "Let America."
10. King, "I Have a Dream."

King's speech amended American history and held the American Dream to account, insisting that the United States must "rise up and live out the true meaning of its creed: 'We hold these truths to be self-evident: that all men are created equal.'" King envisioned an America where people are "not judged by the color of their skin but the content of their character." He still urges us to "hew out of the mountains of despair a stone of hope." Nothing would deter him. Reiterating that "I have a dream today," King resounded his theme: Americans and the American Dream must "let freedom ring . . . from every village and hamlet, from every state and every city." As King himself predicted, he never got to that land. An assassin's bullet in Memphis, Tennessee, saw to that on April 4, 1968, but King's hope and vision live on. His testimony and the American Dream are inseparable.

- On February 18, 1965, James Baldwin debated the conservative icon William F. Buckley Jr. at the University of Cambridge. The contested issue was, "The American Dream is at the expense of the American Negro." Receiving a standing ovation, Baldwin won the debate, arguing the affirmative. "It comes as a great shock around the age of 5, or 6, or 7," Baldwin stated, "to discover that the flag to which you have pledged allegiance, along with everybody else, has not pledged allegiance to you. . . . Until the moment comes when we, the Americans, are able to accept the fact that my ancestors are both black and white, that . . . we are trying to forge a new identity, that we need each other . . . until this moment comes there is scarcely any hope for the American dream."[11]

  The Cambridge debate was scarcely Baldwin's last word about America and the Dream. Ever critical, deeply discouraged especially after King's assassination, Baldwin thought a White America deserved no future, but, he emphasized, "I love America more than any other country in the world, and exactly for this reason, I insist on the right to criticize her perpetually."[12] That spirit kept him working and hoping for the pluralistic America—multiethnic, multiracial, multicultural—that the American Dream at its best envisions and defends.

- In early April 2025, the disqualified Secretary of Defense Pete Hegseth ordered the removal of nearly four hundred books from the library of the US Naval Academy.[13] The banned books included *I Know Why the Caged Bird Sings*, the famous autobiography of the Black American poet Maya Angelou. More than thirty years earlier, Bill Clinton's

11. Baldwin, "American Dream."
12. Baldwin, *Notes of a Native Son*, 1:9.
13. Ismay, "Who's In and Who's Out."

first presidential inauguration took place on January 20, 1993. Three decades prior, John F. Kennedy had invited a poet, Robert Frost, to speak at his inauguration. Clinton revived the practice. What he said on that day has been forgotten, but the voice and words of the poet, Maya Angelou, are better remembered. "On the Pulse of Morning," she called the poem written for that civic-religious occasion when a newly elected president takes the constitutionally prescribed oath of office—with a hand on the Bible and a "so help me God"—to "preserve, protect, and defend the Constitution of the United States."

"A Rock, A River, a Tree," Angelou's poem began.[14] Drawing on the rich religious tradition of the spiritual songs from which she took those images, her words had much for the nation to hear and heed. As Angelou filled their voices, the Tree spoke, the Rock cried out, and the River sang. Their message was realistic and yet hopeful, encouraging though somber, beautiful in spite of tragedy, honest and liberating: We cannot unlive history and its wrenching pain. But if faced with courage, history need not be relived. It can be amended.

In the poet's voice the breaking of hearts could be heard, but also the breaking of the day. No day's beginning could be perfectly new, but in the sense of trying again, sticking at it, refusing to give up, each morning does bring a chance to begin again. Through the poet's voice, the Tree, the Rock, and the River that are our country appealed to us to "give birth again to the dream." We will know if that rebirth takes place because the likes of Donald Trump, Elon Musk, and Pete Hegseth will not plague the land as they are doing during Trump 2.0.

- Black voices so often provide the light and truth we need. That was true on January 20, 2021, when Joe Biden's inauguration included the glowing presence and moving words of the young and brilliant Black poet Amanda Gorman. "The Hill We Climb," her inauguration recitation, ended by countering the darkness that engulfed the United States two weeks earlier—January 6, 2021, a day of infamy—when Donald Trump and his MAGA storm troopers attacked the US Capitol, unleashing their attempted election-overturning carnage. "For there is always light," Gorman said, "if only we're brave enough to see it, if only we're brave enough to be it"[15]

January 6, 2021, was also the feast of Epiphany. That Christian observance commemorates the visit of the magi, the three gift-bearing wise men from the East who, tradition holds, followed a bright star that led them to

14. Angelou, *On the Pulse of Morning.*
15. Gorman, "Hill We Climb."

the infant Jesus. Epiphany honors grace, truth, and light, the opposite of the corruption, falsehood, and darkness that Trump and his unwise apostles, including the White Christian nationalists among them, embody and spread through the United States and thus into the world.

From time to time, Trump and his henchmen have reposted a three-minute video—*So God Made Trump*—that profanely depicts Trump as God's chosen one, as God's authoritarian gift to America.[16] In Trump 2.0, evidence mounts that Trump himself believes such messianic claims.[17] Kings have declared that they rule by divine right, an assertion that has buttressed their claims to unlimited power. *So God Made Trump*, all but proclaiming that assertion and seeking the unbridled dominion embedded in it, endangers American democracy and the American Dream. The Lincoln Project's no-nonsense rebuttal, *God Made a Dictator*, deftly delivers that alert, which is even more timely now than it was in 2024. In a minute-plus, the video warns that a corrupt, lying leader—an ungodly Christofascist who sees himself as exempt from law's reach and who called convicted insurrectionists hostages before pardoning them completely—is a lethal threat to the United States and the world.[18]

If Americans seek and respect it, and especially for Christians, the light has been present all along. It illuminates a key ethical insight: One cannot be loyal to Donald Trump and to Jesus. Indeed, to be loyal to Jesus requires resisting Trump, Trumpism, and Trumpists at every turn. *God Made a Dictator* intensifies the light. "I sent this man to test you," the compelling voice insists. "Until you cast him down, you have failed." Mandates for saving the American Dream rarely get more truthful and decisive than that.

Making Amends

As Sarah Churchwell rightly notes, "The American dream did not have to come true to shape the history of the nation: it merely needed to be reiterated to keep the ideal alive."[19] But saving the American Dream also requires making amends, and acts of amendment, in turn, do require *making*—making situations and relationships, aspirations and opportunities better. Such making requires attention to history and to the American novelist William Faulkner's warning that "the past is never dead. It's not even past."[20] Such mak-

16. Dilley Meme Team, *So God Made Trump*.
17. Kruse, "Does Trump Actually Think He's God?"
18. Lincoln Project, *God Made a Dictator*.
19. Churchwell, *Behold, America*, 304.
20. Faulkner, *Sanctuary*; *Requiem for a Nun*, 73.

ing also depends on acknowledging that failure, inescapable and pervasive, riddles existence. Failure abounds especially in the multiple shortfalls and shortcomings of thought, character, decision, and action that tempt us human beings to betray what is good and incite us to inflict incalculable harm.[21]

A contemporary American poet, Paul Hunter, helps to show a better way. Living and working in Seattle, Washington, he is a self-described "grassroots art activist" and "shade-tree mechanic."[22] He spent formative years on farms, Kentucky fields among them. "It's the lens through which I see the world," I heard him say on a PBS *News Hour* poetry spot. Hunter's diverse interests and talents include repairing things, often things that have been thrown away because, apparently, they have no value. "For most of my adult life now," he says, "I've been finding broken instruments or people give me broken instruments, and I fix them, and they get another life. There's a part of me that's so cheered by that, and it may be part of the same thing that happens with words, with language, that you take a phrase, you take a set of phrases that are shopworn, that people have had around them and not recognized, and take them and put them into a context that gives them a sharpened meaning of freshness." The American Dream can be a phrase like that.

Hunter's experiences and the moods attending them find expression in poetry that often concentrates on failures, on mendings of the shopworn that can approach miraculous, and on what he calls *Ripening*, the title of one of his books. Two samples focus insights about the American Dream. First, in a poem called "This Failure," Hunter takes his reader into a farm field that won't yield a crop this year. Too much rain or not enough has fallen. The sun has been too hot, or the temperature has dipped too low. Cultivation hasn't worked. Bugs and blights have ruined too much. What's to be made of this loss? If loss is not the end, concludes Hunter, someone must "mow rake and burn off this failure."[23]

The outlook in "This Failure" is augmented by "For the Miracle."[24] This time Hunter envisions not a barren field but a cluttered workshop. The partners of its grease-stained bench and well-worn but ever-ready vise jaws are old coffee cans filled with assorted nails and screws, mixed bolts and nuts, waiting to be of use. On the floor are broken, shopworn things, odd parts of this and that, stuff in the way that got consigned to this place by

21. Roth, *Failures of Ethics*. See also Feltham, *Failure*.

22. Hunter, "Hunter Discusses."

23. Hunter, "This Failure," in Hunter, *Ripening*, 37. See also Hunter, "Hunter Discusses."

24. Hunter, "For the Miracle," in Hunter, *Breaking Ground*, 40. See also Hunter, "Hunter Discusses."

someone, sometime, for who knows what. Hunter sees these things—maybe trash, good for nothing, to some—as basic elements waiting for the caring, imaginative, creative, resisting, and even joyful touch that could beneficially salvage and reconfigure them.

Saving the American Dream: Hunter reminds us that what is fragmented, what has been ripped apart, let go, broken, heaved, tossed aside, disrespected, and dumped may sometimes have new life and be of use again. But this repairer-of-brokenness should not be misunderstood. Not everything can be fixed and made whole again. Hunter evokes "the muck of history," the sadness, melancholy, and grief that swirl through it.[25] Nevertheless, he advocates doing the best one can to defy the odds that would wear the world out. What's more, he encourages what I call an *in-spite-of joy*, the deep-down sense of significance and meaning—part of the pursuit of happiness even—found when what we do protects, preserves, and enhances precious human life. Such action requires protest and resistance; it embraces the contradiction of holding together persistent melancholy and tenacious hope—hope that Israeli writer David Grossman calls "the hope of nevertheless," which "does not disregard the many dangers and obstacles, but refuses to see only them and nothing else."[26]

Far away from Paul Hunter's Washington state, one of North America's breathtaking sights is the Niagara River as it becomes Niagara Falls. One can scarcely watch that transformation without feeling terror as well as awe. The beauty of the place can be chilling as it makes one consider the fate to be met by whatever is swept over the escarpment, plunged into the mist, and dashed on the rocks below.

As I write about saving the American Dream, I also think about the Niagara River not because I have recently been to Niagara Falls but because of a California poet named Kay Ryan. Former poet laureate of the United States and a Pulitzer Prize–winner, she was a stranger to me until I heard her interviewed and listened to her read from *The Niagara River*, a collection of her poems published in 2005. That book, I found, is full of poetic provocations.

Ryan's title poem in *The Niagara River*, for instance, envisions people floating on the Niagara River, conversing, picnicking, and observing the shoreline as they go with the river's flow. They know, the poem says, that they are on the Niagara River. But do they understand, Ryan warns in closing, "what that means"?[27] She responds in a poem called "Salvage."

25. See Hunter, *Ripening*, 83.

26. Grossman, "On Hope and Despair."

27. K. Ryan, "Niagara River," in *Niagara River*, 1.

Unthinkable disaster has struck, but the salvage begins, the resolute crew determined to keep the wreckage at bay. Invoking a spirit of *in-spite-of joy*, Ryan's poem asks its reader to hear the salvage squad "whistling as / they work."[28] Can that mood—resistant and resilient—expand so that the salvage crews needed to save the American Dream become larger, stronger, and better equipped to deal with what's headed our way?

Assisting Gen Z

Responses to that question are crucial for all Americans but especially for Gen Z, the young Americans born between 1997 and 2012. Born in 2003, my granddaughter Keeley Brooks belongs to that generation, and this book is dedicated to her and her Gen Z friends. They are energetic and resilient, and they need to be because they share moods about the Dream like the ones asserted by the dispossessed and disillusioned women and men in Archibald MacLeish's *Land of the Free*: They wonder and don't know about their future. Their asking includes the question intensified in the journalist Kofi Mframa's essay "Has Gen Z Given Up on the American Dream?"[29]

Gen Z has plenty of reasons to do so. Scarcely a day of their lives has not been clouded by Donald Trump. From his lethal mismanagement of the COVID-19 crisis and his deeply corrupt criminality to his tariff-fueled inflationary havoc on the economy, the savage DOGE decimation of the federal government, and his disastrous denial of climate change, Trump and his MAGA crowd have put Gen Z, even those among them who supported him, in dire straits. Largely priced out of a future in which homeownership is affordable and good schools for children are available for everyone, Gen Z is tech savvy and nimbly resourceful, but heavy lifting awaits them, especially during Trump 2.0. Gen Z's parent and grandparent generations must do all we can to keep young Americans from forsaking the American Dream. We must do the making that amends our politics and policies so that the liberty is not done and the dreaming is not finished.

Be Bold America! is the name my friend Jill Cody gave the podcast she hosted for many years. She always ended the program by asking her guests three key questions: What should we keep doing? What should we stop doing? What should we start doing? To save the American Dream, we must keep protesting and resisting Trump 2.0, doing so especially by encouraging and supporting qualified candidates to run for national, state, and local offices in 2026 and 2028 and by doing all that we can—everyone

28. K. Ryan, "Salvage," in *Niagara River*, 35.

29. Mframa, "Has Gen Z Given Up," 7A.

can do something—to ensure that those elections are free and fair. To save the American Dream, we must stop taking good things for granted. Democracy, health care, economic prosperity, education, science, honesty, truth—all these good things and more are imperiled. If we realize how fragile and essential, how crucial and endangered they are, we will wake up and rise to the occasion to defend them against Trump's dictatorial onslaught. To save the American Dream, we need to start acting *now* with increased urgency, intensified persistence, and communal solidarity to oust the disqualified persons who presently abuse their political and economic power in ways that will ruin our country.

James Truslow Adams's definition of the American Dream remains as good as any: It is the Dream of life that is better, more abundant, and fuller for every American, with opportunity according to ability, including a person's potential, and achievement. Specifying the meaning of the key terms in that definition is an ongoing responsibility. Like the US Constitution itself, the American Dream enshrines moral visions and ethical commitments. The two aim to show how Americans should and should not act. Neither the Constitution nor the Dream is static. Both are and must be dynamic. The constant, core values—primary among them democracy, opportunity, liberty, equality, justice, and government loyal to the Constitution—must be interpreted, adapted, and amended to sustain their influence and impact in changing times and fraught circumstances.

Ten Priorities

Adams's definition of the Dream is as valid today as it was in 1931. But an accurate and credible understanding of the imperatives and responsibilities that the Dream confers upon us depends on how "We the People" defend its core values amid our current events, needs, and hopes for the future. For the mid-2020s and beyond, sound interpretation of Adams's definition entails making good on at least ten American Dream priorities, which are especially relevant for Gen Z and their children.

1. *Enrich life.* Poverty erodes and destroys the American Dream. So do immense gaps between the ultrarich and most Americans. The American Dream for our times ought to prioritize policies that diminish poverty, grow jobs, and enlarge pay. Those policies should ensure that the discouragement-breeding, opportunity-destroying gap between the ultrarich and most Americans closes in ways that, as the Constitution says, "promote the general Welfare."

2. *Build homes.* Home-owning should continue to be an American Dream aspiration for as many Americans as possible, because home-owning creates stakeholding, which deepens commitment to our country. Homes cannot be owned, however, if there is not an affordable supply of housing. With the median home price at approximately $400,000, which would require an annual income of about $125,000 to meet mortgage costs, the need to increase the affordable housing supply is critical for the American Dream today. No less important is awareness that, as the saying goes, a house is not necessarily a home. American Dream building in the mid-2020s and beyond requires due diligence about the conditions necessary for life-enriching homes. These conditions include affordable childcare, food security for all Americans, a pollution-free environment, high-quality schools safe from gun violence, and a sane balance between work and leisure.

   Sarah McBride, the nation's first openly transgender member of Congress, aptly summed up the right aspiration when she said we must make sure "that everyone can pursue the American dream, which has become increasingly unaffordable and inaccessible; that everyone should be able to get the health care they need; be able to buy a home; be able to send their child to child care without breaking the bank, if they can even get a spot. That needs to be our focus."[30]

3. *Empower education.* In our high-tech, AI-driven, interconnected world, the American Dream can survive only if we empower education. That commitment entails putting more, not fewer, resources into teacher recruitment, training, and retention. It requires assuring that all Americans, young and old, can access excellent schooling that equips them to try their best to be their best.

   In the United States, support for first-rate public schools in every state remains essential. Not only do preschool and K–12 education require care and nurture. Higher education in an amazing national network that reaches from community colleges to research universities deserves increased support and esteem. Attacks on higher education are among the most irresponsible, counterproductive actions taken by Trump 2.0. They are carried out under the pretense of curbing antisemitism on college and university campuses, but the truth is that attacks on universities, which are always in the authoritarian playbook, never curb antisemitism and do not benefit Jews. On the contrary, such attacks are among the most common cudgels wielded against that community.

30. McBride, "Sarah McBride."

Empowered education bans no books or critical inquiries. Instead, such education defends academic freedom and rejects government-dictated control over education's content, especially where honesty about American history is at stake. The stronger democracy is, the stronger its education will be. That relationship works the other way as well. To empower education is to strengthen democracy and vice versa. When Trump 2.0 attacks education, it attacks democracy too.

4. *Support science.* Trump 2.0 is utterly hostile to science. The result is that climate change is denied. Lifesaving vaccines are deplored. Essential statistics, especially when they do not fit Trump's wishes, are trashed. Life-enriching and job-creating research is senselessly crippled by DOGE-fueled cuts that decimate the National Institutes of Health and the National Science Foundation. The ensuing brain drain weakens national security and allows quacks such as the unqualified Robert Kennedy Jr. and the problematic Mehmet Oz to jeopardize the nation's health.

   The excellence of American scientific research has been a sparkling jewel in the national crown. The American Dream rises or falls with the quality of that research. Related to that quality are ethical decisions that must be made as well. They must consider abuses as well as positive opportunities that science creates, including the development and deployment of Artificial Intelligence and the ways that autocracies can use technology and information science for nefarious and corrupt purposes. Much of the American Dream's future hinges on enhancing the uses and curbing the abuses of scientific discovery and technological creation.

5. *Promote pluralism.* People and communities are different. Difference can lead to division, conflict, and violence, but it need not go in those directions. It can lead instead to a creative and constructive affirmation of pluralism. Pluralism connotes variety, diversity, expansiveness, openness, and inclusion. It is a fact of life, a fundamental aspect of American experience and reality itself. Pluralism is at the heart of the motto *e pluribus unum* (out of many, one), which far from silencing, repressing, and erasing pluralism, seeks to honor its role and to celebrate its irreplaceable additions to "a more perfect Union."

   Trump 2.0 fanatically insists on destroying diversity, equity and inclusion (DEI) initiatives that promote fair treatment and full participation of all Americans in the Dream. Trump 2.0 has also corrupted, vilified, and weaponized the virtue of being "woke," a concept that rightly connotes the importance of vigilance against, for example, racial injustice and unmerited White advantage. If such initiatives make mistakes and overreach, those errors can be corrected, but, at their best, efforts to support DEI and to be "woke" are integral to a credible American Dream for our times.

Multiethnic, religiously and culturally diverse, rarely of one mind—that is who we Americans are. The American Dream calls us, requires us, to make the best and the most of that fact, because the great Black novelist Ralph Ellison got it right when he wrote: "America is woven of many strands; I would recognize them and let it so remain. Its 'winner take nothing' that is the great truth of our country or of any country. . . . Our fate is to become one, and yet many—This is not prophecy but description."[31]

6. *Energize equality.* More than sixty years ago, on June 4, 1965, President Lyndon B. Johnson delivered the commencement address at Howard University, one of the nation's leading historically Black colleges and universities. Two months later, on August 6, he would sign into law the Voting Rights Act of 1965. At the Howard commencement, Johnson emphasized freedom but said it is "not enough. . . . We seek not just freedom but opportunity. We seek not just legal equity but human ability, not just equality as a right and a theory but equality as a fact and equality as a result."[32] Johnson's dream and the American Dream are inseparable. Making progress toward those aspirations gives Americans much amending to do. Johnson referenced especially the obstacles to equality of opportunity confronting Black Americans—primary among them poverty driven deep by "the devastating heritage of long years of slavery; and a century of oppression, hatred, and injustice."

   Although Johnson did not use the phrase, he was speaking nevertheless about energizing equality, giving it the priority and the pride of place it must enjoy in the American Dream. In the dark times of Trump 2.0, energizing equality especially requires commitment to voting rights and to the rule of law. Both are jeopardized by Trump's election-rigging and corruption. Equality of opportunity depends on fair and free elections in which every qualified American voter is not only free to vote without restrictions but also assured that her vote will be recorded promptly, counted accurately, and reported honestly. Absent those conditions, elections are held hostage to special interests—particularly Trump's interests and those of his cronies and followers. Equality of opportunity never fares well in such circumstances.

31. Ellison, *Invisible Man*, 577.

32. Johnson, "Commencement Address."

No one is above the law. Unless this binding American principle is truly binding, the odds favoring disrespect for and abuse of the law will favor lawlessness and dishonesty, which are rife in Trump 2.0. That administration's cronyism, corruption, and its quid pro quo transactionalism cripple equal opportunity for individuals and communities, including those in the business world. Restoration of the rule of law, renewed respect for the principle that no person is above the law—nothing is more important in the crucial task of saving the American Dream by energizing equality.

7. *Combat corruption.* Quoting the historian Matthew Dallek—"Trump is the most brazenly corrupt national politician in modern times, and his openness about it is sui generis [in a class by itself]"—the editorial board of the *New York Times* published, on June 7, 2025, "A Comprehensive Accounting of Trump's Culture of Corruption."[33] The editorial board concurred with Dallek, adding that Trump's culture of corruption is "part of Mr. Trump's larger efforts to weaken American democracy and turn the federal government into an extension of himself." The editorial documented the multifaceted "range of self-dealing since he took office four months ago."

What can be done about the corruption? No use counting on quiescent Congressional Republicans, the editorial concluded. In addition, legal remedies are scarce, because the Supreme Court "made it virtually impossible to hold a president criminally liable for actions even distantly related to his official duties." The editorial judged that voters are likely "the remaining remedy."

For that remedy to work, however, the American electorate must be informed and energized not to shrug off the corruption—it's just "Trump being Trump"—and to take action that includes public protest and ousting Trumpists from office. To advance that cause, nothing is more important than investigative journalism, putting the media's bright light on the malfeasance, and producing podcasts that hold Trump's feet to the fire of accountability. The *Times* editors rightly underscored that "historically, when corruption becomes the norm in a country, economic growth suffers, and living standards stagnate." Left unchecked, they might have added, Trump's corruption will destroy the American Dream. Saving the Dream depends hugely on defending and supporting the First Amendment right to freedom of the press, and amending our ways in order to heed the anticorruption calls that we need from it.

33. *New York Times* editorial board, "Comprehensive Accounting."

8. *Democratize democracy*. The American Dream and democracy are inseparable. So, if American confidence in democracy sags, the Dream falters. Saving the American Dream requires rebuilding confidence in democracy, which entails democratizing democracy. Steps that can be taken in that direction are numerous and diverse. Three deserve special emphasis: (1) Various organizations encourage nontraditional candidates to run for office. They merit support to match the expansion of democracy they offer. One example is Run for Something, founded in 2017, which recruits and supports young candidates to run for state and local office, building a new generation of political candidates for higher office in the future. Another example is Emily's List, which recruits, trains, and supports pro-choice women to run for office up and down the ballot. (2) The National Popular Vote Interstate Compact (NPVIC) seeks to annul the antidemocratic Electoral College, which dishonors a fundamental principle of democracy—one person, one vote—permitting the American president to be elected by a minority of American voters. Absent the archaic Electoral College, Donald Trump would not have defeated Hillary Clinton in 2016, and the United States might have avoided his malign presidential influence. Recognizing how difficult it is to amend the Constitution, the NPVIC is an agreement among a group of American states and the District of Columbia to award all their electoral votes to the presidential ticket that wins the overall popular votes in the fifty states and the District of Columbia. (3) Apart from Donald Trump and his 2.0 administration, no institution has harmed American democracy more than the current version of the John Roberts Supreme Court. Stacked with dubious Trump appointees, the Court immunized Trump from criminal accountability and has been tainted by the corrupt practices of Samuel Alito and Clarence Thomas. The performance of this SCOTUS cries out for reform. Two key steps in the right direction would be to establish (a) term limits and (b) a binding code of ethics for the justices.

9. *Deepen patriotism*. Being patriotic differs from being nationalistic and from embracing Trumpist, America First policies that are alliance-destroying and tariff-disruptive. A nationalist says, "My country right or wrong." "My country first, last, and always." "My nation's might makes right." By contrast, as the historian Timothy Snyder observes, a patriot "wants the nation to live up to its ideals, which means asking us to be our best selves."[34]

34. Snyder, *On Tyranny*, 111.

Our best selves want to be better, much better, than our worst impulses and actions, which Trump 2.0 embodies and legitimates. Our best selves resist autocracy, oligarchy, and kleptocracy. They do not equate wealth with intelligence, let alone with virtue. They protest against conspiracies to overturn fair and free elections. Our best selves reject antisemitism and racism; they oppose hypocrisy and lying. Our best selves do not join ICE and deport people without due process of law, let alone kill American citizens as happened in Minneapolis on January 7, 2026, when agent Jonathan Ross senselessly shot to death thirty-seven-year-old Renee Nicole Good, the mother of three.[35] Our best selves do not, as Trump 2.0 has done, federalize the National Guard or deploy the US military to threaten American citizens who defend civil rights and deplore illegal anti-immigration policies. Our best selves hold leaders accountable; they bring tyrants to justice. Our best selves never say "I alone can fix it"; they work together to solve problems. Our best selves neither take human rights away nor withhold international aid so that impoverished, starving children die needlessly and senselessly. Our best selves never stop asking critical questions, including, Are we doing the best we can? Our best selves never give up trying to be our best. Our best selves never cease defending and expanding the American Dream.

10. *Reclaim our country and its reputation.* Donald Trump postures as strong, but he is not. The absurdity of his self-serving lies shows how desperate and vulnerable he is. For example, on August 6, 2025, Trump lashed out when questioned about the Epstein/Maxwell case. "The whole thing," Trump preposterously proclaimed, "is a hoax. It's put out by the Democrats because we've had the most successful six months in the history of our country. And that's just a way of trying to divert attention to something that's total bullshit."[36] Not even Trump's MAGA base is persuaded by such vulgar nonsense.

    Nor were most Americans impressed two months later, on September 30, 2025, the day before Trump 2.0 failed to prevent a needless government shutdown. Summoned from around the world to Quantico, Virginia, hundreds of the nation's top military officers sat largely silent and stoic while the pathetically macho Secretary of Defense Pete Hegseth and an incoherent President Donald Trump harangued them about intensifying "warrior ethos" and stopping the "enemy from within" by using American military might to thwart dissent against

35. Graham, "None of This."
36. CNN, "Trump Lashes Out."

Trump's despotism.[37] Intending to flex muscle, Hegseth and Trump showed insecurity, weakness, and vulnerability in a strutting yet fumbling spectacle that was as embarrassing and laughable as it was threatening and dangerous.

No one can be sure that limits exist to rein in the likes of Hegseth or to check Trump's power grabbing, but support for Trump is scarcely staunch. Increasingly, his policies and practices produce protest not affirmation, resistance not approval, and rejection not acceptance. He and his administration remain dangerous, and the damage they have done to the United States and its reputation is enormous and not easily rectified. But Trump 2.0 is neither impenetrable nor invincible. Public protest, civil disobedience, and successful election rebuttals in 2026 and 2028 can advance the tide-turning already underway.

Trump's cynicism and corruption, his inability to influence or divorce from Vladimir Putin and other dictators, and his chaotic tariff debacle have wreaked havoc on the nation's reputation at home as well as abroad. So have Trump's military attempts to quell the rising protests that the American people are making against him. No one can or should place much faith in the current American government's reliability as an ally of democracy or as a defender of the Constitution.

Trump 2.0 will inflict more damage and pain before it is consigned to the dustbin of history, which will eventually be its fate. The most important steps in that direction will take place in the approaching elections. If those elections succeed, as they must, weakening Trump 2.0 in 2026 and sidelining his legacy in 2028, stability can return to a chaotic economy and strength can be added to national security by rebuilding alliances in the North Atlantic Treaty Organization (NATO) and with Asian partners (the AP4)—Japan, South Korea, Australia, and New Zealand.

Absent solid national security, the American Dream founders. Reliable international relations that defend against autocracy, oligarchy, aggression, corruption, and carving the world into American, Russian, and Chinese spheres of influence can re-create the global context in which the American Dream can flourish at home and help to support and sustain democratic values abroad.

Ten American Dream priorities: the future of the American Dream, which is so vital for Gen Z and their children, requires making good on them. Toward these goals and aspirations, repairing movement and

37. Lamothe et al., "Trump, Hegseth Lecture"; Debussman and FitzGerald, "US Cities."

amending action depend on how Americans vote 2026 and 2028. Taking back our country, reaffirming the American Dream, and reclaiming our nation's reputation hinge on those crucial results. Backing high-quality, pro-democracy, and anticorruption candidates, expanding the right to vote, advancing voter registration and turnout, and defending election integrity—these actions must have priority in order to save the American Dream in the near term and for the future.

Words to Remember

Too much has happened since these meditations for dark times began with memorable words from Psalm 43, Alexander Hamilton, Annie Dillard, Paul Fussell, and James Baldwin. The psalmist asked for light and truth. The United States needs such an outpouring more than ever. That is true because Hamilton's challenge remains ours: Good government by reflection and choice or the misfortune of political constitution by accident and force? How will "We the People" decide? When Annie Dillard asked Paul Glenn how his work was going, Glenn had this to say: "The current's got me. Feels like I'm about in the middle of the channel now. I just keep at it. I just keep hoping the tide will turn and bring me in."[38] The curmudgeonly veteran Paul Fussell counseled against taking things for granted: "If you live in the actual world," he warned, "you can't have your own way."[39] James Baldwin stood with Hamilton, Glenn, and Dillard when he said that "we are the generation that must throw everything into the endeavor to remake America into what we say we want it to be." He also echoed Fussell with a warning of his own: "Not everything that is faced can be changed; but nothing can be changed until it is faced."[40]

Light and truth—how much we Americans need them because our country, its Constitution and its Dream, are at stake. F. Scott Fitzgerald ended *The Great Gatsby* by evoking a haunting image and a melancholy mood. Nick Carraway, the novel's narrator, contemplates Jay Gatsby's unhappy attempt to fulfill his version of the American Dream. Gatsby, he thinks, must have felt his dream "so close that he could hardly fail to grasp it." But as "the dark fields of the republic rolled on under the night," Carraway discerned that our aspirations, especially our best ones, elude fulfillment, no matter how hard we try or how fast we run to attain them.

38. See Dillard, *Writing Life*, 85–88.
39. Fussell, Thank God, 104.
40. Baldwin, "As Much Truth."

"So we beat on," *The Great Gatsby* concludes, "boats against the current, borne back ceaselessly into the past."[41] The American Dream can never be saved completely let alone achieved fully. Beating on, the effort to save it will ceaselessly bear us back into the past without completion. Fitzgerald's counsel, however, is not to give up in despair. Nothing worth doing—like saving the Dream or loving one's country—can be finished in a lifetime, at least not fully. But that fact makes it more important to do the best we can to secure, as the Constitution says, "the Blessings of Liberty to ourselves and our Posterity."

One of Kay Ryan's *Niagara River* poems ends by saying, "Things shouldn't / be so hard."[42] She's right. Saving the American Dream should not be as difficult and discouraging as it became in the mid-2020s. Confronting that predicament, however, is where "We the People" find ourselves. Decisions await. Despairing and giving up are not good options. They only ensure failure. A better way is making amends, trying for new beginnings, showing that we are "better than that."

Another contemporary American poet, Maggie Smith, warns that "life is short," and conservative estimates find that the world's "at least half terrible."[43] Those phrases come from her "Good Bones," which turns a real estate idiom into moving poetry. Sometimes a place badly maintained, decrepit and dismal, still has good bones, a sound foundation and structural framework. It might be salvageable. A cosmic realtor, Smith wants to sell us on the world, a place with abundant "good bones," because it "could be beautiful, / right?" What she says applies to the United States and the American Dream as well. Life is short. Our times and places are at least half terrible, but nevertheless the United States has "good bones." The American Dream at its best is proof of that. "We the People" can recover, reclaim, and rebuild. We can make our country and its Dream beautiful again.

The great nineteenth-century American poet Emily Dickinson lived a reclusive life in Amherst, Massachusetts. It is unlikely that she ever visited Long Island, where Fitzgerald situated *The Great Gatsby*, or saw Kay Ryan's Niagara River. Nor did she have children to receive the "good bones" that Maggie Smith bequeaths to hers. But before Fitzgerald, Ryan, and Smith said so, Dickinson knew that living in America was hard. She saw that the world was at least half terrible. She fathomed that life's current bears us back ceaselessly into the past and toward death. But also—like Fitzgerald, Ryan, and Smith—Dickinson knew that she could and must make beauty and thereby

41. Fitzgerald, *Great Gatsby*, 110–11.

42. K. Ryan, "Things Shouldn't Be So Hard," in *Niagara River*, 41.

43. Smith, "Good Bones."

help to save the world and the good dreams it can inspire. Fitzgerald, Ryan, and Smith rightly echo Emily Dickinson. I will do what I can, Dickinson affirmed. "That I cannot," she insisted, "must be / Unknown to possibility."[44]

Informed by favorite American writers of mine and especially by the Constitution of the United States, these meditations for dark times have tried to send out light and truth to guide and encourage all who seek "a more perfect Union." They end with cautious hope. The hope should not be confused with optimism. It is closer to what the Black voice of W. E. B. Du Bois called "a hope not hopeless but unhopeful," an outlook that says in spite of all the cruelty, corruption, and carnage of Trump 2.0, I will not give up on the Dream.[45]

American life has never fully been what it ought to be. It regularly falls far and horrifically short of that ideal. That fact, however, results in yearning for better times and better selves. Emily Dickinson called hope "the thing with feathers" that perches deep down within us and never stops its singing.[46] Fragile and frustrated though hope may be, it persists and resists no matter what. So, this book's ending must be a beginning. Its abiding conviction is that "We the People" will find our way to make the amendments we need in order to save the American Dream, our democracy, and our country.

44. Dickinson, "What I can do—I will" (361).

45. Du Bois, *Souls of Black Folk*, 227–28.

46. Dickinson, "'Hope' Is the thing with feathers" (314).

Bibliography

Adams, James Truslow. *The Epic of America*. 1931. Reprint, Boston: Little, Brown, 1934.

Ahn, Ashley, and Maxine Joselow. "Where Charlie Kirk Stood on Key Political Issues." *New York Times*, September 22, 2025. https://www.nytimes.com/2025/09/11/us/charlie-kirk-views-guns-gender-climate.html.

Aleaziz, Hamid. "Florida Builds 'Alligator Alcatraz' Detention Center for Migrants in Everglades." *New York Times*, June 23, 2025. Updated July 1, 2025. https://www.nytimes.com/2025/06/23/us/politics/florida-alligator-alcatraz-migrant-detention-center.html;

Alfaro, Mariana. "Ernst Posts Snarky Reply After Telling Town Hall 'We All Are Going to Die.'" *Washington Post*, June 1, 2025. https://www.washingtonpost.com/politics/2025/06/01/joni-ernst-medicaid-comments.

Alien and Sedition Acts (1798). Milestone Documents, National Archives. https://www.archives.gov/milestone-documents/alien-and-sedition-acts.

Allison, Natalie, et al. "Inside Laura Loomer's Rise: 'Obsessive' Research, Oval Office Visits." *Washington Post*, August 5, 2025. https://www.washingtonpost.com/politics/2025/08/05/loomer-trump-influence/

Alter, Charlotte. "Mallory McMorrow Wants Democrats to Reclaim the American Dream." *Time*, April 2, 2025. https://time.com/7273181/mallory-mcmorrow-interview-senate-campaign.

Alter, Jonathan. "Trump's Huge Tariff Exemption Grift." *Old Goats*, Substack, April 13, 2025. https://oldgoats.substack.com/p/trumps-huge-tariff-exemption-grift.

American Association of Colleges and Universities. "A Call for Constructive Engagement." April 22, 2025. https://www.aacu.org/newsroom/a-call-for-constructive-engagement.

American Historical Association. "Historians Defend the Smithsonian." March 31, 2025. https://www.historians.org/news/historians-defend-the-smithsonian.

Anderson, Zac. "'I'm Not a Dictator': Trump Defends Using National Guard for Crime Crackdown." *USA Today*, August 25, 2025. https://www.usatoday.com/story/news/politics/2025/08/25/donald-trump-national-guard-dictator-comments/85816670007.

———. "Trump Signs Megabill That Slashes Taxes, Medicaid While Boosting National Debt." *USA Today*, July 4, 2025. https://www.usatoday.com/story/news/politics/2025/07/04/donald-trump-signs-megabill-taxes-medicaid-border/84470497007.

Angelou, Maya. *On the Pulse of Morning.* New York: Random House, 1993. For the inauguration reading, see the William J. Clinton Presidential Library YouTube channel: https://www.youtube.com/watch?v=59xGmHzxtZ4.

Anishanslin, Zara. "What We Get Wrong about Ben Franklin's 'a Republic, if You Can Keep It.'" *Washington Post*, October 29, 2019. https://www.washingtonpost.com/outlook/2019/10/29/what-we-get-wrong-about-ben-franklins-republic-if-you-can-keep-it.

Appelbaum, Anne. "America's Future Is Hungary." *Atlantic*, March 31, 2025. https://www.theatlantic.com/magazine/archive/2025/05/viktor-orban-hungary-maga-corruption/682111.

———. "The Most Corrupt Presidency in American History: Anne Applebaum on America's Backsliding Democracy." Interview by David Frum. *The David Frum Show* (podcast), *Atlantic,* May 7, 2025, 57:50. https://www.theatlantic.com/podcasts/archive/2025/05/the-david-frum-show-the-most-corrupt-presidency-in-american-history/682720.

Astor, Maggie. "Trump Declines to Back Away from 'You Don't Have to Vote Again' Line." *New York Times*, July 30, 2024. https://www.nytimes.com/2024/07/30/us/politics/trump-christians-vote-ingraham.html.

Attrino, Anthony G. "American Dream Says Decorative Helicopter Crash Cost Mall $20.5M." NJ.com, June 5, 2025. https://www.nj.com/bergen/2025/06/american-dream-says-decorative-helicopter-crash-cost-mall-205m.html.

Avett, Seth, and the Avett Brothers. "We Americans." Track 3 on *Closer Than Together*, by the Avett Brothers. New York: Republic Records/American Recordings, 2019 (CD and digital audio file). For the lyrics to "We Americans." see the Genius website: https://genius.com/The-avett-brothers-we-americans-lyrics. For the official music video for "We Americans." see the Avett Brothers YouTube channel: https://www.youtube.com/watch?v=0MKm9TB9b6s.

Axelrod, Tal, and Zachary Basu. "Trump's Identity Project." *Axios*, August 24, 2025. https://www.axios.com/2025/08/24/trump-american-identity-citizenship-immigration.

Baldwin, James. "The American Dream and the American Negro." *New York Times*, March 7, 1965. https://archive.nytimes.com/www.nytimes.com/books/98/03/29/specials/baldwin-dream.html.

———. "As Much Truth as One Can Bear." *New York Times Book Review*, January 14, 1962. https://timesmachine.nytimes.com/timesmachine/1962/01/14/118438007.pdf?pdf_redirect=true&ip=0.

———. *Notes of a Native Son.* In *Collected Essays*, edited by Toni Morrison, 1:1–129. 3 vols. Library of America 98. New York: Library of America, 1998.

Barajas, Joshua. "Trump Gets an 'F' on His First 100 Days from Plurality of Americans, Poll Finds." *PBS News Hour*, April 29, 2025. https://www.pbs.org/newshour/politics/how-americans-grade-trumps-first-100-days.

Barnes, Julian E., et al. "Strike Set Back Iran's Nuclear Program by Only a Few Months, U.S. Report Says." *New York Times*, June 24, 2025. https://www.nytimes.com/2025/06/24/us/politics/iran-nuclear-sites.html.

Barrett, Devlin, and Chris Cameron. "What to Know About the Epstein Files, a Perfect Recipe for Conspiracy Theories." *New York Times*, July 24, 2025. https://www.nytimes.com/article/jeffrey-epstein-files-trump.html.

Barrett, Devlin, and Perry Stein. "Garland Names Special Counsel for Trump Mar-a-Lago, 2020 Election Probes." *Washington Post*, November 19, 2022. https://www.washingtonpost.com/national-security/2022/11/18/justice-trump-garland-special-counsel.

Bedigan, Mike. "'These Are the Most Magnificent Poles Made': As Middle East Rages, Trump Brags About New Flag Poles at the White House." *Independent*, June 18, 2025. https://www.the-independent.com/news/world/americas/us-politics/trump-new-flagpoles-middle-east-b2772338.html.

Bellinger, John B., III. "Does Trump Have the Authority to Strike Iran?" Council on Foreign Relations, June 22, 2025. https://www.cfr.org/expert-brief/does-trump-have-authority-strike-iran.

Bennett, Brian. "Exclusive: Inside the Preparations for Trump's Next Supreme Court Nominee." *Time*, July 29, 2025. https://time.com/7305987/donald-trump-supreme-court-justices.

Berman, Mark, et al. "Ghislaine Maxwell 'Answered Every Single Question' in Two Days of Interviews, Lawyer Says." *Washington Post*, July 25, 2025. https://www.washingtonpost.com/national-security/2025/07/25/justice-blanche-florida-ghislaine-maxwell-epstein-trump.

Bessent, Scott. Interview by Kristen Welker, *Meet the Press*, April 6, 2025, on the NBC News YouTube channel (interview runs from about minute 5 to minute 17): https://www.youtube.com/watch?v=wClpU3DNcpM.

Bigg, Matthew Mpoke. "Asked About 'TACO' and Tariffs, Trump Lashes Out at Reporter." *New York Times*, May 30, 2025. https://www.nytimes.com/2025/05/29/us/politics/trump-taco-trade-question.html.

Biss, Jonathan, and Christopher Serkin. "A Pianist and a Law Professor Meet at the Bar . . ." *New York Times*, May 3, 2025. https://www.nytimes.com/2025/05/03/opinion/constitution-supreme-court-classical-music.html.

Bivens, Josh. "I'm an Economist. The GOP Budget Undeniably Takes from the Working Class and Gives to the Rich." *Time*, July 3, 2025. https://time.com/7299897/gop-budget-gives-to-the-rich.

Blackerby, Christine. "The Oath of Office: The First Act of the First Congress." Pieces of History, National Archives, May 30, 2014. https://prologue.blogs.archives.gov/2014/05/30/the-oath-of-office-the-first-act-of-the-first-congress.

Blake, Aaron. "The Cracks in Trump's Base." CNN, December 6, 2025. https://www.cnn.com/2025/12/06/politics/donald-trump-republicans-base-divide.

———. "5 Big Questions About Trump's Ties to Epstein." CNN, July 19, 2025. https://www.cnn.com/2025/07/19/politics/epstein-trump-ties-analysis.

Blight, David W. "What If History Died by Sanctioned Ignorance?" *New Republic*, August 7, 2025. https://newrepublic.com/article/198354/history-died-sanctioned-ignorance.

Blinder, Allen, and Michael C. Bender. "Trump Administration Renews Attacks on Harvard with Negotiations Uncertain." *New York Times*, July 9, 2025. https://www.nytimes.com/2025/07/09/us/politics/trump-harvard-data-accreditation.html.

Blinder, Alan, et al. "Harvard and White House Move Toward Potential Landmark Settlement." *New York Times*, August 11, 2025. https://www.nytimes.com/2025/08/11/us/trump-harvard-settlement-negotiations.html.

Bomboy, Scott. "Supreme Court Tackles History with Trump's Immunity Case." National Constitution Center, April 26, 2024. https://constitutioncenter.org/blog/supreme-court-tackles-history-with-trumps-immunity-case.

Bonhoeffer, Dietrich. *"After Ten Years": Dietrich Bonhoeffer and Our Times.* Edited with an introduction by Victoria J. Barnett. Translated by Barbara and Martin Rumscheidt. Minneapolis: Fortress, 2017.

Bonica, Adam. "The 96% Rebellion: District Courts Mount Historic Resistance, But the Supreme Court Looms." *On Data and Democracy*, Substack, May 24, 2025. https://data4democracy.substack.com/p/the-96-rebellion-district-courts.

Booker, Cory. "Cory Booker: A National Crisis and a Global Crisis." Interview by Tim Miller, *The Bulwark Podcast*, season 2, episode 1028, April 24, 2025, transcript. https://podscripts.co/podcasts/the-bulwark-podcast/s2-ep1028-cory-booker-a-national-crisis-and-a-global-crisis.

———. "Senator Booker's Speech." https://www.booker.senate.gov/senator-bookers-marathon-speech.

Borelli, Gabriel. "Americans Are Split over the State of the American Dream." Pew Research Center, July 2, 2024. https://www.pewresearch.org/short-reads/2024/07/02/americans-are-split-over-the-state-of-the-american-dream.

Bouie, Jamelle. "Madison Saw Something in the Constitution We Should Open Our Eyes To." *New York Times*, November 12, 2021. https://www.nytimes.com/2021/11/12/opinion/gerrymandering-guarantee-clause.html.

Bowley, Graham, et al. "Historians Alarmed by White House Plan to Oversee Smithsonian Exhibits." *New York Times*, August 13, 2025. https://www.nytimes.com/2025/08/13/arts/design/trump-smithsonian-exhibits-review-historians-alarmed.html.

Bray, Samuel. "The Supreme Court Is Watching Out for the Courts, Not for Trump." *New York Times*, June 28, 2025. https://www.nytimes.com/2025/06/28/opinion/birthright-citizenship-supreme-court-injunction.html.

Brenan, Megan. "Trump's Approval Rating Drops to 36%, New Second-Term Low." Gallup, November 28, 2025. https://news.gallup.com/poll/699221/trump-approval-rating-drops-new-second-term-low.aspx.

Brookings Institution. "Reference Sheet on the Insurrection Act and Related Authorities." https://www.brookings.edu/wp-content/uploads/2020/12/ReferenceSheet_InsurrectionActAndRelatedAuthorities.pdf.

Brooks, David. "I Should Have Seen This Coming." *Atlantic*, April 7, 2025. https://www.theatlantic.com/magazine/archive/2025/05/trumpism-maga-populism-power-pursuit/682116.

———. "The Rise of Right-Wing Nihilism." *New York Times*, August 21, 2025. https://www.nytimes.com/2025/08/21/opinion/rufo-yarvin-trump-nihilism.html.

———. "'We Are the Most Rejected Generation.'" *New York Times*, May 15, 2025. https://www.nytimes.com/2025/05/15/opinion/rejection-college-youth.html.

Brown, Haynes. "Why Trump Thinks He Can Get Away with It." MSNBC, February 7, 2025. https://www.msnbc.com/opinion/msnbc-opinion/russel-vought-trump-omb-unitary-executive-rcna190807.

Browning, Christopher R. "Hitler's Enablers." *New York Review*, November 7, 2024. https://www.nybooks.com/articles/2024/11/07/hitlers-enablers-the-death-of-democracy-benjamin-carter-hett.

———. "How Hitler's Enablers Undid Democracy in Germany." *Atlantic*, October 8, 2022. https://www.theatlantic.com/ideas/archive/2022/10/nazi-germany-hitler-democracy-weimar/671605.

Bump, Philip. "Trump's 2024 'Mandate' Isn't as Robust as Biden's Was in 2020." *Washington Post*, November 18, 2024. https://www.washingtonpost.com/politics/2024/11/18/trumps-2024-mandate-isnt-robust-bidens-was-2020.

Burch, Audra D. S. "What Has Happened to the American Dream?" *New York Times*, May 3, 2025. https://www.nytimes.com/interactive/2025/05/04/us/trump-american-dream-voters.html.

Burns, Ken, et al., dirs. *The American Revolution*. Written by Geoffrey C. Ward. Produced for PBS. 6 two-hour episodes (aired in late 2025 and available online). https://www.pbs.org/kenburns/the-american-revolution.

Cameron, Chris. "Deploy National Guard to Chicago? Trump Says He Has 'the Right to Do Anything I Want to Do.'" *New York Times*, August 26, 2025. https://www.nytimes.com/2025/08/26/us/politics/trump-national-guard-chicago-dictator.html.

———. "Stephen Miller Asserts U.S. Has Right to Take Greenland." *New York Times*, January 5, 2026. https://www.nytimes.com/2026/01/05/us/politics/stephen-miller-greenland-venezuela.html.

Cameron, Chris, and Hamed Aleaziz. "Over 60,000 Are in Immigration Detention, a Modern High, Records Show." *New York Times*, August 11, 2025. https://www.nytimes.com/2025/08/11/us/politics/immigration-detention-numbers.html.

Carter, Jimmy. President's Commission on the Holocaust Remarks on Receiving the Final Report of the Commission. Online by Gerhard Peters and John T. Woolley, The American Presidency Project https://www.presidency.ucsb.edu/node/248475.

Casselman, Ben. "Trump Fired America's Economic Data Collector. History Shows the Perils." *New York Times*, Published August 3, 2025. Updated August 4, 2025. https://www.nytimes.com/2025/08/03/business/trump-bls-firing-economic-reports.html.

———. "Trump Says a Recession Might Be Worth the Cost. Economists Disagree." *New York Times*, March 18, 2025. https://www.nytimes.com/2025/03/18/business/economy/trump-recession-tariffs-inflation.html.

Casselman, Ben, et al. "Trump's Pick to Lead Labor Data Agency Adds to Fears of Political Interference." *New York Times*, August 12, 2025. https://www.nytimes.com/2025/08/12/business/trump-bls-ej-antoni.html.

Chait, Jonathan. "The Largest Upward Transfer of Wealth in American History." *Atlantic*, May 22, 2025. https://www.theatlantic.com/ideas/archive/2025/05/big-beautiful-transfer-of-wealth/682885.

———. "Trump's Epstein Answers Are Getting Worse." *Atlantic*, July 16, 2025. https://www.theatlantic.com/ideas/archive/2025/07/trump-epstein-obama-boring/683546.

Charalambous, Peter. "220 Lawsuits in 100 Days: Trump Administration Faces Unprecedented Legal Blitz." ABC News, April 29, 2025. https://abcnews.go.com/US/220-lawsuits-100-days-trump-administration-faces-unprecedented/story?id=121252266.

Chemerinsky, Erwin. *No Democracy Lasts Forever: How the Constitution Threatens the United States*. New York: Liveright, 2024.

———. "A Stunning and Tragic Supreme Court Decision." *Los Angeles Times*, June 27, 2025. https://www.latimes.com/opinion/story/2025-06-27/nationwide-injunction-supreme-court-birthright-citizenship.

Child, Fred. "Copland's 'Lincoln Portrait.'" NPR, November 10, 2004. https://www.npr.org/2004/11/10/4165357/coplands-lincoln-portrait.

Cho, Kelly Kasulis. "Trump Directs Justice Dept. to Probe Officials Who Opposed Him in First Term." *Washington Post*, April 10, 2025. https://www.washingtonpost.com/nation/2025/04/10/trump-probe-chris-krebs-miles-taylor.

Churchwell, Sarah. *Behold, America: A History of America First and the American Dream*. London: Bloomsbury, 2019.

———. "A Brief History of the American Dream." *Catalyst*, Winter 2021. https://www.bushcenter.org/catalyst/state-of-the-american-dream/churchwell-history-of-the-american-dream.

CNN. "Trump Lashes Out Over Epstein Case." August 6, 2025, CNN YouTube channel: https://www.youtube.com/watch?v=WrtyQ6iOQLo.

Cohen, Eliot A. "Hegseth's Headlong Pursuit of Academic Mediocrity." *Atlantic*, August 6, 2025. https://www.theatlantic.com/national-security/archive/2025/08/military-education-reforms/683760.

Cohn, Marjorie. "By Ruling Against Nationwide Injunctions, SCOTUS Affirms the Imperial Presidency." *Truthout*, June 30, 2025. https://truthout.org/articles/by-ruling-against-nationwide-injunctions-scotus-affirms-the-imperial-presidency.

Coleman, A. D. Introduction. In *Land of the Free*, by Archibald MacLeish, v–x. New York: Da Capo, 1977.

Collinson, Stephen. "Trump's Day of Tariff Mayhem Contains a Scary Lesson for His Second Term." CNN, April 10, 2025. https://www.cnn.com/2025/04/10/politics/trump-tariffs-china-recession-bond-market-navarro-bessent/index.html.

Colvin, Jill. "Trump Is Selling 'God Bless the USA' Bibles for $59.99 as He Faces Mounting Legal Bills." AP, March 6, 2024. Updated March 26, 2024. https://apnews.com/article/trump-god-bless-usa-bible-greenwood-2713fda3efdfa297d0f024efb1ca3003.

Committee for a Responsible Federal Budget. "Interest on the Debt to Grow Past $1 Trillion Next Year." February 6, 2025. https://www.crfb.org/blogs/interest-debt-grow-past-1-trillion-next-year#:~:text=Net%20interest%20has%20been%20exploding,a%20share%20of%20the%20economy.

Complaint for Declaratory and Injunctive Relief, President and Fellows of Harvard College v. U.S. Department of Health and Human Services et al. No. 1:2025cv11048 (D. Mass. Apr. 21, 2025), https://www.harvard.edu/research-funding/wp-content/uploads/sites/16/2025/04/Harvard-Funding-Freeze-Order-Complaint.pdf.

Contorno, Steve, and Casey Tolan. "Trump Said He Hadn't Read Project 2025—But Most of His Early Executive Actions Overlap with Its Proposals." CNN, January 31, 2025. https://www.cnn.com/2025/01/31/politics/trump-policy-project-2025-executive-orders-invs.

Copeland, Joseph. "Favorable Views of Supreme Court Remain Near Historic Low." Pew Research Center, September 3, 2025. https://www.pewresearch.org/short-reads/2025/09/03/favorable-views-of-supreme-court-remain-near-historic-low.

Cortellessa, Eric, and Sam Jacobs, "Full Transcript of Donald Trump's '100 Days' Interview with TIME." *Time*, April 22, 2025. https://time.com/7280114/donald-trump-2025-interview-transcript.

Cramer, Ruby. "Trump Is 'Fascist to the Core,' Milley Says in Woodward Book." *Washington Post*, October 12, 2024. https://www.washingtonpost.com/nation/2024/10/12/mark-milley-donald-trump-fascist.

Cranston, Matthew. "Will 'Muzzle Velocity' Backfire on Trump?" *Financial Review*, February 8, 2025. https://www.afr.com/world/north-america/will-muzzle-velocity-backfire-on-trump-20250205-p5L9m8.

Crimson News Staff. "Read Harvard's Complaint Against the Trump Administration." *Harvard Crimson*, April 22, 2025. https://www.thecrimson.com/article/2025/4/22/read-harvard-trump-complaint.

Cullen, Jim. *The American Dream: A Short History of an Idea That Shaped a Nation*. New York: Oxford University Press, 2004.

Cummings, E. E. "'next to of course God america i.'" In *Is 5*. 1926. Reprint, Liveright paperbound ed. New York: Liveright, 1970. For the full text of the poem, see the All Poetry website: https://allpoetry.com/next-to-of-course-god-america-i. For Cummings's reading of the poem recorded by the BBC (date unknown), see The Poetry Archive website: https://poetryarchive.org/poet/e-e-cummings.

Dale, Daniel. "Fact Check: Trump Falsely Claims His Highly Unpopular Big Bill Is the 'Single Most Popular Bill Ever Signed.'" CNN, July 4, 2025. https://www.cnn.com/2025/07/04/politics/fact-check-trump-bill-unpopular.

Daniels, Cheyanne M. "Trump Reiterates That He Has the Authority to Pardon Ghislaine Maxwell." *Politico*, July 28, 2025. https://www.politico.com/news/2025/07/28/trump-ghislaine-maxwell-pardon-jeffrey-epstein-00479862.

Dans, Paul, and Steven Groves, eds. *Mandate for Leadership: The Conservative Promise 2025*. Washington, DC: Heritage Foundation, 2023. https://static.heritage.org/project2025/2025_MandateForLeadership_FULL.pdf.

Debussman, Bernd, Jr., and James FitzGerald. "US Cities Should Be Military Training Grounds, Trump Tell Generals." BBC, September 30, 2025. https://www.bbc.com/news/articles/cvgq044n72po.

Delbanco, Andrew. *The Real American Dream: A Meditation on Hope*. 1st paperback ed. The William E. Massey, Sr. Lectures in the History of American Civilization 1998. Cambridge: Harvard University Press, 2000.

Dennie, Madiba K. *The Originalism Trap: How Extremists Stole the Constitution and How We the People Can Take It Back*. New York: Random House, 2024.

De Visé, Daniel, and Carlie Procell. "The American Dream Now Costs $5 Million. Here's a Breakdown." *USA Today*, September 22, 2025. https://www.usatoday.com/story/money/2025/09/21/american-dream-costs-home-college/86186607007.

Dickinson, Emily. "'Hope' is the thing with feathers" (314). The Poetry Foundation. https://www.poetryfoundation.org/poems/42889/hope-is-the-thing-with-feathers-314.

———. "I dwell in Possibility" (466). The Poetry Foundation. https://www.poetryfoundation.org/poems/52197/i-dwell-in-possibility-466.

———. "What I can do—I will" (361). Hello Poetry. https://hellopoetry.com/poem/3964/what-i-can-doi-will.

Dillard, Annie. *The Writing Life*. New York: HarperPerennial, 1990.

Dilley Meme Team. *So God Made Trump*, video (2:47), published in January 2024. https://www.youtube.com/watch?v=1D71GoBC2t8&list=RD1D71GoBC2t8&start_radio=1.

Doggett, Lloyd. "Trump's Economic Promises Timeline." April 9, 2025. https://doggett.house.gov/issues/trumps-economic-promises-timeline.

Du Bois, W. E. B. *The Souls of Black Folk*. Signet Classics. New York: New American Library, 1969. First published in 1903 by McClurg (Chicago).

Durkheim, Émile. "Value Judgments and Judgments of Reality" (1911). In *Sociology and Philosophy*, translated by D. F. Pocock, 80–97. With an introduction by J. G. Peristiany. Reprint with additions. New York: Free Press, 1974.

Eisenhower, Dwight D. Exec. Order 10730, 3 C.F.R. 389 (1954–1958), Providing Assistance for the Removal of an Obstruction of Justice Within the State of Arkansas. Online by Gerhard Peters and John T. Woolley, The American Presidency Project. https://www.presidency.ucsb.edu/node/210621.

Elliott, Philip. "Cory Booker Reminds Democrats What Fighting Back Looks Like." *Time*, April 1, 2025. https://time.com/7273556/cory-booker-filibuster-speech-takeaways.

Ellison, Ralph. *Invisible Man*. 2nd Vintage ed. New York: Vintage, 1995. First published in 1952 by Random House (New York).

Encyclopedia of Arkanasas. "Desegregation of Central High School." Last updated November 21, 2025. https://encyclopediaofarkansas.net/entries/desegregation-of-central-high-school-718.

Everett, Percival. *James*. New York: Doubleday, 2024.

Ewing, Giselle Ruhiyyih. "Musk Said Wisconsin Would Decide the Fate of Western Civilization. Now He Says He 'Expected to Lose.'" *Politico*, April 2, 2025. https://www.politico.com/news/2025/04/02/elon-musk-wisconsin-loss-reaction-00006129.

Farrell, Steven, et al. "Trump Announces Sudden Reversal on Tariffs, Lowering Most to 10% But Hiking China's to 125%." Reuters, April 9, 2025. https://www.reuters.com/world/trump-tariffs-live-markets-selloff-us-reciprocal-tariffs-kick-2025-04-09.

Faulders, Katherine, et al. "Timeline: Special Counsel's Probe into Trump's Efforts to Overturn 2020 Election." ABC News, October 14, 2025. https://abcnews.go.com/US/timeline-special-counsels-probe-trumps-efforts-overturn-2020/story?id=101537003.

Faulkner, William. *Requiem for a Nun*. New York: Vintage, 1954.

Feltham, Colin. *Failure*. The Art of Living Series. Durham, UK: Acumen, 2012.

Feuer, Alan. "Abrego Garcia Was Beaten and Tortured in El Salvador Prison, Lawyers Say." *New York Times*, July 2, 2025. https://www.nytimes.com/2025/07/02/us/politics/kilmar-abrego-garcia-el-salvador-trump-deportation.html.

Fiallo, Josh. "Stephen Miller Explicitly Ordered ICE Raid Home Depots." *Daily Beast*, June 11, 2025. https://www.thedailybeast.com/stephen-miller-explicitly-ordered-ice-raid-home-depots.

Findell, Elizabeth, et al. "The White House Marching Orders That Sparked the L.A. Migrant Crackdown." MSN, June 9, 2025. https://www.msn.com/en-us/news/us/the-white-house-marching-orders-that-sparked-the-l-a-migrant-crackdown/ar-AA1GoJCO.

Firestone, David. "The Supreme Court's Intolerable Ruling." *New York Times*, June 27, 2025. https://www.nytimes.com/2025/06/27/opinion/birthright-citizenship-case-supreme-court.html.

Fitzgerald, F. Scott. *The Great Gatsby*. Amazon Kindle, 2022. First published 1925 by Scribner (New York).

Fossum, Robert H., and John K. Roth. *The American Dream*. BAAS Pamphlets in American Studies 6. Liverpool, UK: British Association for American Studies, 1981.

———, eds. *American Ground: Vistas, Visions & Revisions*. St. Paul: Paragon, 1988.

The Franklin D. Roosevelt Presidential Library and Museum. "'Action, and Action Now': FDR's First 100 Days; A Special Exhibition Commemorating the Seventy-fifth Anniversary of the New Deal." Press release, February 10, 2008. https://www.fdrlibrary.org/documents/356632/390886/oheightone.pdf/86017c2f-ec9e-4eb3-a060-04282aed2ce4.

French, David. "MAGA Is Tearing Itself Apart over Jeffrey Epstein." *New York Times*, July 13, 2025. https://www.nytimes.com/2025/07/13/opinion/epstein-files-trump-maga.html.

French, David, and Vishakha Darbha. "The Worst Part of Pete Hegseth's Group Chat Debacle." *The Opinions* (podcast), *New York Times*, March 25, 2025, 10:49. https://www.nytimes.com/2025/03/25/opinion/pete-hegseth-security-breach-resign.html.

Fritze, John, et al. "Takeaways from the Supreme Court's Ruling on Power of Judges and Birthright Citizenship." CNN, June 27, 2025. https://www.cnn.com/2025/06/27/politics/takeaways-birthright-citizenship-supreme-court-decision.

Fussell, Paul. "The Last Curmudgeon." Interview by Anne Murphy Paul, *Psychology Today*, July 1, 1998. Last reviewed on June 4, 2025. https://www.psychologytoday.com/za/articles/199807/the-last-curmudgeon.

———. *Thank God for the Atom Bomb, and Other Essays*. New York: Summit, 1988.

Gamio, Lazaro, et al. "Tracking U.S. Military Killings in Boat Attacks." *New York Times*, January 10, 2026. https://www.nytimes.com/interactive/2025/10/29/us/us-caribbean-pacific-boat-strikes.html.

Garber, Alan M. "The Promise of American Higher Education." Harvard University, April 14, 2025. https://www.harvard.edu/president/news/2025/the-promise-of-american-higher-education.

Gecker, Jocelyn, and Linley Sanders. "Most Americans Disapprove of Trump's Treatment of Colleges, a New AP-NORC Poll Finds." AP, May 9, 2025. https://apnews.com/article/poll-college-trump-harvard-higher-education-109dae2e19d5fe570a7c02e105bab6e6.

Gessen, M. "Beware: We Are Entering a New Phase of the Trump Era." *New York Times*, May 28, 2025. https://www.nytimes.com/2025/05/28/opinion/trump-danger-normalization-shock.html.

The Gilder Lehrman Institute of American History. "My Country, 'Tis of Thee." 2012. https://www.gilderlehrman.org/sites/default/files/inline-pdfs/05508.230.01_FPS.pdf.

Glaude, Eddie S., Jr. *Begin Again: James Baldwin's America and Its Urgent Lessons for Our Own*. New York: Crown, 2020.

Goldberg, Jeffrey. "The Trump Administration Accidentally Texted Me Its War Plans." *Atlantic*, March 24, 2025. https://www.theatlantic.com/politics/archive/2025/03/trump-administration-accidentally-texted-me-its-war-plans/682151.

Goldberg, Jeffrey, and Shane Harris. "Here Are the Attack Plans That Trump's Advisors Shared on Signal." *Atlantic*, March 26, 2025. https://www.theatlantic.com/politics/archive/2025/03/signal-group-chat-attack-plans-hegseth-goldberg/682176.

Gooding, Dan, and Gabe Whisnant. "Linda McMahon Says Colleges Must Be 'In Sync' with Trump Administration." *Newsweek*, May 28, 2025. https://www.newsweek.com/linda-mcmahon-says-colleges-must-sync-trump-administration-2078065.

Gorman, Amanda. *The Hill We Climb: An Inaugural Poem for the Country*. Foreword by Oprah Winfrey. New York: Viking, 2021.

Graham, David A. "Donald Trump Doesn't Want You to Read This Article." *Atlantic Daily* (newsletter), August 6, 2025. https://www.theatlantic.com/newsletters/archive/2025/08/trump-epstein-saga-tactics/68377.

———. "Donald Trump's Plan to Subvert the Midterms Is Already Under Way." *Atlantic*, October 28, 2025. https://www.theatlantic.com/magazine/archive/2025/12/2026-midterms-trump-threat/684615.

———. "None of This Should Have Happened." *Atlantic*, January 13, 2026. https://www.theatlantic.com/newsletters/2026/01/escalation-ice-renee-good-minneapolis-shooting/685605.

Greathouse, Lowell. *Navigating Trumpworld: A Spiritual Guide for Turbulent Times*. Eugene, OR: Resource Publications, 2025.

Grissom, Grant. "A Plea for Donald Trump to Resign." *USA Today*, April 4, 2025, 6A. Copy possessed by John K. Roth.

Grob, Leonard, and John K. Roth. *Warnings: The Holocaust, Ukraine, and Endangered American Democracy*. Eugene, OR: Cascade Books, 2023.

Gross, Jenny. "Rights Groups Condemn Trump for Using 'Palestinian' as a Slur Against Schumer." *New York Times*, March 13, 2025. https://www.nytimes.com/2025/03/13/us/politics/trump-schumer-palestinian.html.

Grossman, David. "On Hope and Despair in the Middle East." *Haaretz*, July 8, 2014. https://www.haaretz.com/2014–17-08/ty-article/on-hope-and-despair/0000017f-dba1-d3ff-a7ff-fba18ac80000.

Groves, Stephen, and Ben Finley. "House Passes Defense Bill to Raise Troop Pay and Overhaul Weapons Purchases." AP, December 10, 2025. https://apnews.com/article/defense-bill-congress-trump-dd67d203accfb65b7604072ebb5da153.

Groves, Stephen, and Lisa Mascaro. "Pete Hegseth Faces Deepening Scrutiny from Congress Over Carribean Boat Strikes." PBS, December 3, 2025. https://www.pbs.org/newshour/politics/pete-hegseth-faces-deepening-scrutiny-from-congress-over-caribbean-boat-strikes.

Haberman, Maggie, and Tyler Pager. "6 Takeaways from Trump's Meeting with Putin." *New York Times*, August 16, 2025. https://www.nytimes.com/2025/08/15/us/politics/trump-putin-meeting-takeaways.html.

Haidar, Mark, and Aidan Calvelli. "A Landslide? Just 0.15 Percent of All Voters Determined Trump's 2024 Victory." *The Hill*, January 20, 2025. https://thehill.com/opinion/campaign/5094602-a-landslide-just-0-15-percent-of-all-voters-determined-trumps-2024-victory.

Halligan, Lindsey, et al. "Internal Review of Smithsonian Exhibitions and Materials." The White House, August 12, 2025. https://www.whitehouse.gov/wp-content/uploads/2025/08/Letter-Sec.-Bunch-Smithsonian-8.12.2025.pdf (dead link).

Hamilton, Alexander. *The Federalist*, no. 78: The Judiciary Department. https://avalon.law.yale.edu/18th_century/fed78.asp.

Hansen, Ronald J. "Elon Musk Doubles-down on Calling Sen. Mark Kelly a 'Traitor.'" *Arizona Republic*, March 28, 2025. https://www.azcentral.com/story/news/politics/arizona/2025/03/28/elon-musk-doubles-down-on-calling-sen-mark-kelly-a-traitor/82707328007.

Harris, Kamala. Address Conceding the 2024 Presidential Election, November 7, 2024. Online by Gerhard Peters and John T. Woolley, The American Presidency Project. https://www.presidency.ucsb.edu/node/375124.

Harwood, John. "Trump Is Objectively Bad for America. Why Won't More Journalists Say So?" *Zeteo*, June 18, 2025. https://zeteo.com/p/trump-is-objectively-bad-for-america.

Hassett, Kevin. Interview by George Stephanopoulos, *This Week*, April 6, 2025, on the ABC News YouTube channel (interview runs from about 7:48 to about 17:41): https://www.youtube.com/watch?v=JgFaIz_-qwg.

———. Interview by George Stephanopoulos. In "'This Week' Transcript 4-6-25: White House NEC Director Kevin Hassett, Sen. Cory Booker & Larry Summers." published by ABC News. https://abcnews.go.com/Politics/week-transcript-4-6-25-white-house-nec/story?id=120524384.

Hathaway, Oona A. "Trump's Strikes on Iran Were Unlawful. Here's Why That Matters." *New York Times*, June 23, 2025. https://www.nytimes.com/2025/06/23/opinion/international-world/trump-iran-strikes.html.

Hauhart, Robert C., and Mitja Sardoč, eds. *Routledge Handbook on the American Dream*. 2 vols. New York: Routledge, 2022–2023.

Hawthorne, Nathaniel. "Earth's Holocaust." Project Gutenberg. Release date: September 6, 2003. eBook #9231. Most recently updated: November 9, 2022. https://www.gutenberg.org/files/9231/9231-h/9231-h.htm.

Hett, Benjamin Carter. *The Death of Democracy: Hitler's Rise to Power and the Downfall of the Weimar Republic*. New York: Holt, 2018.

Ho, Vivian, et al. "The Chain Saw, the Salute and Other Moments from Musk's Time in Government." *Washington Post*, May 29, 2025. https://www.washingtonpost.com/politics/2025/05/29/elon-musk-doge-moments-trump-administration.

Holmes, Oliver Wendell. "Learning and Science" (1895). In *Collected Legal Papers*, 138–39. 1920. Reprint, New York: Smith, 1952.

Hubler, Shawn, et al. "Calif. Senator Forcibly Removed and Handcuffed After Interrupting Noem." *New York Times*, June 12, 2025. https://www.nytimes.com/2025/06/12/us/politics/senator-alex-padilla-handcuffed.html.

Hughes, Langston. "Harlem." In *American Ground: Vistas, Visions & Revisions*, edited by Robert H. Fossum and John K. Roth, 351. New York: Paragon, 1988.

———. "Let America Be America Again." In *American Ground: Vistas, Visions & Revisions*, edited by Robert H. Fossum and John K. Roth, 348–50. New York: Paragon, 1988.

Hunter, Paul. *Breaking Ground*. Eugene, OR: Silverfish Review, 2005.

———. "Hunter Discusses Reshaping 'Shopworn' Language." Interview by Gwen Ifill. *PBS News Hour*, July 9, 2007. https://www.pbs.org/newshour/show/hunter-discusses-reshaping-shopworn-language#transcript.

———. *Ripening: Poems*. Eugene, OR: Silverfish Review, 2007.

Hutzler, Alexandra. "Trump and the 'Unitary Executive': The Presidential Power Theory Driving His 2nd Term." ABC News, February 7, 2025. https://abcnews.go.com/Politics/trump-unitary-executive-presidential-power-theory-driving-2nd/story?id=118481290.

———. "Trump Vowed to Be a 'Peacemaker' but Iran and Other Conflicts Only Ramping Up on His Watch." ABC News, June 21, 2025. https://abcnews.go.com/Politics/trump-vowed-peacemaker-foreign-conflicts-ramping-watch/story?id=122937241.

Hutzler, Alexandra, et al. "Trump Says 'It's Going Very Well' After Tariffs Roil Markets." ABC News, April 3, 2025. https://abcnews.go.com/Politics/trust-president-trump-white-house-defending-tariffs-amid/story?id=120449641.

Ismay, John. "Who's In and Who's Out at the Naval Academy's Library?" *New York Times*, April 11, 2025. https://www.nytimes.com/2025/04/11/us/politics/naval-academy-banned-books.html.

Jackson, Jon, and Gabe Whisnant. "Donald Trump Tells National Prayer Breakfast: 'Bring God Back.'" *Newsweek*, February 10, 2025. https://www.newsweek.com/donald-trump-tells-national-prayer-breakfast-bring-god-back-2027362.

Jacoby, Jeff. "Elie Wiesel's Love of America." First published in the *Boston Globe*, July 4, 2016. https://jeffjacoby.com/18964/elie-wiesel-love-of-america.

James, William. "The Teaching of Philosophy in Our Colleges." *Nation* 23 (1876): 178–79.

Jenkins, Jack. "At Inauguration, Trump Says He Was 'Saved by God to Make America Great Again.'" *Religion News Service*, January 20, 2025. https://religionnews.com/2025/01/20/at-trumps-inauguration-president-says-he-was-saved-by-god-to-make-america-great-again.

Johansen, Ben. "Trump Says He Would 'Love' to Send Violent American Citizens to Foreign Prisons." *Politico*, April 25, 2025. https://www.politico.com/news/2025/04/25/trump-americans-foreign-prisons-interview-00309297.

Johns Hopkins Bloomberg School of Public Health. "2025 National Survey of Gun Policy." https://publichealth.jhu.edu/center-for-gun-violence-solutions/data/national-survey-of-gun-policy.

Johnson, Lyndon B. Commencement Address at Howard University: "To Fulfill These Rights." June 4, 1965. Online by Gerhard Peters and John T. Woolley, The American Presidency Project. https://www.presidency.ucsb.edu/node/241312.

Jones, Jeffrey M. "American Pride Slips to New Low." Gallup, June 30, 2025. https://news.gallup.com/poll/692150/american-pride-slips-new-low.aspx.

Jordan, Miriam. "What the Supreme Court's Ruling Will Mean for Birthright Citizenship." *New York Times*, June 29, 2025. https://www.nytimes.com/2025/06/27/us/politics/27nat-birthright-citizenship-impacts.html.

Jouvenal, Justin, et al. "GOP Lawmakers Take Aim at Anti-Trump Rulings, Nationwide Injunctions." *Washington Post*, April 1, 2025. https://www.washingtonpost.com/politics/2025/04/01/trump-judges-injunctions-congress-impeach.

———. "Supreme Court Appears Skeptical of Legality of Most of Trump's Tariffs." *Washington Post*, November 5, 2025. https://www.washingtonpost.com/politics/2025/11/05/tariffs-trump-supreme-court-arguments.

Jurecic, Quinta. "Emil Bove Is a Sign of the Times." *Atlantic*, July 30, 2025. https://www.theatlantic.com/ideas/archive/2025/07/the-route-to-a-plum-judicial-appointment/683706.

Kaloi, Stephanie. "'American Fiction' Author Percival Everett Explains Why N-Word Is 'Inoffensive' in the Right Context." *Yahoo*, March 24, 2024. https://www.yahoo.com/entertainment/american-fiction-author-percival-everett-011302413.html.

Kamarck, Elaine. "How DOGE Cutbacks Could Create a Major Backlash." Brookings Institution, February 14, 2025. https://www.brookings.edu/articles/how-doge-cutbacks-could-create-a-major-backlash.

Kanno-Youngs, Zolan, and Luke Broadwater. "Trump Gives Clemency to More Than Two Dozen, Including Political Allies." *New York Times*, May 28, 2025. Updated May 30, 2025. https://www.nytimes.com/2025/05/28/us/politics/trump-pardons-hoover-grimm-chrisley.html.

Khardori, Ankush. "The Epstein Files Timeline Raises Real Questions for Trump." *Politico*, July 25, 2025. https://www.politico.com/news/magazine/2025/07/25/trump-epstein-files-timeline-column-00475334.

———. "The Supreme Court May Not Step In and Save Trump's Tariffs." *Politico*, May 29, 2025. https://www.politico.com/news/magazine/2025/05/29/trump-tariffs-court-defeat-00374194.

Kiley, Jocelyn, et al. "Trump's Job Approval and Views of His Personal Traits." Pew Research Center, August 14, 2025. https://www.pewresearch.org/politics/2025/08/14/trumps-job-approval-and-views-of-his-personal-traits.

Kim, Seung Min. "Lovefest or Cabinet Meeting? For Donald Trump, It's Both." AP, April 30, 2025. https://apnews.com/article/trump-cabinet-meeting-stocks-detainees-rubio-musk-3fdf4f5019bf5b578c466e32aee2ae79.

King, Jon. "Democrat Mallory McMorrow Is the First to Announce a 2026 Run for Michigan's Open US Senate Seat." *Michigan Advance*, April 2, 2025. https://michiganadvance.com/2025/04/02/democrat-mallory-mcmorrow-is-the-first-to-announce-a-2026-run-for-michigans-open-us-senate-seat.

King, Jordan. "Erika Kirk and Donald Trump Had Very Different Memorial Messages." *Newsweek*, September 22, 2025. https://www.newsweek.com/erika-kirk-donald-trump-message-charlie-kirk-memorial-2133593.

King, Martin Luther, Jr. "I Have a Dream." In *American Ground: Vistas, Visions & Revisions*, edited by Robert H. Fossum and John K. Roth, 365–66. New York: Paragon, 1988.

Kingsberry, Janay, and Kelsey Ables. "Trump Says Smithsonian Is Too Focused on Slavery. Scholars See Sanitizing." *Washington Post*, August 21, 2025. https://www.washingtonpost.com/entertainment/art/2025/08/20/trump-smithsonian-slavery-historians.

Kirkpatrick, David D. "The Number: How Much Is Trump Pocketing off the Presidency?" *New Yorker*, August 11, 2025. https://www.newyorker.com/magazine/2025/08/18/the-number.

Klein, Ezra, and Derek Thompson. *Abundance*. New York: Avid Reader, 2025.

Kochi, Sudiksha. "Treasury Secretary Defends Tariffs, Says Cheap Goods Not 'Essence of the American Dream.'" *USA Today*, March 7, 2025. https://www.usatoday.com/story/news/politics/2025/03/07/scott-bessent-trump-tariffs-american-dream-goods-prices/81943904007.

Kristof, Nicholas. "The Waste Musk Created." *New York Times*, June 21, 2025. https://www.nytimes.com/2025/06/21/opinion/waste-musk-trump.html.

Kristofferson, Kris. "The Pilgrim, Chapter 33." Track 9 on *The Silver Tongued Devil and I*. Monument Z 30679, 1971, LP; mp3 audio file, Apple Music, © Sony Music Entertainment.

Kristol, William. "Bill Kristol: March to Dictatorship." Interview by Tim Miller. *Bulwark Podcast*, August 25, 2025, 50:00. https://www.thebulwark.com/p/bill-kristol-march-to-dictatorship.

———. "Bill Kristol: Trump Is a Moral Monster." Interview by Tim Miller. *Bulwark Podcast*, July 28, 2025, 1:05:00. https://www.thebulwark.com/p/bill-kristol-trump-is-a-moral-monster.

———. "Bill Kristol: A Weekend of Tragedy." Interview by Tim Miller. *Bulwark Podcast*, December 15, 2025. https://podcasts.apple.com/us/podcast/bill-kristol-a-weekend-of-tragedy/id1447684472?i=1000741435097.

———. "Democracy Dies in Daylight." *Bulwark*, August 4, 2025. https://www.thebulwark.com/p/killing-democracy-not-bothering-hide-it-epstein-trump-maxwell-texas-redistricting-gerrymander-democrats-abbott-labor-statistics-jobs-report.

———. "Toward Darkness or Dawn." *Bulwark*, August 5, 2025. https://www.thebulwark.com/p/maybe-the-american-experiment-isnt-dead-trump-poll-epstein-inflation-tariffs-unpopular.

Kruse, Michael. "Does Trump Actually Think He's God?" *Politico Magazine*, May 30, 2025. https://www.politico.com/news/magazine/2025/05/30/trump-god-messiah-assassination-attempt-00362322.

Kunzelman, Michael. "Immigration Officials Can't Re-detain Kilmar Abrego Garcia Without a Hearing, Federal Judge Orders." PBS News, December 12, 2025. https://www.pbs.org/newshour/nation/immigration-officials-cant-re-detain-kilmar-abrego-garcia-without-a-hearing-federal-judge-orders.

Lalljee, Jason. "Crypto, Wallets, Bibles: Trump's Assets Top $1.6 Billion in Latest Disclosure." *Axios*, June 16, 2025. https://www.axios.com/2025/06/16/trump-mobile-crypto-merch-earnings-disclosure.

Lampe, Joanna R. "Nationwide Injunctions from January 20, 2025, Through March 27, 2025." Congressional Research Service, May 16, 2025. https://www.congress.gov/crs-product/R48476.

———. "Nationwide Injunctions: Law, History, and Proposals for Reform." Congressional Research Service, September 8, 2021. https://www.congress.gov/crs-product/R46902.

Langfitt, Frank. "Hundreds of Scholars Say US Is Swiftly Heading Toward Authoritarianism." Interview by Scott Detrow. *Trump's Terms* (podcast), NPR, April 22, 2025, 10:00. https://www.npr.org/2026/01/01/1267665416/us-scholars-trump-authoritarianism.

Lardner, Richard, and Dake Kang. "Thousands of Trump Bibles Were Printed in China as He Campaigned Against Trade Practices." *PBS Newshour*, October 9, 2024. https://www.pbs.org/newshour/politics/thousands-of-trump-bibles-were-printed-in-china-as-he-campaigned-against-trade-practices.

Lebowitz, Megan. "Vance Says U.S. 'Not at War with Iran, We're at War with Iran's Nuclear Program.'" NBC News, June 22, 2025. https://www.nbcnews.com/politics/trump-administration/vance-says-us-not-war-iran-re-war-irans-nuclear-program-rcna214329.

Legum, Judd. "7 Things Everyone Should Know About Trump's Megabill." *Popular Information* (newsletter), June 30, 2025. https://popular.info/p/7-things-everyone-should-know-about.

Lamothe, Dan, et al. "Trump, Hegseth Lecture Military Leaders in Rare, Politically Charged Summit." *Washington Post*, September 30, 2025. https://www.washingtonpost.com/national-security/2025/09/30/hegseth-military-meeting-trump-generals.

Leonhart, David. *Ours Was the Shining Future: The Story of the American Dream*. New York: Random House, 2023.

Lepore, Jill. "The Failed Ideas That Drive Elon Musk." *New York Times*, April 4, 2025. https://www.nytimes.com/2025/04/04/opinion/elon-musk-doge-technocracy.html.

———. "How Originalism Killed the Constitution." *Atlantic*, September 22, 2025. https://www.theatlantic.com/magazine/archive/2025/10/constitutional-originalism-amendment/683961.

———. *We the People: A History of the U.S. Constitution*. New York: Liveright, 2025.

Lerer, Lisa. "Clinton Wins Popular Vote by Nearly 2.9 Million." AP, December 22, 2016. https://apnews.com/article/2c7a5afc13824161a25d8574e10ff4e7.

Levinson, Adam. "Presidential Election Day Act of 1845 and the Election of 1840." *Statutes and Stories* (blog), August 3, 2020. https://www.statutesandstories.com/blog_html/presidential-election-day-act-of-1845-and-the-election-of-1840.

Levitsky, Steven, et al. "How Will We Know When We Have Lost Our Democracy?" *New York Times*, May 8, 2025. https://www.nytimes.com/2025/05/08/opinion/trump-authoritarianism-democracy.html.

Library of Congress. "Today in History—June 14." Library of Congress. https://www.loc.gov/item/today-in-history/june-14.

Lincoln, Abraham. Second Annual Message to Congress. December 1, 1862. Online by Gerhard Peters and John T. Woolley, The American Presidency Project. https://www.presidency.ucsb.edu/node/202180.

The Lincoln Project. *God Made a Dictator*. video (1:19). Published on The Lincoln Project website in January 2024. https://action.lincolnproject.us/god_made_a_dictator.

Liu, Jennifer, and Amanda Gorman. "Read the Full Text of Amanda Gorman's Inaugural Poem 'The Hill We Climb'" For the inauguration reading, see "WATCH: Amanda Gorman Reads Inauguration Poem, 'The Hill We Climb'" on *PBS Newshour* YouTube page: https://www.youtube.com/watch?v=LZ055ilIiN4.

Lopez, Ashley. "How We Know Voter Fraud Is Very Rare in U.S. Elections." NPR, October 11, 2024. https://www.npr.org/2024/10/11/nx-s1-5147732/voter-fraud-explainer.

Luttig, J. Michael. "President for Life: Donald Trump Is Trying to Amass the Powers of a King." *Atlantic*, October 28, 2025. https://www.theatlantic.com/magazine/archive/2025/12/trump-third-term-authoritarianism/684616.

———. "The Self-Evident Truths of Freedom—and of Tyranny." Telos.News, July 2, 2025. https://www.telos.news/p/luttig-the-self-evident-truths-of-freedom.

MacLeish, Archibald. *Land of the Free*. New York: Da Capo, 1977. First published 1938 by Harcourt, Brace (New York).

Mandavilli, Apoorva, et al. "Trump Administration Abruptly Cuts Billions from State Health Services." *New York Times*, March 26, 2025. https://www.nytimes.com/2025/03/26/health/trump-state-health-grants-cuts.html.

Matthews, Alex Leeds, et al. "School Shootings in the US: Fast Facts." CNN, December 13, 2025. https://www.cnn.com/us/school-shootings-fast-facts-dg.

McBride, Sarah. "Sarah McBride on Why the Left Lost on Trans Rights." Interview by Ezra Klein. *Ezra Klein Show* (podcast), *New York Times*, June 17, 2025, 1:35:00. https://www.nytimes.com/2025/06/17/opinion/ezra-klein-podcast-sarah-mcbride.html.

Mframa, Kofi. "Has Gen Z Given Up on the American Dream?" *USA Today*, May 28, 2025, 7A. https://www.pressreader.com/usa/usa-today-us-edition/20250528/281663965935586.

Milman, Oliver. "Ted Cruz Ensured Trump Spending Bill Slashed Weather Forecasting Funding." *Guardian*, July 9, 2025. https://www.theguardian.com/us-news/2025/jul/07/ted-cruz-trump-weather-forecasting-cuts.

Milton Bradley. *The American Dream Game*. Springfield, MA: Milton Bradley, 1979.

Montoya-Galvez, Camilo. "Trump Invokes 1798 Alien Enemies Act, Orders Deportation of Suspected Venezuelan Gang Members." CBS News, March 16, 2025. https://www.cbsnews.com/news/trump-invokes-1798-alien-enemies-act.

Moore, Elena, et al. "Trump on Fourth of July Signs 'One Big Beautiful Bill' to Implement His Agenda." NPR, July 4, 2025. https://www.npr.org/2025/07/03/nx-s1-5454841/house-republicans-trump-tax-bill-medicaid.

Mullin, Benjamin. "NPR and PBS Vow to Fight Trump's Order to Cut Funding." *New York Times*, May 2, 2025. https://www.nytimes.com/2025/05/02/business/media/npr-pbs-federal-funding.html.

Mullin, Markwayne. Interview by Shannon Bream, *Fox News Sunday*, April 6, 2025. https://www.foxnews.com/video/6371134022112.

Nadell, Pamela S. *Antisemitism, an American Tradition*. New York: Norton, 2025.

Nakashima, Ellen, et al. "Trump Ousts Members of National Security Council Staff." *Washington Post*, April 3, 2025. https://www.washingtonpost.com/national-security/2025/04/03/trump-national-security-council-firings.

Nakashima, Ellen, et al. "National Security Agency Chief Ousted After Far-right Activist Urged His Removal." *Washington Post*, April 4, 2025. https://www.washingtonpost.com/national-security/2025/04/03/nsa-director-fired-tim-haugh.

NBC 5 Chicago staff, and JB Pritzker. "Full Text: Illinois Gov. JB Pritzker's 'State of the State' Address." February 19, 2025. https://www.nbcchicago.com/news/local/chicago-politics/full-text-illinois-gov-jb-pritzkers-state-of-the-state-address/3678119.

Nehamas, Nicholas, and Erica L. Green. "Trump Says He'll Protect Women, 'Like It or Not,' Evoking His History of Misogyny." *New York Times*, October 31, 2024. https://www.nytimes.com/2024/10/31/us/politics/trump-women-like-it-or-not.html.

Nevins, Allan. *James Truslow Adams: Historian of the American Dream*. Urbana: University of Illinois Press, 1968.

New York Times. "President Trump's Approval Rating: Latest Polls." *New York Times*, August 10, 2025. Updated daily. https://www.nytimes.com/interactive/polls/donald-trump-approval-rating-polls.html.

New York Times editorial board. "A Comprehensive Accounting of Trump's Culture of Corruption." *New York Times*, June 7, 2025. https://www.nytimes.com/2025/06/07/opinion/trump-corruption.html.

Ngo, Madeleine, and Margot Sanger-Katz. "Richest Gain Most and Poorest Face Steepest Cuts Under G.O.P. Law, Analysis Finds." *New York Times*, August 11, 2025. https://www.nytimes.com/2025/08/11/us/politics/trump-gop-policy-bill-rich-poor.html.

Niiya, Brian. "Civilian Exclusion Orders." *The Densho Encyclopedia*. https://encyclopedia.densho.org/Civilian_exclusion_orders.

NPR Network. "The Fight Is On. How Redistricting Could Unfold in 8 Entangled States." NPR, August 14, 2025. https://www.npr.org/2025/08/14/nx-s1–5501537/texas-california-gerrymandering-redistricting.

Obama, Barack. *We're a Nation of Tinkers and Dreamers*. video (1:29). Published on The Obama White House Facebook on April 13, 2016. https://www.facebook.com/watch/?v=10154293478494238.

Olmsted, Edith. "The Sickening Living Conditions at 'Alligator Alcatraz.'" *New Republic*, July 9, 2025. https://newrepublic.com/post/197740/donald-trump-alligator-alcatraz-already-massive-disaster.

Olson, Trygve. "Trump Isn't an Anomaly: He's a Warning." *Seaching for Hope*, Substack, May 31, 2025. https://trygveolson.substack.com/p/trump-isnt-an-anomaly.

Orden, Erica. "Ghislaine Maxwell Transferred to Less Restrictive Prison after DOJ Meeting." *Politico*, August 1, 2025. https://www.politico.com/news/2025/08/01/ghislaine-maxwell-prison-doj-meeting-00488424.

Ordoñez, Franco. "Trump Pardons Honduran Ex-president Who Was Convicted of Drug Crimes." NPR, December 2, 2025. https://www.npr.org/2025/12/02/nx-s1-5628382/trump-pardons-honduran-ex-president-juan-orlando-hernandez.

Orth, Taylor, and David Montgomery. "Donald Trump Approval, Ghislaine Maxwell, Gerrymandering, Inflation, and Unemployment: August 9–11, 2025 Economist/YouGov Poll." YouGov, August 12, 2025. https://today.yougov.com/politics/articles/52753-donald-trump-approval-gerrymandering-texas-redistricting-jeffrey-epstein-ghislaine-maxwell-inflation-economy-unemployment-august-9-–11-2025-economist-yougov-poll.

Pager, Tyler, et al. "Trump's Relationship with Musk Remains Icy as Public Spat Goes Private." *New York Times*, June 6, 2025. Updated June 13, 2025. https://www.nytimes.com/live/2025/06/06/us/elon-musk-trump-feud.

Paine, Thomas. *The American Crisis*, No. 1 (1776). In Project Gutenberg's *The Writings of Thomas Paine*, Vol. 1. Release Date: February 7, 2010 [EBook #3741]. Last Updated: November 15, 2012. https://www.gutenberg.org/files/3741/3741-h/3741-h.htm.

———. *Common Sense* (1776). Release Date: n.d. [EBook #147]. Project Gutenberg: https://www.gutenberg.org/files/147/147-h/147-h.htm.

Parker, Ashley, and Michael Scherer. "'I Run the Country and the World.'" *Atlantic*, April 28, 2025. https://www.theatlantic.com/magazine/archive/2025/06/trump-second-term-comeback/682573.

Patel, Vimal. "Thousands Ask Harvard Not to 'Give in' and Pay Fine to Trump." *New York Times*, August 14, 2025. https://www.nytimes.com/2025/08/14/us/harvard-petition-trump.html.

———. "What the Republicans' New Policy Bill Means for Higher Education." *New York Times*, July 3, 2025. https://www.nytimes.com/2025/07/03/us/trump-bill-education-college-student-loans.html.

PBS. "American Revolution Facts: Battles, Casualties, and More." https://www.pbs.org/kenburns/the-american-revolution/american-revolution-facts-battles-casualties-and-more.

Peller, Lauren, et al. "'Immoral': Democrat Hakeem Jeffries Blasts Trump Megabill in Record-breaking, 8-hour-plus Speech." ABC News, July 3, 2025. https://abcnews.go.com/Politics/democrat-hakeem-jeffries-marathon-magic-minute-speech-blasts/story?id=123444742.

Perry, Stephanie, and Marc Trussler. "Poll: Trump's MAGA Base Is Still Behind Him—But Cracks Are Showing Ahead of 2026." NBC, December 14, 2025. https://www.nbcnews.com/politics/politics-news/poll-trumps-maga-base-still-cracks-are-showing-ahead-2026-rcna248722.

Pew Research Center. "Economic Ratings and Concerns." April 23, 2025. https://www.pewresearch.org/politics/2025/04/23/economic-ratings-and-concerns-2025.

Psaki, Jen. "The Architect of Trump's Immigration Policy Could Be Profiting Off ICE's Cruelty." MSNBC, June 25, 2025. https://www.msnbc.com/top-stories/latest/stephen-miller-palantir-profit-ice-raids-rcna215021.

Putnam, Robert D. *Our Kids: The American Dream in Crisis*. New York: Simon & Schuster, 2015.

Quinn, Melissa. "Trump Wants to Punish People for Flag Burning. Is Burning the American Flag Illegal?" CBS News, August 25, 2025. https://www.cbsnews.com/news/trump-flag-burning-executive-order.

Rahman, Khaleda. "Trump Calls on Pam Bondi to Take Action Against Opponents 'Now.'" *Newsweek*, September 22, 2025. https://www.newsweek.com/trump-calls-pam-bondi-take-action-against-opponents-now-2133221.

Rampell, Catherine. "Trump's Big Budget Bomb." Interview by Ezra Klein. *Ezra Klein Show* (podcast), *New York Times*, May 23, 2025, 1:05:00. https://www.nytimes.com/2025/05/23/opinion/ezra-klein-podcast-catherine-rampell.html.

Rattner, Steven. "How Bad Is This Bill? The Answer in 10 Charts." *New York Times*, July 3, 2025. https://www.nytimes.com/interactive/2025/07/03/opinion/domestic-policy-bill-in-charts.html.

Rauch, Jonathan. "One Word Describes Trump." *Atlantic*, February 24, 2025. https://www.theatlantic.com/ideas/archive/2025/02/corruption-trump-administration/681794.

Ravitch, Diane, ed. *The American Reader: Words That Moved a Nation*. New York: HarperCollins, 1991.

Reed, Rachel. "Are Presidents Above the Law? 50 Years Ago the Supreme Court Said No." Interview with Neil Eggleston. *Harvard Law Today*, July 31, 2024. https://hls.harvard.edu/today/are-presidents-above-the-law-50-years-ago-the-supreme-court-said-no.

Richardson, Heather Cox. "July 14, 2025." Sustack, *Letters from an American*, July 14, 2025. https://heathercoxrichardson.substack.com/p/july-14–2025.

Rittner, Carol, and John K. Roth, eds. *Stress Test: The Israel-Hamas War and Christian-Jewish Relations*. Poughkeepsie, NY: iPub Cloud International, 2025.

———, eds. *This Time: Teaching the Holocaust Today*. Poughkeepsie, NY: iPub Cloud International, 2026.

Roberts, Molly. "Trump's New Crypto Business Is a Religion." *Washington Post*, May 30, 2025. https://www.washingtonpost.com/opinions/2025/05/30/trump-crypto-bitcoin-treasury.

Robinson, Edwin Arlington. "Richard Cory" (1897). The Poetry Foundation. https://www.poetryfoundation.org/poems/44982/richard-cory.

Robledo, Anthony. "SpaceX Starship Rocket Breaks Up Again After Last 2 Attempts Ended in Explosions." *USA Today*, May 27, 2025. Updated May 28, 2025. https://www.usatoday.com/story/news/nation/2025/05/27/spacex-starship-rocket-launch/83884398007.

Romm, Tony, and Ana Swanson. "Trump Says Tariffs Will Stay Until Trade Deficit Disappears." *New York Times*, April 6, 2025. https://www.nytimes.com/2025/04/06/us/politics/trump-tariffs-aides-recession.html.

Roosevelt, Franklin D. Address at Dedication of Great Smoky Mountains National Park. September 2, 1940. Online by Gerhard Peters and John T. Woolley, The American Presidency Project. https://www.presidency.ucsb.edu/node/209936.

———. Exec. Order No. 9066, 3 C.F.R. 111 (1942), Authorizing the Secretary of War To Prescribe Military Areas. Online by Gerhard Peters and John T. Woolley, The American Presidency Project. https://www.presidency.ucsb.edu/node/210838.

Rose, Andy. "Attacks on Harvard by Trump Administration Have Built for Months. A Timeline of the Dispute." CNN, July 23, 2025. Updated September 30, 2025. https://www.cnn.com/2025/04/26/us/harvard-university-trump-timeline.

Ross, Garrett, et al. "Playbook: Homan Makes Himself Heard." *Politico*, July 13, 2025. https://www.politico.com/newsletters/playbook/2025/07/13/homan-makes-himself-heard-00450236.

Roth, John K. *The American Dream*. Springfield, VA: The Teaching Company, 1992.

———. *American Dreams: Meditations on Life in the United States*. San Francisco: Chandler & Sharp, 1976.

———. *A Consuming Fire: Encounters with Elie Wiesel and the Holocaust*. 1979. Reprint, Eugene, OR: Wipf & Stock, 2016.

———. *The Failures of Ethics: Confronting the Holocaust, Genocide, and Other Mass Atrocities*. Oxford: Oxford University Press, 2015.

———. *Holocaust Politics*. 2001. Reprint, Eugene, OR: Wipf & Stock, 2016.

———. *Private Needs, Public Selves: Talk About Religion in America*. Public Expressions of Religion in America. Urbana: University of Illinois Press, 1997.

———. *Sources of Holocaust Insight: Learning and Teaching About the Genocide*. Eugene, OR: Cascade Books, 2020.

Ryan, Allan A., Jr. *Quiet Neighbors: Prosecuting Nazi War Criminals in America*. San Diego: Harcourt Brace Jovanovich, 1984.

Ryan, Kay. *The Niagara River: Poems*. New York: Grove, 2005.

Saad, Lydia. "Surge in U.S. Concern About Immigration Has Abated." Gallup, July 11, 2025. https://news.gallup.com/poll/692522/surge-concern-immigration-abated.aspx.

Safdar, Khadeeja, and Joe Palazzolo. "Jeffrey Epstein's Friends Sent Him Bawdy Letters for a 50th Birthday Album. One Was from Donald Trump." *Wall Street Journal*, July 17, 2025. https://www.wsj.com/politics/trump-jeffrey-epstein-birthday-letter-we-have-certain-things-in-common-f918d796?gaa_.

Safina, Carl. "To Take on Trump, Think Like a Lion." *New York Times*, May 27, 2025. https://www.nytimes.com/2025/05/27/opinion/trump-movement-lions-opposition.html.

Samuel, Lawrence R. *The American Dream: A Cultural History*. Syracuse: Syracuse University Press, 2012.

Sanchez, Ray, et al. "Federal Funding Freeze on Nation's Oldest University Likely to Stay in Place Well into Summer after First Court Hearing." CNN, April 28, 2025. https://www.cnn.com/2025/04/28/us/harvard-trump-court-hearing.

Sands, Philippe. "How Far Does Trump's Immunity Go?" *Atlantic*, October 6, 2025. https://www.theatlantic.com/ideas/archive/2025/10/trump-presidential-immunity/684413.

Sanger, David E., et al. "Trump Lays Out a Vision of Power Restrained Only by 'My Own Morality.'" *New York Times*, January 8, 2026. https://www.nytimes.com/2026/01/08/us/politics/trump-interview-power-morality.html.

Savage, Charlie. "Was Trump's Iran Attack Illegal? Presidential War Powers, Explained." *New York Times*, June 23, 2025. https://www.nytimes.com/2025/06/23/us/politics/trump-iran-war-powers-constitution.html.

Savage, Charlie, and Luke Broadwater. "Trump's Order on Flag Burning Reveals Its Own Limits." *New York Times*, August 25, 2025. https://www.nytimes.com/live/2025/08/25/us/trump-news#trump-flag-burning-executive-order.

Scanlon, Kyla. "How the Attention Economy Is Devouring Gen Z—and the Rest of Us." Interview by Ezra Klein. *Ezra Klein Show* (podcast), *New York Times*, July 8, 2025, 1:05:00. https://www.nytimes.com/2025/07/08/opinion/ezra-klein-podcast-kyla-scanlon.html.

Scherer, Michael. "Trump Says He Decides What 'America First' Means." *Atlantic*, June 14, 2025. https://www.theatlantic.com/politics/archive/2025/06/trump-interview-iran-israel/683192.

Schliefer, Theodore, et al. "Young Aides Emerge as Enforcers in Musk's Broadside Against Government." *New York Times*, February 7, 2025. https://www.nytimes.com/2025/02/07/us/politics/musk-doge-aides.html.

Schmidt, Michael S., and Michael C. Bender. "University of Virginia President Resigns Under Pressure from Trump Administration." *New York Times*, June 27, 2025. https://www.nytimes.com/2025/06/27/us/politics/uva-president-resigns-jim-ryan-trump.html.

Schmidt, Michael S., and Alan Blinder. "Harvard Leaders See Only Bad Outcomes Ahead as They Battle Trump." *New York Times*, May 8, 2025. Updated May 13, 2025. https://www.nytimes.com/2025/05/08/us/harvard-trump-court-case-negotiation.html.

Schmidt, Michael S., et al. "Why Trump and Harvard Have Not Reached a Deal." *New York Times*, December 3, 2025. https://www.nytimes.com/2025/12/03/us/politics/trump-harvard.html.

Schwabish, Jonathan. "The Implications of Shrinking the Federal Workforce by DOGE's Recommended 75 Percent." Urban Institute, January 30, 2025. https://www.urban.org/urban-wire/implications-shrinking-federal-workforce-doges-recommended-75-percent.

Sereny, Gitta. *Into That Darkness: An Examination of Conscience*. 1974. New York: Vintage, 1983. First published 1974 by McGraw-Hill (New York).

Serwer, Adam. "The New Dark Age." *Atlantic*, May 27, 2025. https://www.theatlantic.com/ideas/archive/2025/05/trump-defund-schools-research-republicans/682742.

Shane, Peter M. "This Is the Presidency John Roberts Has Built." *Atlantic*, July 21, 2025. https://www.theatlantic.com/ideas/archive/2025/07/supreme-court-roberts-trump-dictator/683576.

Sheth, Sonam. "Mitch McConnell Says People Worried About Medicaid Cuts Will 'Get Over It.'" *Newsweek*, June 24, 2025. https://www.newsweek.com/mitch-mcconnell-medicaid-get-over-it-report-2090245.

Shuham, Matt. "Anti-Muslim Extremist Laura Loomer Flew to Debate with Trump." Huffpost/Yahoo News, September 11, 2024. https://ca.news.yahoo.com/anti-muslim-extremist-laura-loomer-005426647.html.

Sisak, Michael R., et al. "Guilty: Trump Becomes First Former US President Convicted of Felony Crimes." AP, May 31, 2024. https://apnews.com/article/trump-trial-deliberations-jury-testimony-verdict-85558c6d08efb434d05b694364470aa0.

———. "What to Know about the Justice Department's Jeffrey Epstein Files." AP, December 10, 2025. https://apnews.com/article/epstein-justice-department-trump-fbi-files-7b7e45b283a8344b05f3a47640a960ae.

Smialek, Jeanna, and Steven Erlanger. "Now Europe Knows What Trump's Team Calls It Behind Its Back: 'Pathetic.'" *New York Times*, March 25, 2025. https://www.nytimes.com/2025/03/25/world/europe/signal-jeffrey-goldberg-message-hegseth.html.

Smith, Jack. *Final Report of the Special Counsel Under 28 C.F.R. § 600.8*. Published by the United States Department of Justice, January 7, 2025. https://www.justice.gov/storage/Report-of-Special-Counsel-Smith-Volume-1-January-2025.pdf.

Smith, Maggie. "Good Bones." *Waxwing Literary Journal*, Issue IX, Summer 2016. https://waxwingmag.org/items/Issue9/28_Smith-Good-Bones.php#top.

Smith, Talmon Joseph. "America Has Never Been Wealthier. Here's Why It Doesn't Feel That Way." *New York Times*, March 31, 2025. https://www.nytimes.com/2025/03/31/business/economy/wealth-cash-inequality.html.

Snyder, Timothy. *On Tyranny: Twenty Lessons from the Twentieth Century*. New York: Duggan, 2017.

———. "Trump's Hitlerian Month: A September to Remember." *Thinking About*, Substack, September 29, 2024. https://snyder.substack.com/p/trumps-hitlerian-month.

Sontag, Frederick, and John K. Roth. *The American Religious Experience: The Roots, Trends, and Future of Theology*. New York: Harper & Row, 1972.

Sottile, Zoe. "Marine Corps Veteran Says He Feels Betrayed after His Father Was Arrested by Masked Federal Agents in Southern California." CNN, June 23, 2025. https://www.cnn.com/2025/06/23/us/narciso-barranco-father-detained-santa-ana.

Srinivasan, Hiranmayi, and Amanda Morelli. "The American Dream Now Costs $4.4 Million." *Investopedia*, September 4, 2024. https://www.investopedia.com/cost-of-the-american-dream-2024-8705906.

Stafford, William. *Even in Quiet Places: Poems*. Lewiston, ID: Confluence, 1996. Lanham, MD: Distributed by National Book Network, 1996.

———. *The Methow River Poems*. Poetry in the Environment. Lewiston, ID: Confluence, 1995.

Stanton, Elizabeth Cady, et al. "The Declaration of Sentiments and Resolutions (1848)." Reprinted from Stanton et al., eds., *A History of Woman Suffrage*, vol. 1, n.p. 2nd ed. (1889) on the United States National Park Service website: https://www.nps.gov/common/uploads/teachers/lessonplans/Declaration%20of%20Sentiments.pdf.

Styron, William. *Sophie's Choice*. New York: Random House, 1979.

Sunstein, Cass R. "This Theory Is Behind Trump's Power Grab." *New York Times*, February 26, 2025. https://www.nytimes.com/2025/02/26/opinion/trump-roberts-unitary-executive-theory.html.

Svitek, Patrick. "Trump Suggests 'Bad Genes' to Blame for Undocumented Immigrants Who Commit Murders." *Washington Post*, October 7, 2024. https://www.washingtonpost.com/politics/2024/10/07/trump-undocumented-immigrants-bad-genes.

Swan, Jonathan. "Trump Says 'I Don't Know' When Asked About Due Process and Upholding Constitution." *New York Times*, May 5, 2025. https://www.nytimes.com/2025/05/04/us/politics/trump-meet-the-press-interview-due-process.html.

Swan, Jonathan, et al. "Loomer's Role in Firings Shows Rising Sway of Fringe Figures on Trump." *New York Times*, April 4, 2025. https://www.nytimes.com/2025/04/04/us/politics/trump-nsc-firings-laura-loomer.html.

Tang, Terry. "How 'Woke' Went from an Expression in Black Culture to a Conservative Criticism." AP, September 30, 2025. https://apnews.com/article/woke-wokeness-trump-dei-94ccabbcoaf185b494c273238d3bb50c.

Terkel, Amanda, and Lawrence Hurley. "Trump, Asked If He Has to 'Uphold the Constitution,' Says, 'I Don't Know.'" NBC News, May 4, 2025. https://www.nbcnews.com/politics/trump-administration/trump-asked-uphold-constitution-says-dont-know-rcna204580.

Tharoor, Ishaan. "Leading Genocide Scholars See a Genocide Happening in Gaza." *Washington Post*, July 30, 2025. https://www.washingtonpost.com/world/2025/07/30/israel-genocide-gaza-scholars-historians.

Thompson, Derek. "There Is Only One Way to Make Sense of the Tariffs." *Atlantic*, April 3, 2025. https://www.theatlantic.com/politics/archive/2025/04/tariffs-trump-outcomes-incompatible/682286.

Thompson, Hunter S. *Fear and Loathing in Las Vegas: A Savage Journey to the Heart of the American Dream*. New York: Warner, 1982. First published 1971 by Random House (New York).

Thrush, Glenn. "Trump's Flurry of Pardons Signals a Wholesale Effort to Redefine Crime." *New York Times*, May 29, 2025. https://www.nytimes.com/2025/05/29/us/politics/trumps-pardons-redefine-crime.html.

Thrush, Glenn, and Charlie Savage. "Trump, Arraigned on Election Charges, Pleads Not Guilty." *New York Times*, August 3, 2023. https://www.nytimes.com/2023/08/03/us/politics/trump-arraignment-court.html.

Time staff. "The 'Big Beautiful Bill' Would Pour Billions into ICE's Budget." *Time*, July 2, 2025. https://time.com/7299360/big-beautiful-bill-trump-ice-immigration.

Tomasky, Michael. "Are We About to Have Labor Camps in the United States of America?" *New Republic*, July 7, 2025. https://newrepublic.com/article/197619/trump-immigration-labor-camps.

———. "Trump's Toxic Toolkit: Lies, Corruption, Idiocy, Loyalty, Propaganda." *New Republic*, July 11, 2025. https://newrepublic.com/article/197858/trump-lies-corruption-idiocy-loyalty-propaganda.

Trammell, Alan M. "The Constitutionality of Nationwide Injunctions." *University of Colorado Law Review* 91.3 (Summer 2020) 977–98. https://scholar.law.colorado.edu/lawreview/vol91/iss3/8.

Treisman, Rachel. "Word of the Week: Trump Calls Tariffs 'the Most Beautiful Word.' Here's Its History." NPR, April 9, 2025. https://www.npr.org/2025/04/09/nx-s1-5355661/tariffs-history-meaning.

Trilling, Lionel. *The Liberal Imagination: Essays on Literature and Society*. New York: Viking, 1950.

Trump, Donald J. "'A BIG WIN': Supreme Court Ends Excessive Nationwide Injunctions." The White House, June 27, 2025. https://www.whitehouse.gov/articles/2025/06/a-big-win-supreme-court-ends-excessive-nationwide-injunctions.

———. Exec. Order No. 14158, 3 C.F.R. 8441 (2025), Establishing and Implementing the President's "Department of Government Efficiency." Online by Gerhard Peters and John T. Woolley, The American Presidency Project. https://www.presidency.ucsb.edu/node/375969.

———. Exec. Order No. 14160, 3 C.F.R. 8449 (2025), Protecting the Meaning and Value of American Citizenship. Online by Gerhard Peters and John T. Woolley, The American Presidency Project. https://www.presidency.ucsb.edu/node/375963.

———. Exec. Order No. 14168, 90 Fed. Reg. 8615 (Jan. 30, 2025), Defending Women from Gender Ideology Extremism and Restoring Biological Truth to the Federal Government. Online by Gerhard Peters and John T. Woolley, The American Presidency Project. https://www.presidency.ucsb.edu/node/375968.

———. Exec. Order No. 14248, 90 Fed. Reg. 14005 (Mar. 25, 2025), Preserving and Protecting the Integrity of American Elections. Online by Gerhard Peters and John T. Woolley, The American Presidency Project. https://www.presidency.ucsb.edu/node/376806.

———. Exec. Order No. 14253, 3 C.F.R. 14563 (2025), Restoring Truth and Sanity to American History. Online by Gerhard Peters and John T. Woolley, The American Presidency Project. https://www.presidency.ucsb.edu/node/376812.

———. Exec. Order No. 14333, 3 C.F.R. 39301 (2025), Declaring a Crime Emergency in the District of Columbia. Online by Gerhard Peters and John T. Woolley, The American Presidency Project. https://www.presidency.ucsb.edu/node/378267.

———. "Fact Sheet: President Donald J. Trump Modifies the Scope of Reciprocal Tariffs and Establishes Procedures for Implementing Trade Deals." September 5, 2025. https://www.whitehouse.gov/fact-sheets/2025/09/fact-sheet-president-donald-j-trump-modifies-the-scope-of-reciprocal-tariffs-and-establishes-procedures-for-implementing-trade-deals.

———. The Inaugural Address. The White House, January 20, 2025. https://www.whitehouse.gov/remarks/2025/01/the-inaugural-address.

———. National Security Strategy of the United States of America. November 2025. www.whitehouse.gov/wp-content/uploads/2025/12/2025-National-Security-Strategy.pdf.

———. "President Trump Delivers Remarks on New Tariffs." C-Span, April 2, 2025. https://www.c-span.org/program/white-house-event/president-trump-delivers-remarks-on-new-tariffs/658000.

———. "PROMISES MADE, PROMISES KEPT: Border Security Achieved in Fewer Than 100 Days." The White House, April 28, 2025. https://www.whitehouse.gov/articles/2025/04/promises-made-promises-kept-border-security-achieved-in-fewer-than-100-days.

———. "'Promises Made, Promises Kept': Trump Signs His Legacy, 'Big, Beautiful Bill' Becomes Law on I-Day." *Economic Times*, July 4, 2025. *Economic Times* YouTube channel: https://www.youtube.com/watch?v=Yj6i3hO21MY.

———. "Remarks by President Trump in Joint Address to Congress." March 6, 2025. https://it.usembassy.gov/remarks-by-president-trump-in-joint-address-to-congress.

———. Speech at the Conservative Political Action Conference in National Harbor, Maryland, March 3, 2023. https://www.rev.com/transcripts/trump-speaks-at-cpac-2023-transcript.

———. "Transcript: President Donald Trump Addresses Nation After US Strikes on Iran." ABC News, June 21, 2025. https://abcnews.go.com/Politics/transcript-donald-trump-addresses-nation-after-iran-strikes/story?id=123084288.

———. "Truth Social Posts of April 20, 2025." Online by Gerhard Peters and John T. Woolley, The American Presidency Project. https://www.presidency.ucsb.edu/node/377301.

Turley, Jonathan. "The Mystery of Ghislaine Maxwell: Does Epstein's Associate Have an Untold Story? *Res ipsa loquitor*, July 24, 2025. https://jonathanturley.org/2025/07/24/the-mystery-of-ghislaine-maxwell-does-epsteins-associate-have-an-untold-story.

United States Citizenship and Immigration Services. "Naturalization Oath of Allegiance to the United States of America." https://www.uscis.gov/citizenship/learn-about-citizenship/the-naturalization-interview-and-test/naturalization-oath-of-allegiance-to-the-united-states-of-america.

United States Code, 5 USC 3331. https://www.govregs.com/uscode/expand/title5_partIII_subpartB_chapter33_subchapterII_section3331.

United States Congress. Flag Protection Act of 1989, Pub L. No. 101-131, 101st Cong. 103 Stat. 777, https://www.congress.gov/101/statute/STATUTE-103/STATUTE-103-Pg777.pdf.

———. Joint Resolution of March 22, 1972, Proposing an Amendment to Constitution Relative to Equal Rights for Men and Women. H.J. Res. 208, 92nd Cong. 86 Stat. 1523 (1972). https://catalog.archives.gov/id/7455549.

———. War Powers Resolution, Pub. L. No. 93-148, 93rd Cong. 87 Stat. 555 (1973).

United States Department of Education. "Office for Civil Rights Sends Letters to 60 Universities Under Investigation for Antisemitic Discrimination and Harassment." Press release, March 10, 2025. https://www.ed.gov/about/news/press-release/us-department-of-educations-office-civil-rights-sends-letters-60-universities-under-investigation-antisemitic-discrimination-and-harassment.

United States Department of Health and Human Servicces, Office for Civil Rights, Notice of Violation: Harvard University, OCR Trans. No. DO-25–607541-RV-CRR-Rac., June 30, 2025, https://www.hhs.gov/sites/default/files/harvard-title-vi-notice-violation.pdf.

United States Government Accountability Office. "Defense Workforce." July 26, 2023. https://www.gao.gov/products/gao-23-106966.

United States House of Representatives. Directing the President pursuant to section 5(c) of the War Powers Resolution to remove United States Armed Forces from unauthorized hostilities in the Islamic Republic of Iran, H. Con. Res. 38 (introduced but not [yet] enacted), 119th Cong. (2025). https://www.congress.gov/bill/119th-congress/house-concurrent-resolution/38.

United States National Archives. "Alien and Sedition Acts (1798)." Milestone Documents. https://www.archives.gov/milestone-documents/alien-and-sedition-acts.

———. "Brown v. Board of Education (1954)." Milestone Documents. https://www.archives.gov/milestone-documents/brown-v-board-of-education. Transcript available here: https://docsteach.org/document/opinion-brown-v-board.

———. "Constitution of the United States (1787)." Milestone Documents. https://www.archives.gov/milestone-documents/constitution. Transcript available here: https://docsteach.org/document/constitution.

———. "Declaration of Independence (1776)." Milestone Documents. https://www.archives.gov/milestone-documents/declaration-of-independence. Transcript available here: https://docsteach.org/document/the-declaration-of-independence.

———. "Executive Order 9066: Resulting in Japanese American Incarceration (1942)." Milestone Documents. https://www.archives.gov/milestone-documents/executive-order-9066. Transcript available here: https://docsteach.org/document/executive-order-9066.

———. "Federal Judiciary Act (1789)." Milestone Documents. https://www.archives.gov/milestone-documents/federal-judiciary-act. Transcript available here: https://docsteach.org/document/judiciary-act-1789

United States Senate. 177 Cong. Rec. S1961–S2034 (daily ed. March 31, 2025) (twenty-five-hour floor speech by New Jersey senator Cory Booker).

United States Supreme Court. Brown v. Board of Education of Topeka, 347 U.S. 483 (1954), https://supreme.justia.com/cases/federal/us/347/483.

———. Brown v. Board of Education of Topeka, 349 U.S. 294 (1955), https://supreme.justia.com/cases/federal/us/349/294.

———. Citizens United v. Federal Election Commission, 558 U.S. 310 (2010), https://supreme.justia.com/cases/federal/us/558/310.

———. Dobbs v. Jackson Women's Health Organization, 597 U.S. 215 (2022), https://supreme.justia.com/cases/federal/us/597/19-1392/case.pdf.

———. Dred Scott v. Sandford 60 U.S. 393 (1856), https://supreme.justia.com/cases/federal/us/60/393.

———. Korematsu v. United States, 323 U.S. 214 (1944), https://supreme.justia.com/cases/federal/us/323/214.

———. Marbury v. Madison, 5 U.S. 137 (1803), https://supreme.justia.com/cases/federal/us/5/137.

———. Plessy v. Ferguson, 163 U.S. 537 (1896), https://supreme.justia.com/cases/federal/us/163/537.

———. Roe v. Wade, 410 U.S. 113 (1973), https://supreme.justia.com/cases/federal/us/410/113.

———. Shelby County v. Holder, 570 U.S. 529 (2013), https://supreme.justia.com/cases/federal/us/570/529.

———. Texas v. Johnson, 491 U.S. 397 (1989), https://supreme.justia.com/cases/federal/us/491/397.

———. Trump v. CASA, Inc., docket no.: 24A884 (06/27/2025), https://supreme.justia.com/cases/federal/us/606/24a884/case.pdf.

———. Trump v. United States, docket no. 23-939 (07/01/2024), https://supreme.justia.com/cases/federal/us/603/23-939.

———. United States v. Eichman, 496 U.S. 310 (1990), https://supreme.justia.com/cases/federal/us/496/310.

———. United States v. Nixon, 418 U.S. 683 (1974), https://supreme.justia.com/cases/federal/us/418/683.

———. United States v. Wong Kim Ark, 169 U.S. 649 (1898), https://supreme.justia.com/cases/federal/us/169/649.

———. Worcester v. Georgia, 31 U.S. 515 (1832), https://supreme.justia.com/cases/federal/us/31/515.

Vance, JD. "Transcript: JD Vance's Speech at the Claremont Institute's Statesmanship Award Event." Sinju Post, July 10, 2025. https://singjupost.com/transcript-jd-vances-speech-at-the-claremont-institutes-statesmanship-award-event.

———. "The Universities Are the Enemy." Keynote address at the National Conservatism Conference II, Orlando, FL, November 2, 2021. https://www.youtube.com/watch?v=oFR65Cifnhw.

Van Hook, Jennifer, et al. "Repealing Birthright Citizenship Would Significantly Increase the Size of the U.S. Unauthorized Population." Migration Policy Institute, May 2025. https://www.migrationpolicy.org/news/birthright-citizenship-repeal-projections#:~:text=Each%20year%2C%20over%20the%20next,legal%20status%2C%20the%20research%20shows.

VanSickle, Abbie. "Chief Justice Urges Political Leaders to Tone Down Rhetoric." *New York Times*, June 28, 2025. https://www.nytimes.com/2025/06/28/us/chief-justice-roberts-threats.html.

———. "Supreme Court Agrees to Review Trump Order Restricting Birthright Citizenship." *New York Times*, December 5, 2025. https://www.nytimes.com/2025/12/05/us/politics/supreme-court-trump-birthright-citizenship.html.

Villagran, Lauren. "Over 40 and Eager to Join ICE? Here's Who Can Now Join the Force." *USA Today*, August 6, 2025. Updated August 7, 2025. https://www.usatoday.com/story/news/politics/2025/08/06/ice-deportation-agent-age-apply/85539314007.

Vought, Russell. "Renewing American Purpose: Statesmanship in a Post-Constitutional Moment." *American Mind*, September 29, 2022. https://americanmind.org/salvo/renewing-american-purpose.

Waldvogel, Miriam. "Russell Vought on Trump's Megabill: 'There's Like, No Downside.'" *The Hill*, July 7, 2025. https://thehill.com/homenews/5388842-russ-vought-trump-megabill-no-downside.

Walker, Chris. "House Passes Bill Limiting Judges' Ability to Place Injunctions on Trump Orders." *Truthout*, April 10, 2025. https://truthout.org/articles/house-passes-bill-limiting-judges-ability-to-place-injunctions-on-trump-orders.

Wallace-Wells, David. "The Epstein Story Is Both Conspiracy Theory and Genuine Scandal." *New York Times*, July 16, 2025. https://www.nytimes.com/2025/07/16/opinion/epstein-trump-scandal.html.

Warren, Elizabeth. "One Hundred Days, One Hundred Acts of Corruption." Speech on the United States Senate floor, April 30, 2025. https://www.warren.senate.gov/newsroom/press-releases/icymi-warren-reads-100-acts-of-trump-corruption-into-congressional-record-to-mark-100-days-of-the-trump-administration.

Washburn, Kaitlin. "Guns Are the Leading Cause of Death for American Children. What to Know." Association of Health Care Journalists, December 8, 2025. https://healthjournalism.org/blog/2025/12/guns-are-the-leading-cause-of-death-for-american-children-what-to-know.

Watson, Kathryn. "Which Trump Officials Were in the Signal Chat? Here's Who Was in the Group *The Atlantic* Editor Was Added To." CBS News, March 28, 2025. https://www.cbsnews.com/news/trump-officials-in-signal-group-chat.

Wehner, Peter, and Robert P. Beschel Jr. "Trump's Unforgivable Sin." *Atlantic*, August 10, 2025. https://www.theatlantic.com/politics/archive/2025/08/trump-incompetence/683779.

Whisnant, Gabe. "US Debt Reaches $37 Trillion Years Before Expected." *Newsweek*, August 13, 2025. https://www.newsweek.com/us-government-federal-debt-taxes-budget-economy-2112581.

Wiesel, Elie. Foreword. In *Shadows of Auschwitz: A Christian Response to the Holocaust*, by Harry James Cargas, ix–x. Rev. ed. New York: Crossroad, 1990.

Wiesel, Elisha. "My Father Survived the Holocaust. Why Are Students Taking Part in a New Call to Violence?" *USA Today*, May 2, 2024. https://www.usatoday.com/story/opinion/voices/2024/05/02/protests-universities-students-palestine-antisemitism-extremists/73525814007.

Wire, Sarah D. "Vance: Medicaid Cuts in Senate Tax Bill 'Immaterial' Compared to ICE Increases." *USA Today*, July 1, 2025. https://www.usatoday.com/story/news/politics/2025/07/01/vance-medicaid-cuts-ice-spending-tax-bill/84429757007.

Wolf, Zachary, and Tami Luhby. "Here's How Trump's Megabill Will Affect You." CNN, July 3, 2025. https://www.cnn.com/2025/07/01/politics/congress-senate-bill-tax-spending-trump-gop-explainer.

Wolfers, Justin. "Your Life Will Never Be the Same After These Tariffs." *New York Times*, April 4, 2005. https://www.nytimes.com/2025/04/04/opinion/trump-tariff-economics-cost.html.

Wong, Tessa, and Kayla Epstein. "At a Glance: Trump's Tariffs on China, EU and Rest of the World." BBC News, April 8, 2025. https://www.bbc.com/news/articles/c1jxrnl9xe20.

Wootson, Cleve R., Jr. "Trump Says He 'Couldn't Care Less' If Auto Prices Rise Because of His Tariffs." *Washington Post*, March 29, 2025. https://www.washingtonpost.com/politics/2025/03/29/trump-auto-tariffs-prices-rise.

Wyman, David S. *The Abandonment of the Jews: America and the Holocaust, 1941–1945*. New York: Pantheon, 1984.

———. *Paper Walls: America and the Refugee Crisis, 1938–1941*. Amherst: University of Massachusetts Press, 1968.

Yourish, Karen, et al. "All of the Trump Administration's Major Moves in the First 100 Days." *New York Times*, April 30, 2025 Updated October 22, 2025. https://www.nytimes.com/interactive/2025/us/trump-agenda-2025.html.

———. "These Words Are Disappearing in the New Trump Administration." *New York Times*, March 7, 2025. https://www.nytimes.com/interactive/2025/03/07/us/trump-federal-agencies-websites-words-dei.html.

Zadorozhnyy, Tim. "Russian Media Shows US Armored Vehicle with Russian, American Flags Storming Ukrainian Positions (VIDEO)." Yahoo News, August 18, 2025. http://bit.ly/4qmcORo.

Zagano, Phyllis. "Immigration Policy Has Become a Question of Character." *Religion News Service*, July 8, 2025. https://www.ncronline.org/opinion/guest-voices/immigration-policy-has-become-question-character.

Zimmer, Thomas. "Meet the Ideologue of the 'Post-Constitutional' Right." *Democracy Americana*, Substack, November 27, 2024. https://thomaszimmer.substack.com/p/meet-the-ideologue-of-the-post-constitutional.

Index

www.ingramcontent.com/pod-product-compliance
Lightning Source LLC
LaVergne TN
LVHW100526110826
845146LV00002B/790

* 9 7 9 8 3 8 5 2 4 9 2 0 6 *